TRAVELING THE CONSULTING ROAD

Traveling the Consulting Road: Career wisdom for new consultants candidates and their mentors is a compilation of the author's reflections on a long career in management consulting. The author intends this advice to be helpful to others pursuing a career in this profession.

Memory is imprecise at best, so others who experienced the same events described in the book may remember them differently.

Much has changed in the consulting industry over the years and each individual's experience is different. Consulting is about problem-solving and decision-making and therefore the author encourages readers to treat these reflections as input, but to make their own career decisions and solve their own workplace problems rather than rely exclusively on the author's experiences.

Published by Unusual Wisdom Press LLC
New Jersey, United States of America

ISBN
Paperback: 979-8-9878518-1-4
Hardcover: 979-8-9878518-2-1
E-Book: 979-8-9878518-0-7

Cover and interior design: Lisa Monias, South River Design Team
www.SouthRiverDesignTeam.com

Publisher's imprint logo design: Zac Culler
www.ZacCuller.com/illustration

Author's Photo: Jay Seldin Photography
www.JaySeldinPhotos.com

TRAVELING THE CONSULTING ROAD

CAREER WISDOM FOR NEW CONSULTANTS, CANDIDATES, AND THEIR MENTORS

ALAN CAY CULLER

DEDICATION:

To my wife Billie Smith Culler,
who picks me up when I fall down. I will never forget.

To my parents, Nan and Raymond Culler, my sisters Carolyn (Lynne)
Culler Wilson and Constance Culler Falconer, who raised me to be loving,
kind and to make a difference. I am still working on it.
To my children and grandchildren, sources of never-ending joy.

To every consultant who survived managing me,
or working alongside me. You helped me grow.

To every client who trusted me with improving their organization's results
and all their people who did most of the work.
You kept me learning and shared the pride of achievement.
Thank you! You made this book and so much more possible.

Traveling the Consulting Road

"Whether you're a student thinking about consulting as a career, a recently hired consultant, or you're working your way up the consulting career ladder Alan's advice will help you succeed. Reading *Traveling the Consulting Road* feels like waiting out a rain delay in the Admirals Club at O'Hare, sitting next to a seasoned industry veteran willing to share his accumulated wisdom. From a 30,000-foot overview of topics like client management to specifics on a wide array of consulting frameworks anyone in our profession will find plenty of useful, pragmatic insights well worth bookmarking for future use."

Bob Frisch, Founding Partner of Strategic Offsites Group; former Managing Partner at Accenture and alumnus of Gemini Consulting and The Boston Consulting Group; author of 24 articles for *Harvard Business Review* and the best-selling *Who's in the Room?: How Great Leaders Structure and Manage the Teams Around Them* (Wiley/Jossey-Bass)

"Alan Culler's deeply insightful book *Traveling The Consulting Road* is a great guide for anyone who is looking to excel in consulting, but also looking to build strong workplace skills. His wisdom around all things consulting shines through on every page. Read this unputdownable book for the lessons, but also for the entertaining vignettes, war stories and great writing."

Roopa Unnikrishnan, SVP Strategy and Corporate Development, Idex Corporation, Founding Partner Center 10 Consulting, author of *Career Catapult: Shake Up the Status Quo and Boost Your Professional Trajectory* (Career Press)

Recommendations for Alan Cay Culler

Alan is the most effective management consultant I have encountered, hands down. He was of assistance in focusing management teams in two very different industries - publishing and construction. In both instances his knowledge and interpersonal skills had lasting effects on the success of our management teams. Unlike many others, he was able to become an extension of the management team and someone we could go to for counsel or advice long after the initial assignment had ended. As a repeat client I highly recommend Alan!

> **Bob Yardis, Human Resources Consultant, Global Infrastructure Solutions Inc.; former SVP Corporate Human Resources, Structure Tone; and VP HR, PF Collier.**

Alan's long career as an advisor, wisdom seeker and truth teller has enabled him to excel in the world of consultancy. I have been privileged to work with Alan when he was a Principal at Katzenbach Partners and I was new to the world of Organization Effectiveness at Pfizer. Over the years, I have read and reread his articles, and await his next publications.

> **Kaye Foster, Senior Advisor/ Executive Coach/ CEO Advisory Facilitator, The Boston Consulting Group (BCG); SVP Human Resources, Onya Pharmaceuticals, Johnson & Johnson, and Pfizer.**

When I first worked with Alan a few decades ago, we talked about what it means to remain a student of your profession: always listen, always learn, and be willing to respectfully challenge. Over the years I have often been the beneficiary of Alan's dedication to the consulting service industry; he remains current with what other consultancies are doing through first-hand connections, evaluates competing organizational frameworks for similarities and differences, and leads the way in understanding the change process of both individuals and organizations. Most impressively, he can effectively share this knowledge through the perspective of both client and trained consultant.

Brad Martin, Founding Partner, Next Forge Consulting.

Alan is amazing. His ability to assist clients in cutting through the layers of confusion and redundancy found in most organizations is a real strength. Alan is a great adviser to any organization trying to adjust to, or more importantly stay in front of, a rapidly changing world. I highly recommend Alan as a strategic adviser, trainer and coach.

Jere Cowden, Retired Chairman, Cowden Associates, Inc.

When a company hires an executive consultant for an assignment, you hope that the consultant possesses higher level skill in innovative and provocative thinking, industry knowledge, implementation experience, and organization - in short, a great communicator who can downright just "get things done." With Alan Culler, our organization benefited from all the above. I was head of a team implementing common processes into our global upstream organization, and had the honor of working closely with Alan. I appreciated Alan's talents and dedication to making our company a more successful business. So much so, I appointed Alan to the program leadership board as a full member as I found him to be a great leader as well as motivator. As a result of Alan's guidance, our organization has since become a stronger upstream business with better planning and scheduling capability and we are far more effective at finding and eliminating operational defects. This has allowed the company to mature in thought and aspire to be a leader in green technology in the energy field. Many thanks to Alan for sharing his time and talent in what was a very challenging atmosphere to create process and cultural change. Alan, job well done!

Joe Barnes, former Deputy VP Reliability and Maintenance, BP Exploration & Production, now author of _Developing a High Performing Student_.

I had the privilege to work with Alan when I was in BP leading the Continuous Improvement effort. When we first met, I was immediately drawn to his captivating storytelling ability, his questioning techniques, deep experience in change management, and his knowledge about what makes humans tick. He is approachable, friendly, curious, and humorous, and his desire to make things better is infectious. Alan is one of the best teachers, coaches, and management consultants one would ever find. I am so very grateful I had the opportunity to work with him.

Florence Woo, former VP and Director Continuous Improvement at Cenovus Energy and BP, now an independent consultant.

I worked with Alan at Gemini Consulting. After leaving there, we stayed in contact and when my small business needed help, I called on him to help. We couldn't afford the fees of a large corporation, and Alan worked with us very graciously within a tight budget. Alan is a very trustworthy person and really helped us get things done (plan, do, review) by helping us implement improvements and holding our feet to the fire. I know that this isn't the kind of work he usually does, but it was very valuable and cost-effective too.

Naresh Jessani, Owner and Center Director, Mathnasium of Jersey City.

Two Roads Diverged* ...

... I traveled the Consulting Road ...

... I wish I'd had a map.

* With appreciation and tribute to Robert Frost and his poem
The Road Not Taken

CONTENTS

CONSULTANTS ARE EVERYWHERE

In 1991 I wrote about how I was continually amazed at the ubiquity of consulting and how I found it in the most unexpected situations.

My hair cutter then was an unusual man, a dark-skinned Mediterranean, a guy's guy, a salesman, a dealmaker, quick with a joke or a story. I went to him not just for his stories, but because he cut my hair really well. I found it difficult to find a good cutter, and Mico was a good cutter.

But I did like his stories. I collect stories the way other guys collect beer mats or coins.

One day, Mico started by saying, "You may appreciate this. I mean, because you're a *consultant.*"

I told him once what I did; he remembered a lot, at odd times perhaps, but I was still flattered.

"I was a consultant once, to a college, a community college. . . me, a guy who just made it outta high school. This is one of the only colleges in the country with a course in cosmetology. The state wanted to close them down. They weren't making any money. They'd had these statistical engineers come in. The state sent them . . . they couldn't find out what was wrong."

Mico went on to tell me how he went into the school, observed for two days, then talked to the faculty together and individually and talked to the students together and individually. He explained to each of them:

"This school is yours. When I leave, you're gonna work or go to school here, if <u>you</u> save it."

His real-world experience (he had successfully run his own shop for years) and his down-to-earth manner apparently won over faculty and students alike. He made some suggestions; they made some suggestions. <u>They</u> <u>took</u> <u>action.</u>

"A year later they paid for my ticket to come back and see what they did. They were profitable. The state was happy. They were happy. And it made me feel good, you know. They gave me a lotta credit when I was there. You know, they said I had turned it around. That made me feel good. But <u>they</u> <u>did</u> <u>it.</u> Probably could do it again without me now if they had to. I see why you like what you do . . . You know, I get a lotta guys who don't like what they do and I think . . ."

Mico was off on another tale, but I was back at that community college with him. He had described a near-perfect process intervention that had left the client empowered to continue on after he left.

His principles are the consulting process: **Entry- Diagnosis-Solve - Implement - Disengage**

> Observe with the eyes of the outsider who knows something about what they do.
>
> Gather input from many sources.
>
> Make suggestions.
>
> Give them their ball back, and then
>
> Leave, get out. Fish, relatives, and consultants stink if they're around too long.

Always be prepared to find wisdom in unusual places.

WHAT IS A CONSULTANT?

"Consulting wisdom? Isn't that an oxymoron? I might concede that consultants are smart. Just ask 'em; they'll tell you how smart they are! But wise? Not so sure about that."

This is a conversation I overheard at a business conference once. It was early enough in my career that I didn't think I could engage without being defensive, so I walked on.

Many people's experiences with consultants are quite negative.

"They interviewed me and then presented my ideas as their own." "Can you believe what we are paying these guys? Don't ask about raises or bonuses this year or next!" "They said the industry standard span of control was twelve and I needed to fire two of my managers and five people – they had a list. They've been here less than a week."

Probably all those criticisms are justified. Consultants are sometimes hired as hatchet-men. They're sometimes paid unreasonable amounts compared to internal people. And they are sometimes arrogant and don't give credit where credit is due.

Consultants can also help grow some companies and turn others around. They can set up systems quickly because they have done it before while internal people would need to learn on the job. External consultants can bring needed expertise that would be too expensive to keep on staff.

Consultants help clients and their companies change. Some people react negatively to the word. "Change? You won't change me! We just want a new strategy." The truth is no one ever spent large sums of money to maintain the status quo. Even a new strategy is a plan to do different things. A client hires a consultant to help make that change a reality. The consultant might provide new information about customers and competitors. A consultant might teach you new ways of doing things.

The best consultants give their clients new perspective, skills, and the strength to do what they couldn't do before without taking credit. They are quietly transformative.

Consultants can be helpful or they can be jerks, like most people. Sometimes consultants can be both helpful *and* jerks at the same time.

I wrote this book to encourage consultants to be helpful, like the best medical professional you can imagine.

I came to understand consulting as a helping profession much too slowly. I also wrote this book as the philosophical career guide that I wish I'd had as a "Newbie," a new consultant or even a student investigating the field. I wish I had previewed this book before I became a mid-career consultant trying to balance the needs of clients and my consulting team while deciding if I was on a partner track in an "up or out" environment.

I also wish I'd had this as a senior consultant, struggling to either sell enough to make partner or become independent or start a firm. In my thirty-seven year consulting career, I worked for five consulting firms of various sizes. I founded a small firm, worked as a solo practitioner, and founded a confederation of independent consultants. Most of my early career decisions were made without an understanding of the industry or any idea about why companies hire consultants.

Why do companies hire consultants?

First, companies don't hire consultants; company *executives* hire consultants. That may seem like splitting hairs. After all, company executives work for their companies and are charged with acting in the interest of the companies, right? Right (mostly).

But if one starts with the concept that a client is an individual, even if that client is part of a collection of individuals or a client system, it makes serving clients more personal and the process of acquiring clients, or selling, less of a mystery.

Second, a client hires a consultant to solve a problem or to help make a change. Here some clients might push back because they object to either the word "problem" or "change." They may substitute "opportunity" for problem or words like "improvement" or "innovation" or descriptors like "leap-frogging" or "updating" for the dreaded C-word (change). But no board of directors ever approved a hundred thousand or million dollar expenditure to maintain the status quo.

So some of the problems, issues, and/or concerns that a company executive might hire a consultant to help with include:

Grow revenue, or
Grow profit, or
People stuff.

Wait, that's it? What about a new strategy? (We need more customers than our competition, or innovation, or new products and services to grow revenue.) What about digital transformation? (We need streamlined operations to reduce cost and grow profit; we need better customer information to speed our product to market to grow revenue.)

Actually it's *all* people stuff. Culture, climate, employee benefits, and organization design shouldn't be lumped into a separate category. Simply put, attracting and keeping people = profit growth and/or revenue growth. But often clients who have a "people problem" aren't thinking economically. They can't hire enough people or the right ones, or people are leaving, or unhappy and want a union, or clients don't know who to put in what role or how to organize. So I've listed people stuff separately.

Consultants can bring new ideas or they can legitimize an internal idea. They can bring new processes, methodologies or systems, or help improve existing ones to solve a revenue, profit or people problem. Clients hire consultants as problem solvers. They expect that these consultants have solved their problem before. They may expect problem-solving rigor steeped in data and/or the scientific method. But mostly the client wants a specific result, i.e., more revenue, more profit, or both.

Ideally, this is a true statement. In the real world, however, sometimes a company executive hires a consultant because his or her boss insists on it, or to do an unpleasant task like reducing headcount, or to justify his idea over a rival's. Sometimes a client hires a consultant to try the latest management fad just to "shake things up." In my career I tried to avoid these kinds of projects, because I believe they are a waste of money. I wasn't always successful.

What attracts a person to the consulting road?

For some, it's the money. The consulting profession isn't likely to make you tech entrepreneur or investment banker rich, but it can produce a solidly upper-middle-class lifestyle. For others, it's "glamour and prestige." These folks quickly learn that constant travel is grueling, not glamorous, and talking to CEOs is just a work meeting where pleasing your boss (a consulting partner) and your boss's boss (a client CEO) is a challenge.

I was attracted to consulting for these naive reasons. What kept me in the field was the work of structured problem solving, and the variety of industries and problems I worked in and on. There was a continual steep learning curve and I find learning fun.

There are three typical entry points to the field: post undergraduate, postgraduate, and mid-career directly from a business. Post undergraduate and postgraduate hires are often called "Newbies." Some firms do a better job of training these entrants than others, but most consulting training is focused on this group.

The major consulting firms - McKinsey, Boston Consulting Group Accenture, Bain, and PwC (formerly known as PricewaterhouseCoopers) - recruit top students from top universities as analysts. Often these students join as summer interns between their junior and senior years. These are plum internships because these firms are known as "good places to be from" in the same way that Ivy League universities are. Some undergraduate consulting entrants go to work initially as analysts in investment banking and then move on to consulting two years later. The typical consulting analyst works in the field for two to four years, perhaps to pay down student loans, and then moves on to a job elsewhere. Some analysts choose to get a graduate degree. A few analysts are "sponsored" by the consulting firm to attend business school.

Graduate school recruitment, especially MBA recruitment, used to be the biggest source of new consultants. PhD programs and master's programs in science, technology, engineering, and mathematics (STEM) have been added.

Those who join consulting from industry are often hired as subject matter experts after spending ten-plus years in one discipline in one industry where the firm has substantial client work. Depending on how senior the new hire is, he or she may avoid the typical grind of project work and be brought in to offer expertise and gravitas in client pitches and presentations. Otherwise, they may be used to shorten the learning curve of consultants working in a new industry. Some firms provide these entrants with unique induction training while others treat them the same way they treat Newbies. I too frequently saw poor onboarding for experienced industry hires.

The levels and jobs of a consulting career

There is a life cycle of roles in consulting. I've called these Newbies, Journeymen, and Pros. This sounds like the apprentice, journeyman, master-craftsman of the building trades, but that is a formal process with testing and certifications. The consulting firms I worked in had nothing like that. There are three distinctly different jobs:

1. **Newbies:** a person investigating the field, a new entrant, a

starting analyst, someone who does a lot of the work. Newbies work hard, learn a lot and burn out or get promoted within a few years. There is some Newbie hazing that goes along with the role, and many consultants seemingly look down on Newbies after they have learned the ropes and graduated to a slightly more advanced role. But get a few experienced consultants together talking in a bar and they will speak wistfully about this period in their careers, when "everything was new" and they were "drinking from the fire hose every day." In the best firms there's a Newbie comradery that lasts a long time. "You never forget those you shared a foxhole with." The word "Newbie" may evoke a derogatory connotation; I hated being called a Newbie myself. Some consultants will maintain that Newbie applies only to the first two weeks of a new person's career after which they become a "valued associate." OK, sure. These junior consultants still **do** a lot of the work.)

2. **Journeymen:** these are mid-career consultants who manage the team and keep the client happy day-to-day. Journeymen still do work, sometimes more than is realistic, and they keep the wheels on the bus, solving team and client problems as they go. They may be called senior consultants, senior associates, team leads, engagement managers, project managers, account managers, or principals. I kept the word Journeymen because mid-career consultants are the backbone of any firm. They manage projects, client system interactions, consulting teams, budgets, deliverables, and in some cases results. They're expected to be able to do the work of those below them and direct the judicious application of seniors above them. It's a tough job.

3. **Pros:** this role includes the been-around-the-block senior people, discipline or methodology experts and partners of every

stripe. Pros don't have to be old in years. Some are even in their late twenties or early thirties, but they bring a certain gravitas to every project. Clients listen to them. They also have a completely different job. Their mandate is to bring in business, new clients, new projects from existing clients, extensions on existing projects, in other words . . . **sell**.

Some consultants and some firms dislike the word *sell* because they think selling is beneath the profession. They may call it client development, business development, or "having client conversations," but personal selling is what generates revenue in consulting. It is the major criterion for promotion from manager to partner. Pros sell directly by bringing in new clients, or indirectly by developing new service offerings and methodologies, writing books, speaking and attracting clients. Usually, not always, partners get a share of the revenue they bring in, or a share of the profits based upon the clients they bring, so direct sales pays better than service offering development.

My background

I joined consulting after getting my MBA at the London Business School. I got a summer internship at the London office of Harbridge House (HHI), a Boston-based firm that was ultimately acquired by an antecedent firm of PwC. I did well enough that I ended up working fulltime at HHI during my second year of business school.

At HHI, I worked on three new product introduction studies in the automotive industry. I also learned how to get up to speed in an industry quickly and learn enough to have intelligent conversations with people who had worked in the industry for their entire life. I also learned that consulting is about change and that leadership engagement and commitment are critical.

Soon after LBS and HHI, I went to the Forum Corporation and learned training and organization development approaches. This is where I met

George Litwin, Warner Burke, and a host of other Organizational Development thought leaders. I worked behind George Litwin for ten years, and learned a lot about organizations and how to develop and deliver training.

The turnaround of British Airways (1984-87) was the most significant project of this period. I include a full description of this project in the Appendix because it shaped my view of change and throughout my career kept me looking for the Holy Grail-like combination of successful change elements.

I now realize that BA had the benefit of:

- A burning platform (Margaret Thatcher's privatize-or-close ultimatum).
- Clear business goals, which, in three years, took BA from having the worst customer service and profit record in the industry to the best in both categories.
- A new executive team (John King and Colin Marshall).
- Lots of money (the deep pockets of the British government).

Soon after BA, I became an independent consultant for the first time. Working on my own for eight years taught me that I can survive and improvise, but I eventually wanted large projects and colleagues so I joined Gemini Consulting. I expanded my skill set with Gemini's reengineering methodology and taught Six Sigma at GE Capital. I thrived in the Gemini team environment and ultimately became head of the North American organizational discipline.

From Gemini I went to Katzenbach Partners, a small McKinsey spinoff, to be part of growing something new. I stayed there for four years because of the excitement of the startup environment, despite the fact that the promised blend of organization development process with McKinsey analysis never quite happened.

After leaving Katzenbach, I worked as an independent consultant for another fourteen years in a variety of business structures. The most lasting was the Results-Alliance, a confederation of independent consultants and small firms helping clients develop internal capability to implement sustainable change.

My biases

As will become apparent, along the way I developed certain biases about the field:

- **People focus.** I strongly believe that business is about people. Whether they are called customers, staff, suppliers, or the community, people create and feel the impact of business decisions. Solutions to problems need to factor in both their short- and long-term effect on these groups.
- There are two different approaches to consulting: Content and Process.
- Content consultants are sometimes called expert consultants. They bring ideas, new information and analytical rigor to the client's problem. They provide answers.
- Process consultants help the client solve the problem. They may improve a process, develop people, build a team, or implement a system. They often work with the client longer and do more implementation work than content consultants, and tend to teach the client what they do as they are doing it. Like all teachers since Socrates, they ask questions.
- This fundamental difference defined my career. Over time I gravitated from content to process consulting. I saw firms try to blend these approaches, but they do not mix easily. In this book I try to fairly present both sides, but my bias shows.
- **Ultimately it's the client's business.** Generally, my view is that most problems that consultants are hired to solve could be solved with internal resources. I believe it is the consultant's job to help the client change - to innovate or improve and to integrate what is new into the client's business - without creating a dependency on consultants.

As a consultant I worked to teach clients what I did and to leave an infrastructure in place to allow the client to solve similar problems themselves the next time. Such a strategy meant that I constantly had to look for new clients, but it also increased client self-sufficiency and made consulting a learning experience. As I said, I find learning fun.

Now as a recent retiree, I want to share what I learned traveling the consulting road. Much has changed since I started my journey. I stayed on this path successfully, sometimes in spite of myself. I believe this roadmap will help you avoid some wrong turns I made. My wish for you is that you enjoy the ride as much as I have.

MAPPING A CONSULTING CAREER

T wo roads diverged . . .

Perhaps you read "The Road Not Taken" in school. *"Two roads diverged in a yellow wood and I --- I took the one less travelled by and that has made all the difference."* My English teacher told me this was about Robert Frost's choice to become a poet, which he felt, in retrospect, was a good choice for him.

My "two roads moment" came after nine years as a booking agent for celebrity speakers. I'd kind of stumbled into that career, after not finding work as an actor, but I was good at it. I'd worked at two firms in Boston and was recruited by the lecture bureau attached to New Line Cinema in New York City. I could see how this job might lead to others in entertainment, but I was uncertain about the industry and my wife and I were nervous about moving to New York.

At around this time my brother-in-law Ian got his MBA and went from being an English teacher to a consultant, which seemed like an exciting career. I also knew another booking agent, Jacqueline, who got an MBA and was changing careers, maybe to consulting. In the end, I sold my house, both cars and everything I owned and moved my wife and then two children to London to attend the London Business School. Off I went traveling the consulting road.

That's it, no industry research, no researching individual firms and where and how they recruited, not even much conversation with Ian or Jacqueline. This was the career for me.

I just wish I'd had a map

So this is a map of sorts. It includes a start on the industry research I wish I had done in the late 1970s, an outlined trajectory of a consulting career and some forks in the road, decisions you will face along the way. There is some expansion on why people are attracted to consulting. I'll then go into detail on important early career topics like getting hired, being successful and the first methodologies and tools you will use. I'll go into more depth on the work itself and later career issues. Hopefully you will navigate your career less serendipitously than I did.

CHAPTER 1

INVESTIGATING THE CONSULTING INDUSTRY? WHAT DOES THAT MEAN?

Often when people asked what I did for a living, I would answer, "I'm a consultant." Then they would ask me, "What does <u>that</u> mean?" People understand what a doctor does and generally understand what a lawyer or accountant does, but very few understand what a consultant does. Webster isn't particularly illuminating with its definition of "a person who gives advice professionally." Sometimes I would explain that management consulting is part of professional services available to businesses. Accountants help businesses with records and taxes, lawyers help with the law and consultants help solve problems and make changes.

Most people still didn't get what I did; some launched into consultant jokes. I learned to leave it there, "help solve problems and make changes. It's a big industry."

Industry structure

The global management consulting industry revenue is variously reported as somewhere between $25 billion and $1.3 trillion. Don't you love the precision of such reporting? Of course, it's not clear what this revenue number includes. Do you count only firms of a certain size and leave out the millions of independent consultants? By one 2019 estimate, globally there were 700,000 firms of three or more consultants; and for every consultant that worked for a firm there were between five and fifteen that earned at least some of their income from independent consulting. This translates to at least ten million independent consultants.

How do you count the management consulting revenue of accounting firms and law offices? What about advertising agencies? Do training firms count? What part of the revenue of the large software development and systems integration firms are you counting?

Suffice it to say, there are a lot of management consultants and the industry makes a lot of money.

The consulting industry has many of the characteristics of a fragmented market. It has:

- **Low barriers to entry** – Someone once defined a consultant as "someone with a black briefcase more than fifty miles from home."
- **Many competitors** – there are literally millions of consulting firms globally ranging in size from Deloitte with more than 280,000 employees to millions of small firms with one to three consultants, including independent practitioners.
- **No real economies of scale** - the predominant delivery mechanism in consulting is consultants' time, otherwise known as billable hours. You can't really scale people, there is no multiplier, or as independent consultants frequently moan, "You can't earn money without showing up." The Covid pandemic taught clients and consultants that video conferencing could take the place of some on-site work, but it is still billable hours including all the preparation that goes into a one-hour video call.

Fragmented industries often have significant turnover of firms, lots of startups, many failures, and mergers and acquisitions between smaller and larger players.

The consulting industry also has many of the characteristics of an oligopoly. Much of the revenue, prestige and press are controlled by a few firms. Industry consolidation has meant that the biggest players have gotten bigger, but the top two categories haven't changed much since 1980. This is how the press and so most clients think of the industry.

- **The Big Three** – McKinsey & Company, Boston Consulting Group (BCG), and Bain and Company all got their start as strategy firms but have become more generalist firms. They are the most prestigious firms to hire. The expression "No board every fired a CEO for hiring McKinsey" could easily be applied to the other two firms. The big three have had a golden gloss since the 1970s and so have an edge at attracting both clients and consulting talent.
- **The Big Four** – Deloitte, PricewaterhouseCoopers (PwC) Ernst & Young (EY), and Klynveld Peat Marwick Goerdeler (KPMG) are the consolidated firms of the Big Eight that were around when I started. These firms all started as accounting and auditing firms that moved into management consulting and systems integration.
- **The Third Mega-Tier** – Accenture, Booz Allen Hamilton, Capgemini, Cognizant, Kearny, Hitachi Vantara Consulting, IBM Consulting Services, Infosys, Tata Consulting, and others make up this category. Many of these firms focus on information technology and systems integration. I must note, too, that many of these firms are **huge**, with more employees and greater revenue than firms in the first two tiers, and offer distinct markets and service specialties. Because they aren't top three or former accounting firms, the press describes them as "third tier." I've followed that rubric, but do not discount them. They are formidable.
- **Boutique Firms** - Some of these firms are quite prestigious to work for as they are known for a particular methodology or in-

dustry expertise. There are too many to name all, but a few examples are L.E.K., Roland Berger, Mercer, Huron, Oliver Wyman, The Keystone Group, and Putnam Associates.

Should Accenture, Capgemini, L.E.K., or Kearny be in a separate tier? Are the HR firms like Mercer, Oliver Wyman, Aon Hewitt, Korn Ferry, or Willis, Towers, Watson really boutiques? One could endlessly debate which firm belongs in which groups, and the list here is by no means exhaustive, but the top two groups certainly garner most of the press about the industry. The top groups are most likely to receive a Request For Proposal (RFP) from the largest clients. They often set billing rates and new entrant salaries, and that hasn't changed much since I started.

That is not to say that all the firms in all four groups control a majority of industry revenue. While accurate figures are hard to come by, the millions of small firms and solo practitioners all make a good living. Some even work for large clients right alongside teams from huge consultancies. I know this for a fact because I was often in that situation.

Consulting industry history

Some will point out that there have always been advisors to leaders, the Bible story of Joseph interpreting Pharaoh's dream of seven fat cows and seven lean cows and recommending a warehousing and inventory management solution, for example. It is true that advisors have long existed, but they were usually individuals, independent or internal consultants. Groups of advisors tended to have a religious component to their work. So I will start with the late nineteenth and early twentieth century, the beginnings of the profession as we know it today.

The very beginnings: Arthur D. Little and Frederick Winslow Taylor

Most sources agree that the first consulting firm was started by Massachusetts Institute of Technology chemistry professor Arthur Dehon Little in 1886. His firm Arthur D. Little (ADL) is still around today. When I grew up in Boston in the 1950s Arthur D. Little was mostly a research firm at the forefront of the chemical catalyst and emerging computer and space industries. If someone's father worked at ADL kids would joke about the brains that ran in that family.

From the beginning ADL offered highly analytic problem solving. Evidently Professor Little was against systemization and standardization. He believed each problem was unique and deserved a unique solution.

Frederick Winslow Taylor, the author of *Principles of Scientific Management* (1911), believed in systemization; Taylor was the first industrial operations researcher. He analyzed time and motion of workers to find the "one best way," the most efficient sequence of moves. Then he wrote rules to standardize the process for all workers to follow. As his practice grew he took these standard processes to other clients.

Little and Taylor came to consulting from opposite perspectives. Professor Little was a college professor; Taylor refused to go to Harvard and joined a factory in Philadelphia. Little's clients were executives and technical managers; Taylor's clients were plant managers and he worked directly with front line workers. These two men started two different streams of consulting that still exist today, **content** (Little) and **process** (Taylor):

- Content consulting is embodied in the Strategy firm, which brings new ideas, and is often focused on innovation, new products, markets and technologies (new revenue).
- Process consulting is found in the Operations firm, which focuses on continuous incremental improvement, (repeat buying and share of wallet), and automation technologies (improved cycle time).

There are many overlaps and hybrids over the history of consulting, but stay with me for a bit. Let's look at a few historical events and examples and see how this bears out.

Content stream continues

In 1914 Edwin G. Booz, with a masters in psychology and a bachelors in economics from Northwestern University's Kellogg School, founded

Business Research Service, which became Booz Allen Hamilton. Booz's original mission statement states that senior managers needed "candid advice and an outside perspective on their businesses." The firm became the first to work for both corporations and governments and served both markets until it spun off Booz & Company, the corporate business, to focus on government. (Booz & Co became Strategy &, which acquired Katzenbach Partners long after I left. Both are part of PwC today.)

In 1926 James O. McKinsey, a University of Chicago professor, founded McKinsey and Company Accountants and Consulting Engineers. McKinsey's clients were executives and his first partner was Andrew Thomas Kearney who ran the Chicago office. The firm split up when McKinsey died unexpectedly in 1937.

Marvin Bower, the second McKinsey partner who ran the New York office, ultimately bought the name McKinsey & Company and the Chicago office became AT Kearney, or just Kearney as it is called today.

People at McKinsey have an almost religious reverence for Marvin Bower who resurrected the New York office and built the firm. Bower served as the managing director of McKinsey & Company from 1950 to1967, but had a major role in the firm and remained a director until 1992 even though he voluntarily sold his shares back to the firm at age 60 in 1963. Bower is widely credited with the "professionalization" of the consulting field.

The process improvement stream continues

Frederick Taylor collaborated with Morris Cooke. Cooke had an engineering degree from Lehigh University in Pennsylvania, but went to work as a machinist for his first few years and formed a consulting firm in 1903. Later, he was quite active in the rural electrification projects of the 1920s and 1930s.

Another of Taylor's team was Henry Gantt, another degreed engineer (Johns Hopkins) who worked as a machinist and draftsman. Gantt met Taylor at Midvale Steel and Bethlehem Steel. Gantt is known for the ubiquitous project management tool the Gantt chart, which he created so that workers could understand the timing of their work and relationships to others' tasks.

GANTT CHART

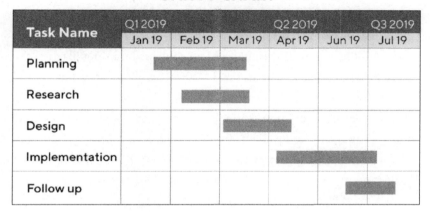

Task Name	Q1 2019			Q2 2019		Q3 2019
	Jan 19	Feb 19	Mar 19	Apr 19	Jun 19	Jul 19
Planning						
Research						
Design						
Implementation						
Follow up						

Frederick Taylor's major competitor was Frank Bunker Gilbreth. Gilbreth founded Frank B. Gilbreth Inc. with his wife Lillian in 1903, and they called themselves consulting engineers or efficiency experts. Like Taylor, Gilbreth began work as a manual laborer, a bricklayer's assistant, but he soon looked for the "one best way." Taylor and Gilbreth had what was often called a "war," so when Gilbreth died in 1924, apparently Taylor rejoiced a bit. Then Lillian Moller Gilbreth took over Frank B. Gilbreth, Inc. and ran it successfully for years. The Gilbreths had twelve children and were the subject of two books by their son Frank and daughter Ernestine, *Cheaper by the Dozen* and *Belles on their Toes*. Both books were made into feature films in the early 1950s (different from the much later Steve Martin movie).

The Gilbreths are widely credited as the parents of process improvement. Process consulting history includes Walter Shewhart of Bell Labs who created statistical process control and Plan-Do-Check-Act in the 1920s. It continues in the work of Dr. W. Edwards Deming and Dr. Joseph Juran, both graduates of the Bell System under Walter Shewhart. Deming focused on statistical process control while Juran discovered the little known work of Vilfredo Pareto, a nineteenth century Italian engineer who discovered that 20 percent of pea pods produced 80 percent of the pea crop; he went on to conduct a study to show that 20 percent of the Italian population controlled 80 percent of the country's wealth. Juran continued this research and demonstrated that 20 percent of causes produced 80 percent of the effects of a problem. Juran popularized the Pareto Principle, also known as the 80/20 rule and the "trivial many and critical few."

Both Deming and Juran, founders of the quality movement, were unsuccessful in attracting clients in the United States, but Japanese man-ufacturers welcomed them with open arms. As a result, they spent the 1950s through much of the 1970s improving Japanese businesses.

The process improvement stream of consulting took on new life in the early 1970s. Dr. Deming's return to the US caused or coincided with the birth of the quality movement of the 1980s which in turn led to the development of Lean and Six Sigma in the 1990s, an approach still in use today. Firms like Alexander Proudfoot, which bought Phil Crosby's firm (*Quality is Free*) begat United Research Company, founded by David Teiger in 1973. In 1989 Teiger bought The Management Analysis Center (The M.A.C. Group) and launched Gemini Consulting where I worked toward the end of the reengineering craze. The 1990s saw an explosion of re-engineering projects for Gemini and competitor CSC Index. Jim Champy wrote the book *Re-Engineering the Corporation* with Michael Hammer in 1993. Jim Champy's Index was bought by Com-puter Sciences Corporation, and CSC Index and Gemini were very hot firms for a while. The Gemini merger was funded by the French com-puter firm Sogeti, which owned the combination of the French computer firm CAP and the US firm Gemini Computer Services. The firm is today called Capgemini, one of the leading firms in the "digital trans-formation" space.

The 1960s and 1970s: BCG and the rebirth of content

During the late 1940s and 1950s McKinsey, Arthur D. Little, and Booz Allen Hamilton seem to have done a lot of export market studies and Organizational Design for US companies. The latter projects often consisted of replicating first the departmental structure learned at DuPont and then the product/market structures learned from Alfred P. Sloan at General Motors, "a car for every wallet."

THE BOSTON BOX

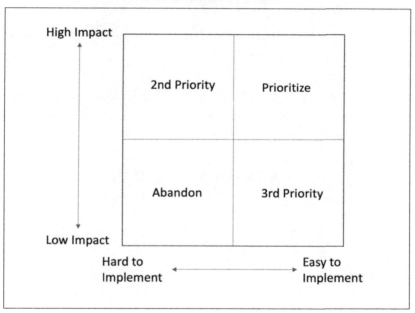

In 1963, Bruce Henderson left ADL to create an internal consulting firm for a bank. After the project was done Henderson formed the Boston Consulting Group (BCG) as a strategy firm. BCG developed several strategic frameworks that seem very simple by today's standards:

The Boston Box was a simple two-by-two matrix used to rationalize current strategic activities.

THE GROWTH SHARE MATRIX

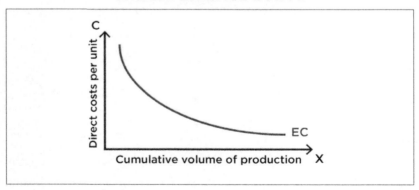

The Growth Share Matrix with its "Milk Cash Cows, Invest In Stars, Divest Dogs, and Fix Problem Children" was used to rationalize a portfolio of businesses.

THE EXPERIENCE CURVE

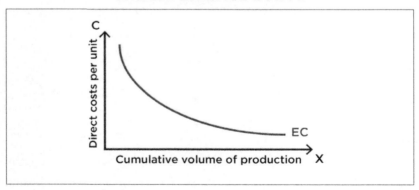

The Experience Curve showed how learning occurred with cumulative production volume thereby reducing costs. It is a simple idea, "practice makes us better," but it was based upon correlation analysis of detailed production and cost data that showed how businesses learned more efficient ways of doing things over time. Some thought this happened automatically; the wise realized that you had to actively manage learning from experience and adopt the lessons to reduce costs.

These simple concepts revolutionized strategy consulting.

As we've already seen, the industry grows when consultants leave and start new firms. (Of course, if the market slows there is consolidation, but when did an entrepreneur ever worry about that?)

In 1973, Bruce Henderson decided to accelerate with internal competition. He created three internal firms, red, blue, green. The leader of the blue team, Bill Bain, developed a different model of consulting with key client Union Carbide. Rather than the usual six- to eight-week study, Bain sold a $25,000 per month retainer and took responsibility for longer-term results. Henderson and other BCG partners objected to the risk. Bill Bain left (with Union Carbide) and formed Bain & Company.

The model was extraordinarily successful; Bain grew exponentially. When I worked for Forum, Bain was a client and we were invited to the Bain holiday party. I remember a lot of people my age passionately singing "BAIN -we're gonna grow forever!" to the tune from the 1980 film *Fame*. Bain is now one of the Big Three, all of whom have some retainer contracts. Bain also created Bain Capital to capitalize on the long-term results they were achieving with a private equity model.

The industry often grows by dispersion: ADL spawned BCG, which spawned Bain, which spawned LEK and Parthenon. McKinsey tended to keep its partners in the firm after the split with AT Kearney, but Jon Katzenbach of Katzenbach Partners left McKinsey when he was over the mandatory retirement age with the firm's blessing. Often spinoff firms run into trouble at the first recession and are acquired. Katzenbach Partners was acquired by Booz in 2007 and is now part of PwC.

The other kind of content firm -Technology and Systems Integrators

I frequently self-describe as the "original late adopter," so I am probably not the best source for the history of technology consulting, despite the fact that my mother became a computer programmer in 1956. Here is my limited understanding of this industry.

These days, Information Technology (IT) consultants may work for the Chief Executive Officer (CEO) or the Chief Information Officer (CIO) delivering such services as IT strategy, IT architecture planning, IT Security, or Enterprise Requirements Planning (ERP) services. Or they may work for various department heads for services such as data analytics, IT implementation, software management and systems integration.

Let's just think for a minute about what has happened to computer technology in the thirty-seven years that I was a consultant.

- **Hardware** – Mainframes, mini-computers like DEC PDP-8 and the IBM 360 (my mother was on the operating system programming team in the early '60s and the 360 was still in operation in the 1980s), Personal Computers (PCs and Macs), laptops, tablets, flip-phones, smart phones.
- **Software** - Operating systems for all of the above written in multiple languages
- **Systems and Systems software** - Financial and Management Accounting, Production Planning, Inventory management, materials requirements planning, Enterprise Requirements Planning (ERP providers like German firm SAP cast a huge shadow) HR Systems (PeopleSoft and the long awaited SAP HR Module) Customer Relationship Management (Oracle, Salesforce.com), Internet, Social Media, media presence and the algorithms and Big Data analytics that go with them.
- **Services** -There were always services firms, large ones like Electronic Data Systems started by H. Ross Perot, sold to GM in the 1980s and spun off in the 90s. There were also thousands of small firms.

Accounting systems were the first to be automated so it is easy to understand how the Big Eight and now Big Four got into IT, including Accenture (which was born after Arthur Anderson spun off the consulting business, post Enron).

Then every technology manufacturer - IBM, Hitachi, NTT - got into consulting. Following them were the Indian Data Center outsourcers such as Infosys and Wipro and multi-industry, multinational Tata. Now even the Big Three, Booz Allen Hamilton and newer firms like Cognizant, and Virtusa are all in IT chasing "Digital Transformation," the latest service offering craze.

The other kind of process firm – Organization or Human Resources consultants

Someone once told me, "You know the problem with organizational consultants? You guys can't get organized." Bada boom.

There is some truth to this. Much of the specialized content of human resource consulting firms comes from academic research applied to businesses by individual professors. Perhaps the most famous of these research studies are what were known as the Hawthorne studies, named for the Hawthorne factory of Western Electric, a part of the Bell System.

At Hawthorne George Elton Mayo, an MIT professor, and Fritz Roethlisberger from Harvard studied workers across the plant from 1924 to 1932. They first studied the effects of lighting and then moved on to other physical environmental factors. What they discovered was that simply paying attention to workers, asking them questions about the best way to do the work and allowing participation, produced gains in productivity far exceeding any physical changes to the environment. Later this was named the "Hawthorne effect."

The Hawthorne studies launched a field of study called the Human Relations Movement. Researchers such as Kurt Lewin studied "group dynamics" through techniques called "action learning." At the Tavistock Institute on Human Relations in the United Kingdom researchers like Elliott Jacques, and Wilfred Bion demonstrated the effects of participation and supervised group dynamics on motivation and performance. Professor George Litwin and his graduate student Bob Stringer at Harvard Business School demonstrated that what Kurt Lewin called "organizational climate" was affected by management practice and instrumental in driving motivation and performance.

Kurt Lewin is considered by many to be the father of the field of Organization Development. Many of these ideas have their roots with earlier researchers such as Mary Parker Follett who worked with Theodore Roosevelt and first posited such ideas as participative management, and horizontal organization, based upon guiding values, groups and teamwork.

Some of the academic findings of the Human Relations and Organization Development Movements made it into what human resource consultants deliver today. Too much has been ignored by business.

Now consultants that deal with the "people stuff" fit into many categories: training consultants; organization development firms; organization design firms; headhunters and recruiters; leadership coaches; human resource, legal, and regulatory advisors; diversity, equity and inclusion advisors; employee benefits firms; industrial and organizational psychologists; and organizational climate and culture specialists, to name a few.

So part of the problem is that organizational and human resource consultants haven't gotten organized, or that the research they espouse is viewed as "squishy" compared to strategy or process improvement. Perhaps human resource consultants struggle to get beyond the boutique level because they have divided into many different specialties with little overlap or synergy among them.

However, there has been some expansion in recent years. Executive recruiters like Heidrick and Struggles and Korn Ferry have expanded into leadership assessment and development. Training firms like Achieve Forum have moved from management and leadership training into leadership coaching and organizational climate work.

I do think that recent mergers have created some inherent conflicts of interest. Employee benefit firm Aon Hewitt is owned by Aon Financial service, Towers Watson is owned by British insurance firm Willis, and Oliver Wyman is owned by Marsh McClelland. It is tough for employee benefit firms to be credible in all other disciplines or to appear objective in recommending health and welfare insurance policies when said recommendations or policies are among the parent insurance company's products.

Looking at the antecedent firms may increase client view of credibility. Oliver Wyman has some credibility due to its heritage firms - Temple, Barker, and Sloane, Strategic Planning Associates. Also Mercer Delta, the firm started by David Nadler, should have greater credibility in organizational development, but its financial industry ownership undermines that in my view.

Much organizational research is still done by university professors. Otherwise, many organizational firms are boutique firms, while some are acquired by the Big Four or other larger firms. Firms in the top three tiers all say they are in organizational consulting.

120 years of consulting history - what does it mean to you?

I once observed two Organizational Development gurus arguing. "Spare me the history," said one. "The only thing that matters is action. What are you going to do?" "No, history is important," said the other. It sets the context for action."

Here are take-aways from this history:

Every firm is different

- **Where a firm came from** and its history and where it sits in the fragmented oligopoly determine how hard it has to work to get clients, what kind of jobs it offers, and how it treats its people.
- **The disciplines and service offerings a firm is known for** (strategy, organization, process improvement, technology, etc.) often dictate hiring and the promotion ladder. These days when every firm seems to do everything, it's worth looking at Wikipedia and the firm's website to understand its history, which will have an impact upon culture and the way certain capabilities are valued.

- **Content consulting and process consulting** focus on different audiences, executives vs. the workforce, respectively. Content sells answers (strategy and innovation), and process trades in questions (methodology and improvement).If a firm says it combine these approaches, be wary; I never saw that work.

How firms differ – organization and job structure

The client industry - discipline matrix

Most consulting firms are structured in a matrix between:

- The client industry, e.g., chemicals, financial services, automotive. This is where business is sold and projects are conducted.
- The discipline, e.g., strategy, organization, finance, technology, etc. This is where service offerings are developed.

A quick look at a firm's website will give you a picture of the work they do. Smaller firms may specialize in one or two industries and limited service offerings. Large firms will list many industries and disciplines. What do they list first - industries or functions? This isn't foolproof, but if they list industries first, it's likely that client industry verticals hold the power; if they list functions or disciplines or services first, that may indicate a more balanced power structure. Also look at their publications or insights page. This will tell you what kind of business they are actively seeking. Does it fit with the firm's history or are they diversifying?

Geography

Larger firms will have geography as a third element to the matrix. Different offices of the same firm can be quite different. Some of that is history. Did they acquire a firm that is the basis of that office? Or it may be that a given office reflects local client industries. There are a lot of Fortune 500 corporate headquarters in New York City for strategy, but local operational work is most likely in financial services or media. Office size will often indicate promotional opportunities; nearby industries are where you will likely go if you transition out to a client.

Specialist -generalist

Some firms expect that new entrants will come in with some industry or discipline expertise and they expect Newbies to "stay in lane." As a result, new entrants tend to work in the same industries over and over and do similar types of projects. Breaking out and extending capabilities is difficult. This "stay in lane" career track happens in manufacturing, chemicals, oil and gas industries and in sales/marketing, technology and human resource disciplines.

Other firms pride themselves in building cross-industry generalists. These firms often have cross-industry, multidisciplinary training for new entrants. They also tend to work in teams with many junior people so that there is always help available.

This type of job structure is hard to research online. Some firms provide this information in recruiting materials and the Join Our Team page of their website, but often the only way to find out is to ask people who work there.

Climate and culture

The late Dr. Sumantra Ghoshal, who taught at the London Business School and wrote many books on leadership and management, used to describe Organizational Climate and Culture as "the smell of the place." He didn't disparage the rigorous research in these areas, but did maintain that many job seekers could "feel" what a business was like to work in by visiting offices and talking to people.

Firm cultures are different. Gemini Consulting was an intense team-centered environment. These days whenever alumni connect in any way they always talk about the "magic culture." You could join a team anywhere in the world and feel instantly at home. In the interview process, I met with a dozen people and was invited to attend and contribute to a discipline meeting. I felt that this was also a team assessment. It turned out I was correct. Gemini had a team consensus decision process for new hires.

Katzenbach Partners was a McKinsey spinoff. One of the founders wrote *The Wisdom of Teams*. Despite that, the firm established fewer team processes and in many ways felt more hierarchical. We did multiple interviews, but rarely saw candidates in a team setting.

Look at how the firm recruits and who they send to recruit (recruiters? consultants? with what tenure?). How does the firm describe itself? How does the recruiter describe the firm? If you are invited to an office, look at how people treat you, where they are sitting, and the design of the offices – in short, the smell of the place.

PROJECT STRUCTURE AS A JOB INDICATOR

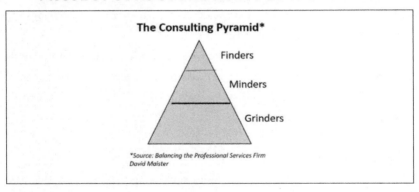

The Consulting Pyramid*

Finders

Minders

Grinders

*Source: Balancing the Professional Services Firm
David Maister

If you can get a look at how the organization structures a project it may give you an indication of what the job will be like. All consulting firms have a similar structure. There are partners, Pros who find the work; mid-career consultants who manage or "mind" the work; and Newbies like you who do the work or "grind it out." Dr. David Maister of Harvard was the first to describe this pyramid. (Maister's Finders, Minders, and Grinders nomenclature is roughly the same structural division as Newbies, Journeymen, and Pros. Maister describes roles by the primary work they do and I describe increasing capability.) Consulting firms now have at least six levels, but the concept remains the same. **The idea is to have the work done by the lowest level possible with the greatest compensation multiplier so the firm makes money.**

The standard is an equilateral triangle with four to five grinders to a minder. A firm can be more profitable with wider pyramids, eight to ten grinders to a minder, but that requires doing the same type of project over and over again and means routinized work. When I entered consulting, Anderson Consulting and their consultants were called "AN-droids" who carried "the book." Accenture, the descendant firm, may operate differently, but the IT work they do and history suggest a similar structure.

PYRAMID SHAPE INDICATES FIRM PROJECT TYPE

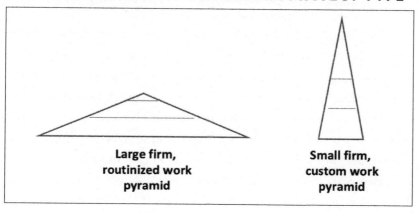

**Large firm,
routinized work
pyramid**

**Small firm,
custom work
pyramid**

If the pyramid is narrow, two grinders to a minder, it's usually in a small firm, where everybody does everything. The work is often customized with every project, but the scope can be narrow with one or two service offerings. Opportunities to learn within the narrow scope are often greatest here, but advancement is limited.

Training, staffing and promotion
The biggest determinants of the consulting job for new entrants is how

the firm trains, staffs projects, and promotes people.

Because the industry consolidates (mergers) and fragments (startups and spinoffs), **the competencies you develop are key to career longevity.** What kind of induction training do they do? How is on-the-job project training handled - is there a buddy system or project mentor, for example? What about ongoing training?

Because I went on to work for five different firms I was a "Newbie" five times. Becoming a new entrant in any firm is tough. Whether you are entering from undergraduate or graduate school or after ten years of experience in an industry you have a lot to learn. Being called a Newbie doesn't help. It may seem like everything you have learned to date - in fact everything that got you hired - is being discarded.

There are some firms that are better than others at "onboarding new hires." (Sorry, you will learn that consultants make nouns into verbs with abandon. So there is teaming, and impacting, as well as onboarding. Consultants are not the only ones who do this, but it is one of our most amusing qualities.)

Onboarding is the process of inducting a new hire and may include initial training and acculturation. Some firms have their own language and give new entrants a dictionary. (Gemini Consulting did that and even gave it to clients at the beginning of engagements. Some clients found that "cute;" others were incredulous, and a few thought us arrogant.)

Gemini actually had one of the best induction processes I experienced. There were two weeks (including a weekend) of intensive residential training called Gemini Skills Workshop. I learned the consulting process by actively working as part of a consulting team, analysis to presentation. There were lectures, tours of the back office at headquarters, and talks by field consultants and clients. I remember not sleeping much and one helluva dinner and party at the end of the second week.

The Forum Corporation was also good at induction training, which you might expect from a training company.

There was training about its sales and management training products. Everyone had to take every course and learn to deliver some training.

They had an induction course called Flipchart 101 that taught us how to write legibly on flipcharts while talking to a group. I took that course four times before they gave up on my magic-marker handwriting. Later, as Forum expanded into consulting, it offered more training and sent me to outside workshops and university programs.

By contrast, when I joined Katzenbach Partners, I was consultant number six and employee number seven. I went directly to work on a project. The three founding partners had worked only at McKinsey and later used the phrase MTA to describe their ideal hire, a McKinsey Trained Associate. They quickly realized I wasn't an MTA and didn't know what to do with me, but were nice about it. As the firm grew, they had training for new associates, some of which I led.

How do they staff projects? Is it by local geography, so you only do projects in the local office? Or is it global, so you could work for six weeks in Egypt and the next month you'll be in Vietnam? Degree of travel will shape the job. Some want to work in consulting for the travel, but many leave the field because it gets old. How honest is the firm about this and how are they managing it? Will you consistently work with new people or largely with the same team?

What are the levels and criteria for promotion? At junior levels the criteria will be the quality of analysis and meeting delivery timelines. What else? When will you be expected to manage team mates? When will you have client relationship responsibilities? What about business development? (As previously noted, some consultants are allergic to the word "selling" even though bringing in new clients is often the most important criterion for promotion to partner.)

These questions are important but rarely described anywhere. You can do a "What's it like to work at _____?" search and find Glass Door, Indeed, or Quora reviews and occasionally some LinkedIn posts. But companies have learned to flood review sites with "happy staffers" to counteract one disgruntled consultant. My advice is to actually talk to some folks.

One final note: Economics 101

Consulting firms, like a lot of B2B services, are sensitive to business cycles. When a recession hits, one of the first reactions at client firms is "cut the consulting budget." This hits smaller consulting firms harder, and consultants tied to recession-sensitive industries like automotive still harder. Big retainer contracts, like Bain's and systems integrators', are less affected by the business cycle.

Bottom line: If you're thinking about a career in consulting, investigate the field. OK, you are reading this book (thank you), but there is a lot more you can do. You will have a great many more resources than I did in 1979 and that might be more difficult because you'll need to evaluate and validate all that you discover. Find out about the work, consider the downsides, research firms, find those that interest you, **talk to people** and apply. Prepare i.e., read a book or watch YouTube videos on case interviewing, and **practice interviewing**. Many university and/or business schools offer short courses on interviewing and getting hired by consulting firms. Take one.

If you do get an offer - or maybe even before you apply - talk with people at the level you are joining. Some firms treat Newbies better than others. Yes, you will be learning a new field, but that shouldn't mean working all the time, being treated like a child, or entering indentured servitude. Ask to see any contracts you might be asked to sign; get an attorney's advice on non-disclosure agreements (NDAs) and "non-compete" clauses. In my experience those are all too often an indicator of firms that use the law to keep people they don't treat well.

Seems obvious, I know, but in the next chapters I will tell you about what I actually did and what I wish I knew when I was starting to go down the consulting road.

CHAPTER 2

TRAJECTORY OF A CONSULTING CAREER

As mentioned earlier, there are three levels in consulting. Others call them analyst, manager, and partner or other similar names. Don't confuse this with the many job titles consulting firms give consultants to give more opportunity for promotion. I've called them Newbie, Journeyman, and Pro to describe the three different jobs –

- Do the work – Newbie
- Manage the work – Journeyman
- Sell the work – Pro

Remember, everyone adds their new responsibility to the previous one, so Journeymen do some work as well as manage and Pros do some work and manage as well as sell.

The drawing below shows a consulting career trajectory including how consultants come into a firm and some of the career path choices they face along the way.

CONSULTING CAREER TRAJECTORY

Becoming a Newbie

As can be seen on the diagram above, there are different paths for Newbies to enter consulting.

Some come into an analyst role directly from an undergraduate program. These folks may start as an intern in the summer after their junior year. Analysts do a lot of Excel data analysis and PowerPoint slide drafting. Some intern analysts are hired upon graduation and work for two years. If they want to stay in consulting, they go to graduate school to get a Master of Business Administration (MBA) or law degree. An infinitesimal percentage are sponsored by the consulting firm for their master's degree provided they return to the firm for an agreed period.

The biggest Newbie path is post-MBA or other graduate degree. A few are hired from industry with four to eight years of experience. Consulting firms also hire people from industry who become industry or discipline specialists, and they hire executives who have worked at senior levels as direct sales partners (rainmakers).

However a Newbie enters, he or she is still a Newbie. That may feel like all previous experience is being disregarded, that the Newbie is treated as ignorant. Some firms are better at "on-boarding" Newbies than others, but consulting is a unique industry and until Newbies demonstrate consulting capability there is a steep learning curve.

Becoming a Journeyman

Journeymen may have the toughest job in consulting. They manage the team, keeping people on task and not burned out. They manage project deliverables, keeping the project on time and on budget. They manage the client, getting the inputs needed and keeping the client appropriately apprised of findings and progress. Finally, they manage the partner.

Partner management may seem inappropriate. The partner is generally more experienced and sold the work based upon his or her relationship with the client. But partners are also frequently off-site selling other work or touching base with other projects and prospects. This means the partner is often out of touch with the day-to-day work. The partner must be updated constantly and consistently and <u>be onsite</u> at just the right time. That takes management skill. Some partners work hand-in-glove with managers. Some are the proverbial "bull-in-a-china-shop."

Promo or no-go

On the Trajectory diagram, there are curved arrows to the left for each role category. These show people leaving the firm both voluntarily and involuntarily. Previously firms had a policy called "up or out." There was a proscribed period young consultants were to spend at each stage of their career – one to two years as analyst, two years as associate, and so on. Anyone who wasn't ready to be promoted was asked to leave.

Balancing staffing is one of the supreme management challenges in a consulting firm. Partners constantly find projects and need staff. New service offerings are created and that requires staff. When a firm is humming, everyone is operating at a level above their current job and there is a full pipeline of new hires flowing. There is little room for the "late bloomer."

Human resources language has reached consulting and "up or out" is now much more staff focused. "Up or out" is called "grow or go" with staff being offered many more learning opportunities before being booted out the door. This is certainly true of The Big Three (McKinsey, Boston Consulting Group, and Bain) and probably true of other large firms (PwC, Accenture, Capgemini, Deloitte, KPMG, EY, etc.). Larger firms also soften the blow with strong outplacement departments. This gives them a future client development advantage as they often sell to alumni of the firm. Smaller firms may be slower or less rigid about deselection, but they rarely have outplacement.

Pros: direct and indirect sellers

All levels do consulting work, even Pros, especially those partners who have risen through the ranks. Those folks are likely to jump on Excel or PowerPoint anytime. But the system is set up so as a consultant rises the portion of the job spent selling increases.

Journeymen sell extensions (same client, more of the same project work) and expansions (different client buying center, same or different project work). Pros bring in new clients. There are two different career paths for Pros that involve two different kinds of selling.

Some Pros pursue direct sales, calling on executives to secure new projects. Other Pros sell through indirect sales and/or thought leadership, attracting new clients through new research, service offerings and publications. This choice begins at the Journeyman level.

Journeymen direct sellers build and maintain client relationships at their level, and as those people rise to senior levels they sell new projects to them directly as Pros. A second group of Journeymen and Pros focus on researching and developing new services offerings. These attract clients indirectly through published articles and books. Some firms, especially smaller firms, expect senior people to follow both paths simultaneously, which doesn't always work.

The secret to a long career as a direct-selling Pro is to pick the people who are rising at corporations, especially those younger than yourself.

The secret to a long consulting career as thought leader is to publish. Pros working into their eighties and nineties - W. Edwards Deming, Joseph Juran, Peter Drucker, Jon Katzenbach, and Tom Peters come to mind - invariably have multiple best-selling books and busy speaking schedules.

There are two choices any consultant will have to make. First, what happens when you are faced with Promo or-no go? And second, if you want to be a Pro, will you be a rainmaker or a thought leader? Both decisions are covered more extensively in the section "Forks in the Road: Later Career Issues."

To be or not to be: that is the question

Whether to suffer the slings and arrows of… being a consultant or not. Choosing to be a consultant will always involve the questions of why, when, what and how.

Why?

You'll probably be asked this in your first interview and you'll say that you "like to solve problems in a fast-paced team environment" or words to that effect. This book isn't interview training. Don't wait for the interview; ask yourself why do you want to be a consultant?

Some good reasons to become a consultant are that you like:

- **Business** and immersion in different types of businesses.
- **Learning.** You are good at absorbing a lot of data and quickly seeing patterns.
- **Solving complex problems.** You enjoy defining a problem, analyzing causes, producing measurable results.
- **To be helpful and don't crave credit.** (It's the client's business.)
- **Working with teams of smart people.**
- **The money.** You need to pay off student loans. (Obviously, don't say this in an interview, but it is a reason many people enter a field where starting salaries are relatively high.)

Some bad reasons to become a consultant:

- **The money**. Yeah, starting salaries are high, but they level out and you will work very hard for what you earn. If you want to be rich, become a tech entrepreneur or an investment banker.
- **The prestige.** OK, the Tumi rolling suitcase and computer bag are cool and telling "client disguised" war stories at parties is fun, but it wears thin quickly, for you <u>and</u> your friends.
- **The travel.** When you realize that you are working in Paris or Bangkok, but only see the inside of office buildings, hotels, rental cars and airports, the magic of travel wears off. Sure you can stay over for personal travel, but most weeks you just want to go home.
- **Easy respect from senior managers.** Consultants get opportunities to talk with executives, but respect comes from the analysis they do and the knowledge and skill they acquire over time.
- **Be a star.** Consultants don't get credit for results; clients do. Standing ovations are so rare as to be non-existent.
- **Learn people management skills**. I saw some great people managers in consulting, but I can count them on my fingers. Constantly changing project teams, speed of delivery, and consultant egos don't create fertile ground to grow people managers.

When?

As shown in the Trajectory diagram, consultants typically enter the field at four junctures. Pick which works the best for you:

- **From undergraduate school**. Undergrad hires have an inside track to the field because, if you are good, you get a lot of experience and exposure early. You can pay off student loans or save for graduate school. You can find out if the field is right for you and if it isn't you'll have an impressive first job on your resume. However, it is a tough job to get and you may not have much of a life outside of work for the first two years.
- **From graduate school.** This used to be mostly MBAs and lawyers, but has expanded to other graduate degrees. You'll have many of

the same advantages and disadvantages as an undergraduate hire, but the expectation to "hit the ground running" is higher and competition is greater.

- **After 5-10 years in industry or academia.** This group is usually hired for industry or discipline expertise (marketing, operations, etc.). They may face a "grow or go" choice in three to five years. The biggest downside is that you may feel like your previous experience isn't respected. You may be staffed with younger people with less real world experience who are treated better because they have learned consulting capabilities.

- **After 10-15 years in industry or academia.** This group may be hired for industry or discipline experience, but is usually hired for their contacts, client acquisition (selling), and/or advanced service offering development. The best rainmakers in consulting learn quickly how a project works and come up the ranks from inside the firm.

What kind of firm?

In the last chapter we talked about the kinds of consulting firms, discipline specialists (strategy, marketing, operations, human resources, technology, etc.) and industry specialists. Choose what interests you and where the greatest opportunities lie.

Large firms offer more training, broader project variety, and a more generalist orientation, but they are often more rigid in promotion criteria for "up or out" or "grow or go" choice points. Large firms have more prestige and are good places to be from as you move into industry. Smaller firms often offer more opportunity more quickly. They may be less rigid in "up or out," but they are also more susceptible to changes in the business cycle.

Firms with a content orientation sell answers and tend to write reports and make recommendations as an end product. Project length is often three to six months. Disciplines (strategy, marketing, certain types of financial analysis) lend themselves to content orientation. On the other hand, process-oriented firms sell the process and tend to stay longer with the client during orientation. Process improvement, organization development, and management accounting lend themselves to a process orientation.

How?

In the last chapter I encouraged you to look at websites and recruiting materials and to read evaluations on sites like Glass Door or Indeed, but mostly to talk to people who work there. Aside from content and process considerations, pay attention to how the firm talks about staffing, training, and promotion.

Unanticipated consequences of a consulting career

Like lawyers, consultants must put up with the jokes about their profession. One joke says a lot about the career.

> "If you introduce yourself to your neighbor three times,
> you might be a consultant."

Constant travel, meeting new people all the time, can be quite disorienting. The lifestyle is a challenge. Finding a spouse, if you're interested, is hard and maintaining relationships is harder Many long-term consultants are divorced. Also, it is difficult to stay in touch with your friends and neighbors when you are home only on weekends. It means no after-work sports or weekday barbeques, no mid-week book clubs, yoga classes, or PTA meetings. Some firms have programs to reduce this strain by reduced travel, family leave, etc. It is worth planning how you'll manage these issues.

I had to pay attention to staying in shape. For me that meant early morning workouts in the hotel fitness room. It wasn't my ideal workout time, but the end of the day was too unpredictable and the inevitable Thursday night team event –"Big Food" – made it absolutely necessary.

Other downsides of a consulting career

The money is good, but not great. The travel isn't what you thought. Being a consultant is tough on relationships. What else?

Work friends are tough to find. Many projects are staffed from several offices, so even if you wanted to spend more time with people you worked with for five days, they go home to a different city on the weekend. Further, while some projects are year-long, most engagements are shorter, so if you work for a big firm your work mates are changing every three months.

Some firms staff groups of people together to combat this. These are usually smaller firms, or those with more local client bases, but that typically means a trade-off for less interesting work.

Upsides of consulting

Why would anyone want this job? Here are my answers to that question:

The variety of the work. Every few months I worked on a different problem - revenue growth, profit growth, people stuff – in different companies and industries. It was always changing.

The challenge of the work. Very few companies hire consultants to solve "dead-easy" problems. Even if they were hiring you as an "extra pair of hands," there was a reason they didn't just hire a Manpower temp. Most work you do is something they tried to figure out or do themselves and had given up. Maybe they couldn't figure it out. Maybe they quit because there was too much disagreement on causes or approach. The net is they just needed help for a tough problem and hiring a consultant was worth the money.

The perpetual learning curve. A consultant always needs to learn something, and quickly. You will need to learn about the client's company, success patterns, culture, and political system (who makes what decision, who must be included, etc.). You might learn new industries for your established methodologies or a new methodology for an industry you worked in several times. Dull and boring it isn't.

The people. The best consultants are smart people, focused on solving

45

problems, open to learning new things all the time. The best clients are very similar. Both consultants and clients work in teams. They have an agreed approach, a collective work product, mutual accountability and aid. They help each other out. Are there jerks? Sure, but I made it my business not to work for jerk clients or with jerk consultants more than once. I managed to (mostly) work with people who knew how to get stuff done and still have fun.

Trajectory variations

This Newbie-Journeyman-Pro trajectory is drawn from the perspective of a consultant in a firm who survives every level of "grow or go" culling and becomes a Pro. I didn't do that. Most consulting careers aren't like that. Consultants change firms a lot. Consultants go back and forth between industry and consulting. Some consultants go into academia, do research, teach and supplement their salary with consulting. Consultants start new firms or become solo practitioners doing sub-contract work to larger firms or working alone. Some independent consultants work with a network of other independents. It is a very fluid industry, with many different ways to structure your work.

The common success factor is simple: consultants have clients who hire them. These clients find the consultant **helpful** in achieving **results** that are greater than the client could achieve without the consultant's help.

Early in my consulting career, a mentor told me, "Alan, <u>you</u> are the product." At that time I took that as an admonition to "be professional." Later I realized it was also career path trajectory advice, with implications for innovation, continuous improvement, and client relationship building. The trajectory of a consultant's career is self-development, increasing capability to remain true to yourself, be helpful to clients and deliver results.

CHAPTER 3

A CAREER IN CONSULTING: GETTING HIRED

"So you want to work in consulting? Why?"

I was sitting in a walnut-paneled conference room in a large one-square-block brownstone mansion overlooking the Boston Public Garden. Facing me was George, the managing partner of Harbridge House, the firm I had worked for in its London office – effectively working fulltime during my second year of the London Business School (an experience with severe marital and health consequences).

George stood six-four, had the right amount of gray at the temples, iced-steel blue eyes, and the kind of perfect teeth you see in ads for cosmetic dentists. He was smiling, but with all the warmth of a typical Boston winter.

I smiled my best enthusiastic smile and said, "I like the variety of the work and learning about different industries."

George said, "So you want us to be an extension of business school for you?"

George's question did not bode well. This wasn't my first consulting interview. I had been in five or six to that point.

Earlier a Bain principal four years my junior told me he had concerns about my "horsepower." I was so nonplussed I blurted out, "You don't think I'm <u>smart</u> enough?" He didn't. "I may not be the smartest person in the class," I replied, "but I do have the ability to translate difficult concepts to the average person." He said it was "a good answer," but it was not good enough.

I also had managed to secure an interview at the London office of McKinsey & Company. When I arrived, I was ushered into a strange reception area, midnight blue carpeting, lit by dimmed down-spots. I sat on the sole dark blue couch, and found my knees were at eye level. After twenty-three minutes of solitary waiting, a previously invisible door opened in the wall and a tall, very proper woman said in the best BBC accent, "The Brigadier will see you now."

Getting up off the sofa was a challenge, but I quickly scrambled toward the door. When I arrived at the threshold, I was greeted by the blinding light of the afternoon sun streaming through the floor-to-ceiling windows. As I stepped from the blue tight-weave carpet of the reception area to the soft inch-thick plush beige floor covering, I stumbled. As I struggled to maintain my balance and get to the waiting Barcelona chair, from over my right shoulder I heard, "Well, Mr. Culler, just what is it that <u>you</u> have to offer a client of McKinsey's?"

The rest of the McKinsey interview went downhill from there.

I believed my Harbridge House interview was my "safety" interview. I had worked on three automotive industry projects for HHI while still in business school. The partner I worked for was pleased with my work. The firm headquarters was in my former hometown. I thought I was a shoo-in; I was wrong.

This was 1981. The automotive market in the US was dominated by the Big 3 and the previous year had seen a nineteen-year low for US car sales. Nobody had told me, and I had done no research to understand that this firm's auto group wasn't hiring. George didn't have a very high opinion of the partner I'd worked for, nor the London office in general.

In his view, the London office never made much profit, and the partner ran "tiny little market studies with students, which undermined the market."

So with the laser-like acuity of hindsight, I offer two tips on getting hired in consulting:

Understand the industry landscape, firms and disciplines.
Understand what you have to offer.

The consulting industry

In 1981, the industry landscape was similar to today, dominated by McKinsey, Boston Consulting Group, Bain, and the Big 8 (accounting/ audit firms with consulting arms that did management accounting and systems-integration projects, now the Big 4). I did very little research and so I would not have known how Harbridge House ranked (definitely lower mid-tier). I interviewed at a few smaller firms, but didn't understand that small firms create opportunity if they grow, but instability if they don't.

Firm organization: client industry and consulting disciplines

When I was joining the consulting industry I was unaware of the matrix organization I described in the last chapter, which combines client industry (automotive, manufacturing, financial services, chemicals, oil and gas, etc.) and consulting discipline (strategy, sales and marketing, operations, finance and accounting, information technology systems). Big firms pigeonhole a new hire somewhere in the matrix; in smaller firms everyone does everything.

What you have to offer

Don't discount anything in your background. "Odd" jobs may be more valuable than you think.

When I was a booking agent, I arranged speaking engagements for celebrities such as Ralph Nader, Margaret Mead, and Ross Perot. From those nine years, I had learned how to sell, and how not to be intimidated by powerful people, valuable skills in consulting. I just didn't realize that at the time.

Later, I learned that "The Brigadier" at McKinsey was Harry Langston, a "really smart and nice guy" who had grown the London office by selling million-dollar projects. His tough question – "What do you have to offer?" and the similar question "Why?" from George Rabstejnek at Harbridge House - are typical. In the years that followed, I asked similar questions to potential new recruits. What I was looking for were people who like to solve problems and get results. I also sought a helpful mindset and client focus. I looked for people who were comfortable with the client getting credit for results of their work.

I've now worked for five firms and most say they are looking for "smart, nice people," smart because client problems are tough, and nice because clients and teammates have to like you. Interviewers often give you cases to test your analytic ability, i.e., "What is the market size for AA batteries in the world?" They expect you to puzzle your way through the problem out loud to show your thinking. Or they give you an outline of a client case and hope you start by looking at the same things they did. Noting volunteer work on your resume or asking questions about team sports are proxies for "niceness" and how you talk about those are quite important.

Between college and my stint as a booking agent there was a year where I was looking for acting work. I drove a cab, worked as an orderly in a hospital intensive care unit, waited tables, tended bar, shoveled snow, cut lawns and worked night shift in multiple factories. I worked so much for Manpower that they stopped hiring me because they'd have to call me a W2 employee. I worked at anything that would leave my days free for the auditions I wasn't getting.

In the beginning I left all this off my resume. Then a woman I was interviewing with asked me about the gap, and I said "various jobs." She asked me about those jobs and the discussion turned out to take most of the interview. I still think it was one reason I got the job.

Consulting firms are also looking for interesting people. A colleague once called this the "Detroit airport rule." "Imagine that you are stuck in the Detroit airport for four hours with a candidate. Would they make you crazy? Or would you have an interesting conversation?"

I had a lot of consulting interviews during my final year of business school. McKinsey made only one offer and one hire, the top student of our year. But I got one of six interviews they gave. In fact, I had seven consulting interviews while most of my classmates had none. Looking back, that was probably because of my "unusual career" as a booking agent, which was on the resume provided to recruiters. I thought my previous career was too weird and <u>never</u> talked about it in interviews. When asked, I generalized about my sales skills and quickly changed the subject to what I had learned in the last six months. I would answer differently today.

"So you want to work in consulting? Why?"

"I like to help other people solve problems and get results. What I learned as a booking agent, selling speaking engagements for celebrities, is that people are people. <u>Everyone</u> appreciates help solving <u>their</u> problems. They want you to <u>listen</u> first, then to work <u>hard</u> to help them get the results they want."

CHAPTER 4

HOW TO BE SUCCESSFUL IN A CONSULTING FIRM

"**I** fight authority; authority always wins."

This is a line from an old John Mellencamp tune "Authority Song." It's not a particularly complex song, just three chords. Nor do I think it is great songwriting, but it always makes me smile. I suppose that smile is in recognition of my counter-dependent way of being in the world.

In the more than fifty years since high school, the longest I ever worked for someone else was six years.

I suppose, like Groucho Marx, I refuse to join any club that would have me as a member.

So, I appreciate the irony of writing about how to be successful in a consulting firm. I will share behaviors of those who *are* successful. Many of these are actions I didn't do myself or took far too long to learn (see problem with authority described above). I was successful in spite of the fact that I didn't always listen to people who in retrospect only had my best interest at heart. My first piece of advice: "A chip on your shoulder cuts off blood flow to the brain."

Get your head on straight, Newbie

You may hate being called a Newbie. I did. Or if the firm is more "sensitive" and people don't call you Newbie, but smile condescendingly like you are "not quite with it," you have two choices:

- You can "bristle" and talk about your accomplishments before consulting. (I bristled; it is less than effective.) or
- You can adopt a learning attitude, be a sponge, soak everything up, do what you are asked to do, and if you see an opportunity to be "helpful," ask before you "help." Help is defined by the recipient.

Truth is <u>you</u> <u>know</u> <u>nothing</u> until proven otherwise, so suck it up and soak it up. Ask questions to understand, not to demonstrate how smart you are.

Oh, and by the way, Newbies in consulting aren't just entry-level analysts. Even if you are hired as a "rainmaker" partner, you're still a Newbie. Hopefully your time in the "not quite with it" cell is shorter than the analyst's, but you'll do time there. So treat people the way you treat clients - you know, smile and listen a lot.

Get your head into the business of consulting

I think it is important to understand how most consulting firms actually make money. There are all kinds of consulting firms, with thousands of service offerings. Some offer products, like software, or pre-packaged research or surveys. Some get paid a percentage of the benefit the client receives.

However, most are **time-based professional services businesses.** They make money based upon the mark up on their people's time. A consulting firm may sell a project based upon time and materials or they may sell a fixed price project, but the price is based upon time: so much time from the partner, so much from the managers, and so much time from the people who do the work. Partner fees are approximately two times what the firm pays the partner. Manager fees are three to four times what the firm pays the manager, and analyst and associate fees are four to six times compensation.

Lesson #1: For the firm to make money the work needs to be done by the least paid qualified resource. You increase your value to the firm by becoming more capable than others at your compensation level.

Lesson # 2: The whole system is based upon time management. Track the time you take to do a task and learn to forecast and improve that time.

So whether Newbie, Journeyman or Pro, a critical success factor is **bringing the project in within the budgeted price**. Most firms expect a project profit of 50-60 percent. The additional 40-50 percent pays for office overhead (rent, power, furniture), firm research and service offering design, marketing and client acquisition, and staff recruiting and development. Most firms expect a net profit of around 20 percent, some portion of which is distributed to partners in addition to salary and bonus.

In order to be successful in this financial environment:
- Learn how long you need to deliver a piece of work
- Negotiate for enough billable time to do the job you are asked to do
- Continuously improve the speed and quality of your work

This will require religiously tracking your hours. When I started in consulting we used weekly handwritten timesheets; these days everyone uses Excel or an online system. But be proactive and consistent about entering your time. As a project manager, I hated chasing people who were always late getting billable hours in on time.

It wasn't until I worked for myself that I internalized the importance of tracking time. It is the basis of how you bill clients and make money; if you do not bill clients, <u>they will not pay you</u>.

Boutique firms staffed by senior people often manage on lower margins. Their pyramids may be narrower, and growth limited, but they are often founded by Pros who still like doing the work. These are great places for a Newbie to learn the methodologies offered, but promotion opportunities are also limited.

A word about expenses

Many consulting contracts are structured as an aggregate fee "plus reasonable materials, travel, and accommodations expenses." Some consultants have used this phrase to fund an extravagant lifestyle on the road. They rationalize this by saying "the client can afford it and, after all, I'm away from home and my family so I deserve a few perks." So some clients have unknowingly funded $500 bottles of wine at dinner, massages described as "miscellaneous hotel services," first class flights of one hour, and a host of other client rip-offs.

My advice: Spend the client's money as if it were your own. And stand up to people who don't. It's the <u>right</u> thing to do, and it will add to your reputation as honorable and client-focused. An honest approach will produce more business for you and your firm.

Get staffed on projects

Because consulting firms make money on billable hours they track the *application rate*, the percentage of time individual consultants are applied to client projects. Firms often have utilization targets based upon the firm's profit model, e.g., 80 percent for associates, 60 percent for managers and 40 percent for partners.

Many firms say unapplied people are "on the beach," which sounds like relaxing time in the sun and surf. It's not a good thing to be on the beach. Consultants who are persistently unapplied or underutilized are the first to go. Find out how staffing works in your firm.

I worked in firms where all partners jointly decided staffing and in firms where staffing was in the industry groups. Gemini Consulting had a staffing group of rotating consultants who wanted to come off the road for a while, perhaps to care for a new baby, to be home with an aging parent, or just for a break from the grind.

Find out how staffing decisions are made. Find out what projects are coming up and express your interest. My experience in consulting firms showed me that those who were staffed continuously took an active role in finding their next project, even in places that had rules against "staffing yourself."

Learn

Being successful inside a consulting firm is about more than just working hard and hoping somebody notices. It is about thinking like an owner of the firm, and learning and growing your own value to clients.

There is a lot to learn in consulting, beginning with basic competencies in research and analysis tools. Being good at Excel and PowerPoint is important even in firms that have internal analytics and graphics departments.

If your firm is structured around types of projects, learn the triggers that demonstrate the need for those services. For example, if your firm specializes in organization design, understand how new global competition might drive an international structure. Or explore how declining customer profitability might drive a relationship management structure to facilitate cross-selling. Learning how a project comes to be will help you anticipate staffing

Then there is client industry knowledge, i.e., knowing which firms are making money and who isn't and why, who is acquiring and who is looking to be acquired. It is also useful to follow the latest academic research and to understand how that might lead to consulting service offerings. What is important will depend on the consulting firm's organization structure and staffing model. If there is a client industry structure that drives staffing, then focus on industry knowledge and the service offerings sold in that industry at the present time. Look at how similar industries have evolved. For example, the oil and gas producers followed the chemicals industry into continuous improvement after oil prices fell and large process safety accidents occurred.

Look for new opportunities to learn. For example, every new project has a steep entry learning curve. Often some consultants are assigned to put together the deck to educate the incoming project team. These consultants research industry dynamics, review relevant academic research and compile a list of the firm's work in the industry or with similar client problems. Volunteer for this work and you will have a great advantage at this project and similar projects going forward.

At some point you may have to choose between becoming a specialist or remaining a generalist. This will depend on whether depth or breadth is more valued at your firm. Look at who is staffed. Look at who is promoted.

Some disciplines lend themselves to industry specialization, like strategy or marketing. Some disciplines work across industries, like organization development and process improvement.

Try not to be pigeonholed by building competence in a skill that others don't want to do. When I was at Gemini, one of my mentees excelled in using the electronic software we used to live-survey groups in large meetings. She was staffed a lot because no one wanted to do this work, but it became so boring for her that she ultimately left the firm.

Find a mentor

This is a tough one. Consultants can be a self-centered lot. Also, professional people prize autonomy. Some firms assign mentors who help with development. In my experience these relationships are less successful than organic relationships where the mentee and the mentor choose each other.

Some people look for mentors who have faced similar challenges. Women, people of color and minorities may look for someone who "looks like me." In my experience the best mentors see potential and <u>want</u> you to <u>grow</u>. My mentors didn't coddle me. One reduced me to tears once. But I grew from that association.

A mentor should help you sort out what is important at the firm, what you should learn, how to get staffed, etc. What should the mentor get in return? The mentor may enjoy helping someone grow, especially someone that reminds her of herself at a younger age. But what the mentor absolutely needs is for your performance to enhance his or her reputation as a leader and as someone who identifies and develops talent.

Sometimes consulting firms can get a tad "political." In many service businesses, the absence of a hard product leads people to over-identify with departmental or personal "tribes," which can result in internecine warfare. In consulting firms with aggressive expectations for consultants to be promoted to a limited number of slots, there are some nasty internal battles.

My advice is to be politically aware, but not political. Don't gather intelligence for your mentor. Don't talk behind anyone's back. As the "Desiderata" said, "As much as is possible without surrender, strive to be on good terms with all persons."

Learn to sell

At lower levels in a consulting firm, promotion is based upon application rate and the manager and partner's perception of the quality of your work. As you rise in a firm, *rebuy rate* - the percentage of your clients who buy another project within a period of time - becomes important. Seeing opportunities to *extend* a project means more revenue, e.g., "As long as we are looking at the invoicing process, shouldn't we also look at collections?" Seeing opportunities to *expand* to another buying center leads to another project, e.g., "We saved the finance department two million dollars. Could we see what we might save in operations?"

Rebuy rate, extensions and expansions are often the criteria not only for bonus but also for promotion from project manager to the first level of partner. New client acquisition is a key criterion for promotion to full partner.

Some firms have the equivalent of tech firms' "technical ladder" that offers advancement opportunities to engineers who don't want to manage. In consulting this takes the form of "thought leadership," a reward for those who create new service offerings or publish books that build the reputation of the firm and attract clients on a more general basis.

But all firms promote the "rainmaker," the man or woman who capitalizes on relationships to bring in big clients. These partners often came up through the ranks of the firm, maintaining their relationships with midlevel clients and former consulting colleagues, so that years later they can bring in project work from those who've risen to a position to buy consulting services. While some firms do hire high-powered sales people from big-ticket industries like mainframe computers or infrastructure engineering, a substantial portion of partners at the major firms are home-grown talent.

Stay client-focused

There are two core values I think are important for consultants:

- Stay focused on results
- Be helpful

Consulting projects are about making a change, doing less of something, or more of something, or doing something differently to achieve a result. The client may take the action to achieve the result, and as a consultant you may be more or less involved in implementation. But getting the result is what is important.

The result is more important than the brilliance of your analysis. The result is more important than the presentation deck. The result is more important than any extension or expansion and there will not be a rebuy rate without it.

It is your job to help the client get the result. Funny thing about help. As American psychologist Carl Rogers told us, "Help is defined by the recipient." The only way you'll understand what the client perceives as helpful is to ask. Sometimes clients won't know what is helpful and the consultant will enter a "guess and test" process. But it is imperative that the consultant maintain the focus on what is helpful to the client not what is convenient to the consultant.

Carl Rogers also told the psychotherapists he trained, "You can't help someone you can't find a reason to like."

Consultants often talk smack about clients. It is understandable; the consultants work at one firm and the clients work at another. The client has a problem that the consultants have been asked to solve. It's easy to call the client "stupid" or "incompetent." I had a boss once who would intervene in these discussions by saying, "Permission requested NOT to client-bash."

Client-bashing lowers the consultant's ability to be helpful. It creates an adversarial relationship that makes it difficult for the client to achieve the desired result.

A few years ago a major strategy firm conducted a study of project success. The research found that clients acted upon only 15 percent of their recommendations. I can only imagine the lack of client focus that probably led to such an outcome.

The arrogant consultant tells the "stupid" client what he should have already known to do. The client smiles through the presentation, says 'thank you" and goes back to business as usual.

Contrast that with the consultant who joins the client to solve a problem, helps the client remove obstacles to implementation, and checks back to ask how it is going. Being helpful and focusing on results are more likely to achieve results.

If you want to be successful in a consulting firm, learn: learn to help the firm make money, learn and grow your own capabilities, learn to build relationships with clients so that they hire you to help them change and get results.

And, of course, if you, like me, have a problem with authority, either get over it or work for yourself. As an explanation for my self-employment, I often joked, "I learned that I'm a lot nicer to clients than I am to bosses." Being independent meant I sometimes had smaller projects and fewer colleagues, but it helped me to be truer to my values. It wasn't easy working for me, though. Some days, I was quite permissive; other days I was a slave driver.

CHAPTER 5

THE ENTRY
LEARNING CURVE

"Tell me, what did you learn?"

It was the last team meeting of my first consulting project. The team was composed entirely of London Business School first year MBA students. We had just spent the summer studying the UK commercial vehicle market to determine the feasibility of two new truck lines. The client was ERF, a Cheshire assembler of heavy duty forty-four-ton articulated lorry cabs (called tractor-trailers or semis in the US). ERF asked us to study whether they should build a thirty-two-ton, eight-wheel vehicle (think garbage truck or road construction dump truck) and a sixteen-ton box van (used for grocery distribution and U-Haul rentals).

As the "data secretary" for the team, I felt that the question was directed at me.

I stumbled a bit over the words but launched into a summary of the findings. "In the market for the sixteen-ton distribution vehicle there is no premium end of the market. There is a substantial penalty for vehicle weight because margins are razor thin. . . ."

"No, what did _you_ learn?"

The questioner, Basil, had been the team's advisor while the project leader, Dick, went to the south of France for four weeks. Basil was a tall lanky man, a bit craggy of face, with a kind, professorial demeanor. In our weekly meetings with Basil, he would quietly listen as we reported findings, his long fingers steepled, touching his lips. He only lowered his hands slightly to make the occasional quiet suggestion; we students were pretty much on our own. I had no idea what he was looking for, but commenced again.

"By contrast, the thirty-two-ton market does offer a premium for durability, and the power of Gardiner drivetrain has a certain cache. . . ."

"No. . . what did you <u>learn</u>?" Someone else jumped in to describe how the British Leyland Chieftain was the clear price leader in the sixteen-ton market and no competitor seemed to be able to underprice them, nor establish a premium, for even six months without dramatically impacting their own sales.

We had compared registrations, longitudinal price data, interviewed dealers and customers for the sixteen ton and thirty-two ton vehicles and compared them to ERF's legacy forty-four ton customer views. We had looked at drive-train combinations in both vehicles. Our brains were barely treading water in waves of data.

"There is no need for the power of the Gardner engine in distribution, lower fuel costs . . ."

"No, no, no. . . well. . ." Basil intoned in a gently condescending way. "Let me tell you what you <u>should</u> have learned. *Perhaps* you learned how, with very little prior industry experience or knowledge, to get yourselves to the point where you could have intelligent business conversations with people who had worked in this industry for their entire careers."

I looked around the room. It was clear that all my fellow students were simultaneously coming to the same realization that we had in fact done that.

"If you did learn <u>that</u>," said Basil quietly, "It will feed you for the rest of your lives."

The meeting went on to prepare us for how to bring Dick up to speed quickly upon his return from Provence, what to put in findings or appendices in the report, and what clients typically wanted in a final presentation. But I have often reflected on Basil's question, "What did you learn?"

For me, the excitement of starting a new project and the steepness of the learning curve are what kept me in consulting for thirty-seven years.

Thinking back on that first project, how did we learn enough about the UK truck market to be credible to industry insiders? Quite simply, we read a lot and we talked to some friendly industry people before we ever talked to a client.

At that point Dick, our project leader, had been a marketing consultant in the auto industry for about ten years. In those days consulting firms had libraries and librarians. Carolyn, the librarian, created a packet for us to read. Our first days on the project were spent reading the reports from previous projects in the truck industry, articles from manufacturer and dealer trade magazines, truck model brochures, and company information from the client.

We were business school students used to reading and analyzing three cases a night. This was a piece of cake. We were told to formulate questions.

Dick and Basil then brought in some content specialists, industry insiders who came in for a paid meeting to answer our questions and help frame the research plan. We started with desk research from the firm library and some local London publication libraries and then went to the Registrar of Commercial Vehicles, the truck equivalent of the DMV (but a lot more helpful).

After further team discussion, we went to see the client. We were told to "be respectful, listen, and ask clarifying questions, but don't try to show off your newfound knowledge. This meeting is for them to frame the question, not to tell them what they already know or embarrass them with anything they haven't seen." The CEO told us a little about the history of the firm, and framed what he wanted to know by asking, "Should we enter these two new markets?" He gave us a young manufacturing manager, Tom, who was close to our age, to help guide us around. He was clear that Earl, the marketing manager, should be kept informed, but added, "Don't let him influence your research. Earl has a point of view here, don't you, Earl?" The marketing manager allowed as how he would try to keep his opinions to himself until "we see the report."

So now we knew something of the politics behind the project and we had a client guide, who, it turned out, was highly invested in learning along with us. We were underway.

Dick and Basil took the train back to London from Strathclyde and Tom took us around headquarters. Earl the marketing manager gave us many marketing brochures and reams of data to get us started and most of the team took a later train back to London. Tom and I were going to tour assembly facilities the next morning. He took me to a local small hotel, waited while I stashed my suitcase and then we went to the pub across next door, where we met Tom's boss Ang, and a crew of young manufacturing men that Tom called the "lads."

Ang spoke first in a thick Northern accent that sounded like Ringo Starr with marbles in his mouth. "*Consooltant*, eh? Good money for auld rope," he said with a smile, but his message was clear: What are <u>you</u> going to teach <u>me?</u> I replied I was "there to learn" and Ang lightened up. It was a fun evening with far too many pints of "heavy" and "bitter." I had the presence of mind to bring a notebook and took notes, but the next morning I was feeling a little rough.

Tom arrived, took one look at me and took me to a local café. "He needs the motor industry breakfast," he said. When the woman brought me a "full Scottish," complete with blood pudding, two other kinds of sausage, kippers, and eggs, Tom intoned, "If you live through that you'll feel a lot better. I ate and to my surprise, I did. I'd passed the first test of consulting: entry engagement.

After so many years in the field, I've recognized that each phase of the consulting process has its own learning requirements:

In the Entry phase the consultant must win over clients such that they work with you to jointly solve the problem. The learning curve is the steepest here because the consultant must learn enough about the industry and company to earn the right to proceed.

THE CONSULTING PROCESS

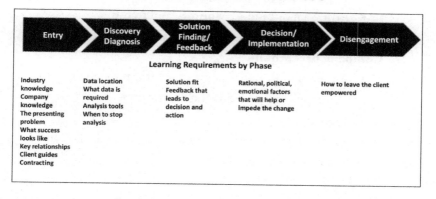

Entry	Discovery Diagnosis	Solution Finding/ Feedback	Decision/ Implementation	Disengagement

Learning Requirements by Phase

Industry knowledge	Data location	Solution fit	Rational, political,	How to leave the client
Company knowledge	What data is required	Feedback that leads to	emotional factors that will help or	empowered
The presenting problem	Analysis tools	decision and action	impede the change	
What success looks like	When to stop analysis			
Key relationships				
Client guides				
Contracting				

From Discovery to Decision the learning requirements are technical and project-specific. Disengagement is hard to do well and many consultants get so wrapped up in the pitch for additional work they forget that the client needs to achieve the results of your work. You ensure that through the way you leave.

I worked with some consulting firms and project managers who were really good at preparing the team to learn quickly. And I worked with some consultants who do this as a matter of course by themselves. Entry phase learning gets easier after the second project in an industry or the second time you work on a similar problem.

I also worked with consulting firms and project managers who didn't spend enough time preparing the team. They sent out consultants to do initial interviews with little prep, and predictably clients felt like the consultants were "borrowing their watch to tell them the time."

In this situation, some consultants feel the need to demonstrate how smart they are, which gives all consultants the reputation for arrogance.

But the consulting firms and project managers who are good at preparing the team all provide some of the same things:

- **An industry pre-read deck**, which includes Information about:
    - Customers and buying criteria
    - Competitors and their products and services

- Relevant previous industry project materials, if available
- Articles about industry history and trends
- *Harvard Business Review* industry notes (or similar)
- **Company background**
  - Annual report and analyst notes if a public company (client-supplied data if a private company)
  - Organization charts
  - Relevant previous company project materials, if available
  - Product/service brochures

- **The project proposal** or statement of work or relevant portions of those documents
- **A contact list** that includes email addresses and telephone numbers for the consulting team, the client team including names and numbers of relevant administrators, and any assigned relationships (e.g., only the project manager is to talk to the CEO)
- **An opening meeting** to discuss questions from the pre-read and the project plan

Many times all this information isn't available at the beginning of the project, but a good project manager creates a template and charges the team to help fill it in. Often some material is confidential and the project manager is clear about "not leaving this stuff in the photocopier or printer, and be careful with email lists and flash drives."

These materials can't cover everything needed to learn to start a project, but it can lessen the magnitude and steepness of the learning curve a little. Not too much of course, because consultants like a steep entry learning curve. The learning provides a lot of the "fun" of consulting. And learning quickly "will feed you for the rest of your lives."

SKILLS, METHODOLOGIES, AND TOOLS

I n the beginning of a consulting career, much of what you will do is data collection and analysis. Some of that work will involve online research, reading industry trade organization data, visiting websites, reading annual reports, chasing down academic papers, etc. You may analyze company, competitor, and supplier data, and any other quantitative data your firm may have gathered from third party sources for this or previous projects. Your Excel skills will get a good workout, but you may use Minitab, or Jump or SPSS or some other statistical analysis software.

You will also collect qualitative data through interviewing, focus groups, surveying or observation to provide a people perspective to quantitative data and build engagement and energy for implementing the solutions you find.

The nature of the problem you are solving will dictate the data you collect and analyze. The consulting approach your firm uses, i.e., content or process, heavily influences how you collect and analyze data. The content consultant sells recommendations, a plan for change that can be acted upon by the client. The process consultant sells a process, teaching the client how to make the change. This has an impact on how tools and methodologies are used and what skills are required.

For example, everyone does interviewing, but these two approaches use interviewing differently. Content consultants tend to use a few interviews to understand the problem so as to frame the analysis. Process consultants tend to do more interviews because they are building engagement in the client system to help find and then implement the solution.

Process consultants are often more focused on implementation. They tend to use client teams to help with analytics, whereas content consultants do analytics completely within their own firm.

Open meeting facilitation is a core skill of process consultants. The role of a facilitator should be to help the group come to the outcome that suits them, not one that the consultant favors. I worked with content consultants who understood the value of open discussion in reaching a decision, but I have also worked with those who manipulated the group to the consultant's desired outcome, which I found an anathema.

Process consultants typically pride themselves in encouraging full participation and transferring the ownership for decisions and follow-up actions to the group. Running a meeting in this way relies on structure and ground rules that the group agrees to and self-enforces.

For content consultants a tool, methodology or a "framework," e.g., a matrix, is a way to structure the analysis of problem solving and deliver findings of that analysis to the client. A process consultant might use the same tool, but typically teaches the tool to the leadership team or another decision-making body, who actively participate in the analysis.

There really is no right approach. Clients and consultants have preferences. I have tried to couch these methodologies in neutral terms such that it could benefit both content and process consultants. (However, it is unlikely I succeed in masking my process bias.)

I have also included some "people stuff" methodologies, surveys and day-in-the-life observation that Newbies may be asked to use.

CHAPTER 6

INTERVIEWING

Following a sales process the client agrees with the consultant on the scope of the work and a price, and this agreement is called a statement of work or SOW. This contract can change as the project progresses, but only with the agreement of both parties. The project doesn't begin until the client agrees to the SOW and to pay for services.

Sometimes, interviews are part of the pre-SOW sales process and are usually conducted by the partner and project leader; other times, interviews are the first tasks of Discovery conducted by the entire team, including Newbies. As we shall see interviews often uncover data that frame the project.

Most interviews, however, are conducted at the beginning of the project in the Entry or Diagnosis phases.

THE CONSULTING PROCESS

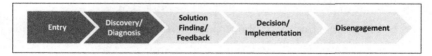

Why do interviews?

All consultants use interviews to introduce themselves in the Entry and Discovery/Diagnosis phases of a project. Some consultants also use interviews in the sales and scoping process.

Content and process consultants tend to use interviews to gather initial data to develop hypotheses about the problem. Sometimes content consultants arrive with an idea of the problem and its solutions, and the interviews are used to confirm their initial hypotheses.

Process consultants are frequently more "on the hook" for implementation and therefore tend to use the interview to build relationships and identify people for a client team that they will work with to implement.

At Gemini Consulting, we were often sent off to do multiple interviews with the instruction, "Go make some friends for Gemini." At Katzenbach Partners, the partners were impressed with my interviewing skills but thought I wanted to do "too many interviews." In their view, interviews were an initial opinion-gathering tool that helped only to frame the problem. By that time I had developed a longer-term implementation focus, which was out of sync with their approach.

Sometimes process consultants will do interviews in the solution-finding stages of innovation or improvement projects. Organization design and systems architecture consultants sometimes use interviews to troubleshoot and test the efficacy of their solutions.

In any case, the questioning strategy and the interview protocol will depend on the content and phase of the project.

Questioning strategy

Most firms have a standard interview protocol. The questions run from the general to the specific. One such framework is SCQA:

- Situation - questions about the environment, changes in technology, competitors, regulations, and existing strategy.
- Complications – questions about obstacles, i.e., what is getting in the way both externally and internally? What strengths do we want to support?
- Questions - What is happening that shouldn't be happening, or

not happening that should be happening?

- Answers – What are current hypotheses about the problem, or suggestions for a solution?

Often the client provides administrative help in scheduling these interviews, but not always.

The amount of time you spend with each interviewee varies by project and by client. I have found most interviews for most projects take between twenty-five and forty-five minutes. Whatever your time commitment is, stick to it. If you are running over time because the interviewee has a lot to say, ask the interviewee for permission to continue.

Types of questions

Questions will vary depending on what the project goals are, but most firms have a boilerplate template of questions that have worked well in the past. If you are working from the template, have a look at the questions.

Do they flow from the general to the specific? Will the interviewee be able to answer? I think it is reasonable to ask front line workers what they know about the strategy or customer needs, but maybe not so reasonable to ask about the capital budgeting process.

Whether you are choosing questions from an existing template or creating a protocol from scratch, think carefully about how you are asking.

First, some questioning basics:

- Open-ended questions begin with What, How, When, Where, and Tell me about. They let the answerer talk.
- Closed-ended questions begin with Do, Did, Will, Have, Is, Should. These questions can be answered yes or no or with short responses. They are used to clarify and summarize. When overused the interview feels like an interrogation.

I think everyone knows this distinction conceptually, but sometimes I find myself asking closed-ended questions unintentionally.

The interview should be structured so that the interviewee does most of the talking, while, at the same time, you get as much detailed information as you can about other people to talk to and where to find certain data. The best interview protocols that meet those objectives contain an open-ended question followed by a series of specific closed-ended probes.

For example,

Please tell me what you know about this firm's existing strategy?

- Is this documented anywhere?
- Have you seen these documents?
- Is this generally known among your peers?

The interviewer doesn't need to ask every probe. They are there as prompts.

If we want people to talk, we need to ask an open-ended question. Often, we want to start with something easy.

"Tell me a little about your background" or "Tell me about your job. What are the critical elements?" or "What's working well today?"

I believe positive questions about organization strengths and what is working well should precede deep dives into problems so the interview doesn't turn into a "bitch session."

Ask easy questions first, slightly harder questions next, and save the hardest for last because it's best to put the subject at ease, build trust before asking them to think deeply. The hardest kind of question, and the one with the biggest payoff, is the open-ended question that calls upon the answerer to:

- **Speculate** about something that is unknown or uncertain. "What level of quality errors do you think would cause a customer to leave?" "What kinds of features would delight a customer to such a degree that she would call all her friends to recommend us?"
- **Compare** two or more unlike things. "How do the problems we are having with delivery compare to something that frustrates you on vacation?" "What is the customer value of our medical device product compared with XYZ pharmaceutical?"
- **Evaluate the impact** of an action or decision over multiple time horizons or groups of people. "What is the difference between the way our suppliers look at this product versus the customer, our

people and the regulators?" "If we looked at this change over ten years, or fifty years, would that make any difference in how we look at it now?"

Use high payoff questions sparingly because they take time and thought both to ask and to answer. They are useful in getting to ideas about potential solutions and can take the discussion to a different level. You will know they are working by the sound of a teeth-sucking inhale ("Ooeesh") or nasal-vocal exhaling ("Hmmmnn") followed by "That's a gooooood question. . . ." But again - use them only occasionally.

Processing interviews and output

I took notes in the interviews I conducted; I always asked for permission to do so, but I always took notes.

In some situations I have even used a tape recorder, saying to the interviewee, "Remember that English teacher who said 'find a note-taking system that works for you and it will be your friend for life?' Well I didn't do that and now I need to record." I reassured the interviewee that no one else but me will ever hear the tape.

We all carry a smart phone, a recorder in our pockets, and there is automated transcription software, so the temptation is to record everything. Remember to build trust first and always to ask permission. Automated transcriptions must be edited, hopefully by the interviewer.

Mostly I wrote things down and typed them later. I have seen people who can legibly write verbatim, but that's not me. I also saw people type verbatim and maintain eye contact with the interviewee, but those people are rare. I heard people _say_ they could do that, but they typically stared at the keyboard, making the interviewee uncomfortable, missed a lot and had no relationship with the subject to build upon later.

Some people don't document interviews or expect teammates to review their scribbles. Some don't believe that interviews need to be shared with a team. But interviews are the first step in diagnosis, and sharing them with the team gets everyone on the same page, which leads to better solutions for the client.

Sometimes I used quotes in client feedback to represent a point of view expressed by many. I never attributed the quote to the person who said it. I also never used the opinions expressed by one or two people as a mainstream view.

One caveat is that interviews can be susceptible to confirmation bias. If you have seen similar problems, or you think you are the smartest person in the room, you may decide on the problem and solution in advance and use interviews to confirm your pre-existing bias. In other words, you find what you are looking for. This is why I recommend that interviews cast a wide net across different departments and with a diverse set of people.

I also recommend that the entire team conducts interviews with some warnings about confirmation bias and other cognitive biases. There are financial biases such as hyperbolic discounting, i.e., taking a smaller short-term reward by discounting larger long-term rewards. There are social biases like the bandwagon effect, doing something because "everybody's doing it." There are short term-ism biases, "if it ain't broke don't fix it," and estimating biases, "future results will be like the past," among others. (Note: for other cognitive biases you should avoid, see https://www.visualcapitalist.com/18-cognitive-bias-examples-mental-mistakes/)

Interviews should inform your hypotheses and direct you to data for analysis. And when interviewees suggest solutions, **always give them the credit for the idea**. Interviews are an exercise in trust.

CHAPTER 7

ANALYTICS

There is a reason why in many firms new entrants are called analysts; their job is to analyze data. Some large firms hire analysts from undergraduate universities and put them in cubicles in the office. These analysts never see a client; they run Excel all day and provide charts to the graphics department to make into PowerPoint slides for "the deck." If you are an undergraduate analyst in these firms you hope to be promoted to go to a client site and do the same work.

Some of these firms start those with graduate degrees the same way with a shorter promotion path to the client site. Analytics is seen as training. Those who break out rarely do so with a particularly elegant pivot table, but rather because they think analytically and, most importantly, they explain the results of analysis in easy to understand terms.

Thinking analytically: The Scientific Method

If I think about consultants I met in my five iterations as a Newbie, they were a pretty analytical group. There were undergraduates from STEM disciplines (science, engineering, technology or mathematics), MBAs, and JDs or other legal degrees. There were Masters or PhDs in STEM disciplines, as well as in social sciences, psychology, sociology, or anthropology, or even humanities degrees like history or semiotics. Most Newbies did research during their education and learned the scientific method.

THE SCIENTIFIC METHOD

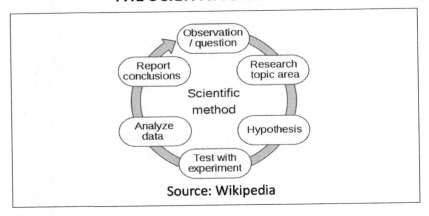

Source: Wikipedia

The scientific method is an empirical "guess and test" problem-solving methodology. Different people are given credit for its invention: Sir Francis Bacon, Galileo, Abū Ali al-Ḥasan Ibn al-Haytham al-Baṣrī (Arab physicist of the first millennium), and Aristotle. It has been around a long time. It may not be obvious how this applies to consulting.

The researcher formulates a question: Why is revenue declining? Then does some research into revenue in the existing firm and competitive and similar firms for the same period. "Competitor A has a new product and their revenue is increasing. Maybe that's the reason. My hypothesis is customers find competitor A's product superior to our own. Let's do a blind test focus group to test that hypothesis." Then we analyze that data and we conclude, "Yes, customers prefer the competitor's product" or "No, customers prefer our product - it must be something else."

The scientific method is an iterative process. The process then begins again with a theory (question and hypothesis) and the replication of experiments that hopefully produce similar analysis results, confirming the theory.

I knew many consultants who talked about the scientific method but were less than scientifically rigorous in their work. I also observed some rigorous analysis and those consultants might explain the scientific

78

method as fitting into the consulting process in this way.

Analytics in content and process consulting

Analytics and the expertise behind them are the foundation of consulting. Content consultants bring this expertise to the client. Process consultants teach this expertise to the client so that the client can use it the next time they face a similar issue. But the analytics and the scientific method remain foundational to consulting regardless of approach.

CONTENT AND PROCESS CONSULTING ANALYTICS

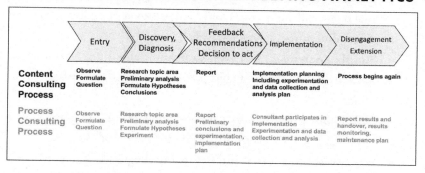

As we've discussed, content consultants believe their role ends with recommendations, that implementation is the client's job. So while they help with implementation planning they disengage earlier.

Some process consultants, especially those in the technology or organization spaces, often extend the experimentation phase thereby remaining with the client longer.

As a process consultant I often used the analogy of the running relay baton hand-off. When the client knew how to control the process and could troubleshoot and improve then I disengaged.

Regardless of the model of consulting, the importance of the scientific method is in the rigor of hypothesis development, experimentation and analysis. And while it may seem like analysis and analytic tools are given to the lowest people in the consulting organization and are therefore unimportant, nothing could be further from the truth. The quality of thinking and the rigor of analysis is central to providing a real and implementable solution to the client's problem, which is the value consultants bring.

Analytic tools

Analyses vary greatly according to project objectives and discipline. There are a few types of analyses and tools that are used in many different types of projects. When I trained or mentored new consultants, my advice was:

- **What is the question you are answering?** Knowing why you are analyzing will help you avoid "going down the rabbit hole" or descending into analysis paralysis.
- **Simple analyses first.** If you can show something with a count stacked bar or a percentage pie chart, why do linear programming?
- **Think about trends over time.** While data for any given year is interesting, trends over multiple periods are more so.
- **Have your output in mind before you begin.** This doesn't mean that you make up your mind about results, just that you understand how you will display the results of your analysis. Knowing that you are building a pie chart rather than a horizontal bar chart will help structure the analysis.

Here are a few analytic tools new consultants may be asked to use.

Accounting Ratios

What is relevant depends on why the client hired you. If the client wants to increase profit you might start with ratios like gross profit, but move to waste or inventory turn in manufacturing or staffing or lead times in services. If you are working with a large public company, these may be done at a firm-wide level before the project begins, but you may find yourself with divisional profit & loss and balance sheets that are not public. Smaller or private companies will give you data when you arrive.

Some basic high level ratios to consider:

- Revenue growth (decline) – Year on year: gross sales by year / previous year; Five-year trend: last year minus the first year divided by the first year. (Note: Be sure a five-year trend doesn't mask year-to-year volatility.)
- Profit growth (decline) - Gross margin = Gross profit/ net sales. Show trends as well.
- Return on assets = Net income/ total assets

If debt or liquidity is an issue, you may be asked to use debt ratio (total assets/total liabilities) or the current ratio (current assets/current liabilities), but those ratios are more relevant at the corporate level. Accounting analysis is mostly useful when comparing with industry data and only called for if the division managers are not financially literate.

If the client asks for changes in staffing or a new organization (people stuff) you will still look at ratios e.g., revenue/employee, and other metrics like customer complaints vs. staffing levels to show possible impact. Remember that metrics drive behavior so tracking call handle time in the complaint center, but not problem resolution, may create quick calls but unhappy customers.

Simple counts

How many customers bought a new service? How many customers does the firm have and how has that changed over time? How many people with college degrees left before completing two years? How many returns or refunds occurred after the last sales promotion?

Counts work best when numbers are small (50 or below) and are usually displayed on stacked bars or pie charts.

Percentage analysis

Percentages are like counts - a simple analysis number by category/total number - and are often displayed the same way, but percentages are more often used when the numbers are higher. When the organization lost seven sales, they might not be concerned, but losing 28 percent of revenue might get more attention.

Pareto analysis

We talked earlier about Pareto Analysis, the 80/20 rule, or "the trivial many and the critical few." This is one of the most useful analytic tools. It analyzes the relationship between two metrics: customers compared to revenue, products compared to profit, overtime compared to workers.

DOWNTIME BY PUMP TYPE PARETO CHART

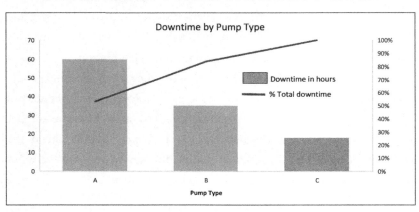

The positive hypothesis is always the 80/20 rule, i.e., 20 percent of customers produce 80 percent of revenue, 20 percent of machines cause 80 percent of downtime, 20 percent of stockkeeping units (SKUs) produce 80 percent of sales. After some relatively easy data preparation this displays in a standard Excel chart. This is extraordinarily actionable in revenue growth and profit improvement projects. I know a turnaround consultant who successfully built her entire practice with core products/ core customers analysis. She did the analysis and encouraged her client to focus on the customers and the products that made money, and get rid of the rest. The output is most often displayed in a Pareto chart like this one:

Graphical analysis

Sometimes just plotting data is incredibly useful. Showing many data points in a scatter plot can demonstrate a relationship trend that isn't apparent from the data. Relating all data points to a single category might show a relationship. On my first project, ERF, we had several years of distribution truck vehicle price data which on a scatter plot looked like there might be a relationship. We gave the British Leyland Chieftain, the segment leader, a score of 100 and related everything to it. In the days before spreadsheets we did this by hand. It would be much easier today, but the graph, like the one at right, showed that British Leyland was the clear price leader. No competitor was able to either undercut them or maintain a price premium and therefore ERF entering the distribution vehicle market as the premium brand was a challenge.

RELATIVE PRICE VS. MARKET LEADER

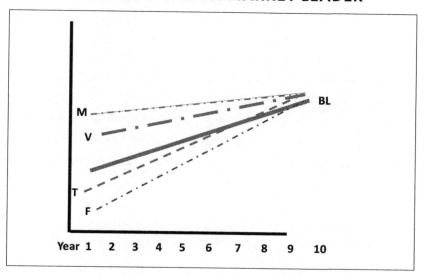

Correlation analysis

This analysis is done to understand a linear relationship of two factors.

For example, a company has an excessive overtime problem, but finds hiring new employees to reduce overtime increases employee turnover, thus increasing their training costs. Are these two factors related? Through correlation analysis they determine that, over the last two years, for every eighteen hours of reduced overtime one senior worker resigns. The problem with this analysis is that the company may immediately try to get below the eighteen hour per week threshold to retain senior workers. But correlation is not causation. There may be many more intervening variables contributing to turnover like salary, benefits, working conditions, closeness to retirement, etc.

Correlation analysis is good for relationships between two variables where no other factors exist or to direct further data collection and analysis. Sometimes simple "ocular analysis," graphing numbers and "eye-balling," to see if they appear to move together can precede correlation analysis or even regression. If it looks like there is a relationship, it bears further analysis.

Regression

Regression analysis is used to find the relationship between two variables with one or more risk factors or confounding variables. This analysis is frequently used in process improvement. Often the largest problem with it is controlling for intervening variables or explaining the output to decision makers such that they take action. Non-linear regression (e.g., multiple variables) produces some interesting graphs, which are often impossible to explain to the client.

Big Data and data mining

Companies in spaces such as retail, ecommerce, financial services, business to consumer, medicine, broadcast or streaming media produce a lot of data. Technology consultants are sometimes hired to create clustering or prediction algorithms. While I understand these concepts, a new consultant hired to do this work probably already knows more than I do.

My only advice is to step back from the screen every now and then and ask, "Does this make sense?" Too often we get caught up in our analysis and forget that real people (customers or marketers) are making real decisions that may not fit the model.

Content analysis

Content analysis is a tool to quantify qualitative data. It isn't well known to all consultants, but it is used by those who do focus group work or massive open-ended interviews and surveys.

The analytic methodology was created in the United States during World War II by the Office of Special Services (OSS), the predecessor to the Central Intelligence Agency (CIA). It is still used in intelligence gathering all over the world.

The methodology counts the number of mentions of certain concepts, ideas or phrases within text or spoken words. During World War II OSS read German newspapers looking for categories that indicated new technologies. They discovered the VR rocket program and the scientists running it. They used it to discover the mood of the German people and predicted a shift in the war after the long conflict on the Russian front.

With focus groups, open-ended interviews or surveys, a small team reads through all the data (or a representative sample) and creates categories. Then a larger team goes back through all the data and places quotes from the qualitative data into specific categories. I've seen this done on flipcharts for small amounts of data, which makes everything instantly visible. For large amounts of data Excel works well and can be quickly merged and counted.

For any quotes that fit in multiple categories the original team makes the call according to pre-established criteria. If a piece of data fits into none of the categories the originating team creates a new category. Doing this work in a team uses diversity to overcome bias.

MECE

Mutually exclusive and collectively exhaustive (MECE) is the objective of all analytics. The term was invented by Barbara Minto who evidently was the first MBA hired by McKinsey in the early 1960s. Minto wrote *The Pyramid Principle: Logic in Writing and Thinking.* "Mutually exclusive data" is data that isn't interrelated or conjoined. For example, "all consultants vs. all Certified Public Accountants (CPAs)" is misleading unless you also show what percentage of consultants are also CPAs. "Collectively exhaustive" means you have gathered all relevant data, e.g., talking about all CPAs without acknowledging that Chartered Accountants from the British system of accounting practice is a misleading representation of the global accounting profession unless you can explain the exclusion of those data. Try as we might, MECE doesn't always happen. In the preceding discussion of analytics, for example, counts and percentages are not mutually exclusive, and the discussion itself is not collectively exhaustive.

However, it is a worthy goal for analytics on a consulting project. Imagine how confused a client might be if two recommendations conflicted. Or imagine the embarrassment of a consulting project manager whose findings prompted the client to say, "I understand that big customers buy a lot, but did you look at what they buy?" Or "The two biggest categories in your content analysis seem to overlap. Did the same people pick both?"

"Er. . ." To whatever extent possible MECE is a good goal.

Outputs and data display

Presentation technology changed radically during my years as a consultant. One thing, however, didn't change:

The outputs of analysis are the story the data tells the client.

Each consulting firm has data display rules and what client presentation slides should look like. At Gemini Consulting the presentation was called a "panel set" and slides were called "panels," which dated from posterboard presentations drawn by artists. Panels used cartoons extensively and had one idea each. The desirable quadrant of a matrix was always upper right.

At Katzenbach Partners, slides were called charts, and never had cartoons. Text was sparse, but complex charts were encouraged. A matrix might have more than one end point.

In both firms slide headlines told the whole story. The "storyboard," headline-only-outline or slide sorter view in PowerPoint, was the first step in building the client presentation, and was approved by the project manager and/or partner before you built the rest of your presentation.

Learn your firm's display style and terminology. Don't get seduced by technology (e.g., Internet links) and remember the story you are telling the client.

CHAPTER 8

THE
MATRIX

E very consultant develops favorite analytical tools and frameworks. Many use a matrix. The matrix is a simple tool that graphically represents data according to two criteria, which can help choose among multiple options.

In the section on industry history we discussed the Boston Square or the Boston Box (after the Boston Consulting Group, which popularized its use in the 1970s). This matrix uses the criteria business impact vs. ease of implementation. Strategies or solution options are evaluated according to their impact on the business or problem (from low to high) and the ease of implementing (hard to easy). This simple tool is best used as a first pass to rationalize a large number of solutions.

This matrix leads to prioritizing *quick wins,* easy solutions or strategies that have the highest impact. What does easy mean? How are we defining impact? This brings us to a critical success factor of using a matrix:

A matrix defines the criteria and the scales. Before placing strategies or solutions on the matrix, come to agreement with the group about what is high impact on the business or problem. How will it affect financials and/or customer satisfaction? Is it a complete or partial problem resolution? Also come to agreement on the ease of implementation: How long will this take to implement? Who are the resources and what is the existing budget?

THE BOSTON BOX

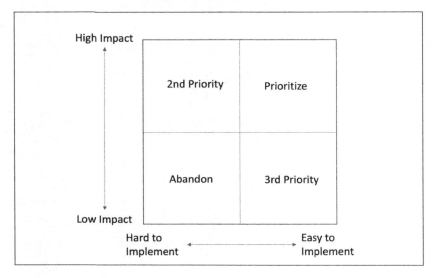

Another use of the matrix is to aid in structuring analysis and display findings. For example, a small business-to-business company was losing money. Analysis showed that a few customers produced most of the profit. The company had many customers who spent $500-$1000 per year and bought only one product but consumed a lot of service time. Therefore these customers didn't cover allocated costs. The most profitable customers tended to buy six products and spend around $15000 per year.

These data were displayed on a matrix. The visual display helped the leadership team make the tough decision to fire some customers (divesting the customers in the lower left corner to a former employee who had started a new business). They then concentrated on growing those in the upper right and cross-selling those in the middle. This strategy not only increased top-line sales but did so much more profitably. The matrix compelled the group to take action in a way that the detailed spreadsheets of the analysis couldn't.

This tool is best used as a facilitated team process. Typically facilitated team processes work best when the group includes knowledgeable people with diverse points of view, and they have the data required to make the decision.

CORE CUSTOMER ANALYSIS

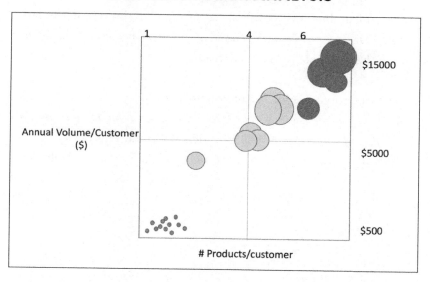

It is also possible to use a matrix in a one-on-one discussion. I have used a matrix that plots what is or is not happening vs. what should or should not be happening to help a client who was having difficulty defining a problem.

How to use the tool

A caveat: Research shows that the very idea of thinking in matrices and other frameworks is unnatural to about 75 percent of the general population. As part of the 25 percent of people comfortable with frameworks or models, consultants must help the other 75 percent navigate the matrix, so take your time with these steps.

1. Be clear about the decision to be made. The objective of the matrix is to facilitate a decision – either filtering what to focus on or coming to a decision based upon data.
2. Select and carefully define criteria. (If the criteria are based upon data, be clear about that in the scale.)
3. Draw the box so that the decision points are represented in the upper right quadrant. This is a convention and not a requirement, but most people are accustomed to this type of display.
4. Discuss ratings and plotted positions. The discussion is what helps people come to a decision.

For further information about potential criteria:

The Power of the 2 x 2 Matrix: Using 2 x 2 Thinking to Solve Business Problems and Make Better Decisions, Alex Hood and Phil Lowry

Exploring: Using 2 x 2 Matrices to Analyze Situations, Ruth Williams

CHAPTER 9

PRESENTING

"**T**he deck is the product."
"No, No. the deck isn't the product. The change, the result is the product. The deck is just a tool to help us get there."
This conversation encapsulates the difference between content consultants, who provide answers, and process consultants, who ask questions to drive change.

Consultants and consulting firms, whether content or process, spend far too much time focused on presenting. There are hours of angst about the deck, the slidepack, the panelset.

This has always been true, even before PowerPoint. In prehistoric times, when I started in consulting, slides were Letraset letters hand-pressed on acetates or "flimsies."

And then there was Alexander Proudfoot and its descendent United Research who hired calligraphers and artists to hand draw "panels," big white poster boards backed and bound into a leather bound book that was flipped through with the client executive team.

So it's clear that presentation delivery technology has changed. Now typos are easily correctable and changes can be made up until the last minute - no, last second – and presentations are digitally produced. But the presentation process is the same:

A presentation must be:

Planned ---- Validated --- Practiced ------ Presented

In my view too much of the focus is on the last step. Consultants want to sound smart and confident. They want to "wow" the client. Presentations are the "Big Reveal," the surprise finish to the project. Consultants dream of a "standing ovation." In my experience, vigorous applause is a rarity and actually worrisome because the focus may be on the consultant's "big idea" and not on achieving results.

Storyboarding: Planning starts with the end.

In an early project, I knew so much about the industry and the product we were studying that I wanted to showcase that knowledge. My project lead, a man who had worked in advertising and entertainment, stopped me cold.

"What do you recommend the client **do**? In one simple declarative sentence, please."

This was a longer painful conversation until I finally got it. I've condensed it below.

"Build one product; ignore the other."

"That's your conclusion!"

Then he asked me, "Which one finding leads you to that conclusion?"

Then, "What are other supporting findings?"

He walked me backwards to the beginning. "What did the client ask us to do?"

Each time he asked he wrote the simple declarative sentence on the top of a blank page.

"That's your story," he said. "Now fill in the data that fits that story, whether it is from interviews, analysis of market data, competitor information. If it doesn't fit the story or has too much detail it goes in the Appendix."

The story is what is important. Simply stated, it should say:

- You asked us to look at this
- Here is what we found
- Here are the implications
- Here are our recommendations and next steps

Some consultants build complex slides that show the depth of their analysis. They feel this justifies their fees. "If the client is confused, they think you are smarter than them" one colleague told me. I put his slides in the appendix.

Pre-presents, validation, and commitment building

As consultants, we look at data that might or might not have been easily available to parts of the client system. We talk to customers, suppliers, and staff who might not have been talked to in a while. We bring industry or management knowledge from other client projects.

All of these data may lead us to our conclusions. What we want is for the client to take action. If we are content consultants, we want clients to act on our recommendations. If we are process consultants, we may work alongside our clients, but we want them committed to action rather than just waiting for us to leave so they can go back to doing what they've always done.

The "Big Reveal" presentation, where we surprise the client and/or embarrass members of her leadership team, runs counter to that.

Never present data that haven't been validated or at least shared with those in the organization accountable for acting upon it.

At Gemini Consulting, we used to call those "pre-presents," which is a silly term that means you present before you present. Where I have worked with extensive client teams, I have built the final presentation with the key members who will act upon it. And in some cases, these key members actually presented the data.

Isn't there a danger that middle managers will fix problems you uncovered? Yes. If it is a simple fix, that isn't a problem; just agree to document the change, giving credit to the one who makes it. If it is part of a systemic change, gain agreement to wait until all the parts of the system are visible. That requires a longer conversation that validates the finding and addresses implications and possible negative effects of acting prematurely.

Practice. Practice. Practice.

In his book *Outliers,* Malcolm Gladwell highlighted and amplified the research of K. Anders Eriksson that posits that anyone who is world class has logged at least 10,000 hours of practice. One might think consultants, who often quote this research, wouldn't say,

"Practice? Nah. I got this. I like to keep it fresh."

As consultants we pride ourselves as being "good on our feet," confident presenters. However, I have found that practice helps and the "freshness" of a first run through is quickly derailed by an inconvenient client question.

The Big Day – Presenting with competence and confidence

A quick Internet search will turn up courses on presentation skills. I learned a great deal from such courses including where to stand, when to use a microphone and what kind of microphone, how to dress, move, gesture, and use the full range of my voice. I won't try to replicate those courses here.

I will impart some principles:

- **Know your audience.** If you have done your work on the project and have taken the appropriate validation steps you have made a good start. If you ever find yourself in the situation where you are presenting to people you do not know, arrive early enough to have conversations with your audience. This also means watch your references and examples. I had a colleague who told me that some movies I referenced were made before she was born. We laughed when later she mentioned some musical artists that left clients my age scratching their heads.
- **Think engagement.** Don't think of a data dump. Remember that your goal is action, not imparting every miniscule esoteric piece

of analysis you have done. Engagement means dressing and acting like the client, maybe a little better. It also means stopping periodically and asking questions of the group, perhaps moving around to be closer to different people. If you think engagement, you'll make eye contact and not turn your back to the group to read from the screen.

- **Capture reactions and questions.** I am a fan of the "parking lot," a flipchart or whiteboard on which to capture questions or reactions in real time. That way you can keep the flow and come back to them later. On multi-consultant teams, whoever isn't speaking mans the parking lot.

- **Be cautious about technology.** Both Bill Gates and Steve Jobs had the same rule: "No Live Demos!" I'm a bit of a technophobe, so I assume Murphy's Law will always apply (whatever can go wrong, will go wrong). So I checked batteries in laser pointers and slide changers, made sure I had an extra bulb for the projector and was leery of on-screen Internet links and videos. I refused to use some tech-effects, checked and rechecked and had backup handouts.

- **Follow up.** The presentation is not the end; it's the beginning. You want action, change, so even if everyone applauded your recommendations, things can go awry. Reconnect with the client later, answer questions, offer suggestions on roadblocks. I've seen what was widely viewed as a disastrous presentation saved by follow-up.

Plan, Validate, Practice, Present. Confidence born of competence. Content before style. Be authentic, helpful where you are asked to be, and focus on action and results. And remember, present only as much as you need to. Nothing is happening when you are talking.

CHAPTER 10

MEETING FACILITATION

Consultants are often asked to facilitate meetings. There can be many different understandings about what that means, and that lack of clarity about objectives and outcomes can lead to a lack of success in the role. Many consultants think that facilitation is an insubstantial skill, which may be the reason why many consultants are not very good facilitators.

Facilitate means literally "to make easier." In consulting parlance it denotes managing the process (not the content) of the meeting. Managing process can be anything from designing a meeting to carefully directing the conversation (to keep the group on time and on task) to simply scribing meeting notes on flipcharts.

Therefore, the first rule about meeting facilitation is to agree with the meeting owner what he or she means by facilitation. This rule applies if a leader or staff member agrees to facilitate a colleague's or boss's meeting. It is useful to discuss with the client why he/she wants to use a facilitator, what kind of meeting it is, what are the expected outcomes, what is the structure of the meeting, and what are the respective roles of the facilitator and the group leader.

Why use a third-party facilitator?

Facilitators are most often used when:

- The group leader has significant content expertise and/or wants to contribute to the meeting freely without having to manage the process (e.g., strategy formulation, discussions).
- There is a requirement for a disciplined or structured process (e.g., formal brainstorming, creative problem solving, focus groups, etc.).
- There is an experiential education component to the meeting (e.g., Continuous Improvement, Innovation, Change Alignment, etc.).
- The issue is sensitive and requires an objective third party (e.g., conflict management, team formation, project troubleshooting, "lessons learned" sessions, alliance building, supplier/customer relationship reviews, etc.).
- The group leader wants to "break set" and try something different.

Types of meetings consultants facilitate

"Meetings! Too many! Too Long! Don't accomplish anything!" These are consistent complaints of business people. Meetings are forums for the two-way exchange of information. That exchange is not necessarily an equal exchange. For example, in announcement meetings, the flow is from the announcer to the group and often the only return flow comes in the form of questions of clarity. Conversely, in pure discovery meetings (e.g., focus groups), the flow is from the group and the return flow comes in the form of initial questions and encouragement to keep the conversation going.

A facilitated meeting may be a staff meeting or change team where we agree who is doing what, how and when. It may be cross-functional or cross-level in nature, where it is critical that all points of view are heard and special expertise is recognized. Training and education facilitation is a set of unique skills that includes an understanding of what knowledge is best learned by discussion and what skills should be practiced.

There are five meeting types or elements that consultants are sometimes asked to facilitate: **Announcements, Discovery, Problem-Solving, Commitment Building, and Decision-Making**. The biggest problem in meetings is trying to do too much at the same time. You can mix announcements with problem-solving, but these elements need to be separated by a break, a change in where people sit, even a visual on a slide or whiteboard.

Each meeting type has a unique objective with its own structure, opening, body, and closure. The chart below outlines these meetings, the facilitator's role, and potential pitfalls.

TYPES OF MEETINGS CONSULTANTS FACILITATE

Meeting Type	Objective	Examples	Opening	Body	Closure	Facilitator Role	Pitfalls
Announcement	To give information	Policy changes, conflict resolutions, New group responsibilities	This is an announcement and this is the process for questions	The announcement and the questions	Summary of announcement, questions and actions required	Capture each question as asked, establish format, document	• Usurping the client's role • Dismissing questions • Being defensive
Discovery	To get information	Focus groups, group Interviews, employee input sessions, idea generation or evaluation	Explain why you are asking for information, how it will be used, process of collection and feedback	Facilitator asks questions, participants respond; facilitator charts answers	Thanks, summaries, what will happen with these data	Sticking to the process, discipline, transparency, objectivity, documenting	• Lack of transparency • Lack of objectivity • Poor documentation
Problem Solving	To solve a problem using a formal problem solving meeting	Project trouble shooting, obstacle anticipation, solving a customer problem	State problem, the problem solving process, expected outcomes, and timeframe	Define problem, gather info, generate options, select solution, test it, plan implementation	Summarize process, solution, actions responsibilities	Adherence to the problem solving process	• Not sticking to the process • Jumping into the content • Failing to plan implementation/ responsibilities
Commitment Building	To build commitment, sell a concept, negotiate a deal	Supplier - customer agreement, dispute resolution, pitch change mgt.	State group's role, ground rules and constraints	Discuss each element of the subject: point - counterpoint- compromise process	Summarize agreements, actions, and individual commitments	Conflict resolution and commitment building	• Lack of clarity • Forcing false commitment • Allowing intractable positions
Decision making	To agree upon a decision	Strategic options, capital budgeting, hiring	Describe decision and process	Structured discussion similar to solution selection in problem solving	Summarize decision, action plan and who will do what by when	Being clear about decision rights, process, and outcomes	• Misaligned goals e.g., group input or group decision • Not surfacing disagreement

General principles and facilitation tips

Here are some ideas to think about in preparing to facilitate:

- **Preparation, preparation, preparation:** First agree the purpose and process, plan the agenda, and then think up three to seven good open-ended questions in advance. Anticipate the "black holes" where the discussion could get derailed and plan how you'll dig out of them.

- **Their needs, not mine:** A good facilitator adopts a truly helpful mindset and puts aside the need to be liked or to control things.
- **Be authentic:** Your objectivity is your best contribution to the process. For example, if you don't understand some of the content and that lack of understanding is getting in the way of your helping the process along, say so.
- **Transparency of process:**
  - Be clear about outcomes and approach.
  - Stay neutral and don't put your own opinions in the room. Sometimes you can step out of your role as facilitator by clarifying that these are <u>your</u> opinions, but this risks the authenticity of your role and is dangerous.
  - Explain why you do things, e.g., "I ask people to make an opening statement so that we set the norm for equal participation in the meeting."
  - Be clear about what will happen with the information or decision after the meeting.
- **When you are in a hole, stop digging:** For example, if you ask a question that leads the group off topic, stop, identify the problem, and guide the group back on track. Or if the group attacks you and you get defensive, stop and explain what you did: "Wait a minute. I guess I'm getting a little defensive here. Can someone bring us back on track?"
- **Don't be afraid to ask the group for help:** e.g., "I just had a mind-blink. Can someone summarize what Bill just said so I can capture it?"

Following these guidelines will make meetings more effective. Facilitation isn't easy, but it is a learnable skill and critical for consultants and leaders alike.

CHAPTER 11

SURVEYS, QUESTIONNAIRES AND THE HELICOPTER VIEW

Surveys are a way of collecting the perspectives and opinions of people, customers, suppliers, shareholders, and those who work at the company. Corporations have gone "a little nuts" with surveys lately.

"After you have [completed this transaction], [used the HR kiosk or website], [updated your corporate MployEPass], or [fill in the blank], would you be willing to fill out a brief survey? Please enter 1 for Yes, 2 for No or 3 for I hate $#@%&*! surveys. Your opinion is important to us. Thank you in advance for your participation."

We are in the age of surveys and all transactions seem to come with something like the above request.

Corporations have always had "employee attitude surveys" and consultants have always shown up with their own versions. There are organizational climate surveys - the combined employee perceptions of the workplace along variables that impact performance. Some consultant use

103

culture surveys that purport to determine the culture and show which elements should be changed. There are also change readiness assessments, which are designed to indicate which change management techniques should be used.

I think surveys can be very helpful if they have clear objectives and valid questions, produce reliable data and are not over-used or misused.

The key issue about surveys is their validity, i.e., do the questions gather data that have an impact on performance? The second issue of surveys is reliability i.e., do the survey questions give the same answer over time and between companies?

If you work for an HR consultancy or an OD firm, your survey might actually be based upon research and may be tested for validity and reliability.

When I first joined Gemini Consulting, the analysis phase employee survey had over one hundred questions and had not been tested for validity and reliability. However many of the survey questions were the same as those in the organization climate model I was familiar with. I emphasized questions I knew had been validated and then organized the output into the climate model graphic. (This would be easier today as many of these questions are now available online.) This allowed me to report the survey according to a model validated for impact on performance.

Organization Climate

Organizational Climate measures people's perceptions that impact performance. When I worked for The Forum Corporation and later with Dr. George Litwin and Dr. Warner Burke, I used an Organizational Climate survey. The survey measured a series of well-tested questions around six variables that affected organizational performance:

- Clarity - What are the goals, strategies, job requirements?
- Commitment –Do workers support the work? Do managers support their people?
- Standards –Is it too easy or too hard to perform?
- Responsibility –Is there personal responsibility - pride in work?

- Recognition —Are the right people recognized?
- Teamwork —Do we help each other or is it everyone for himself?

A scenario marked with low clarity, high standards, low recognition, high responsibility and high commitment is a pressure cooker. Look for burnout. Low in everything except teamwork is a frat party, soon to be busted.

Climate is a short-term variable controlled about 70 percent by management practices and has been proven to have a huge impact upon steady state performance. Surveying climate is most useful to determine causes of current performance problems by assessing how people feel about management, and the systems and structures that define the workplace. Like any survey, longitudinal data, taken at various time points, is preferable to a single data point in time. In a change project, climate data helps to document the as-is state. A secondary measurement taken post change can show success of management actions to improve climate. Asking "How do you feel about the company?" and then either not sharing the data or not taking action is destructive.

SCHEIN MODEL OF ORGANIZATION CULTURE

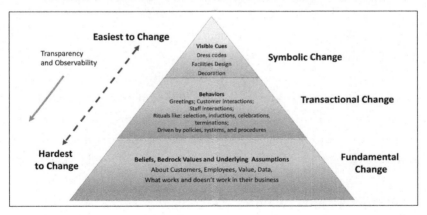

Organization Culture

Organizational culture is a longer-term variable and harder to change. Culture is affected by the history of the firm and the underlying assumptions of the business. It also encompasses beliefs and values, which manifest in norms of behavior, i.e., how we do things around here. As such, organizational cultures tend to be somewhat unique and therefore resistant to the categorization required for survey and cross-company comparison. There have been some attempts for a universal culture survey, but I have yet to see one that I think works.

The late Dr. Edgar Schein was the authority I respect most on organizational culture. Schein described culture as composed of the visible artifacts, the observable behavioral norms and espoused values, and the underlying assumptions that are the hardest to change. They also may represent the "long shadow of the founder," those assumptions that no one can see because they have been around since the organization began. To the best of my knowledge, Dr. Schein never produced a culture questionnaire. Many consultants (including me) have used his model of culture shown here as a way to describe what culture is and how it can be changed.

I once saw an interview with Dr. Schein in which he described culture as a "complex, multifaceted entity, consisting of many elements. It's impossible and unnecessary to influence all of them at the same time. . . consequently we should work to identify those elements that would help or hinder the change we are trying to make."

I facilitated many leadership team "From-To" discussions to achieve this result. The group would brainstorm change ideas, e.g., we are moving "from Top Down to Bottom Up" or we are moving "from Internally Focused to Customer Focused." Then they would discuss what each transition would mean and what actions they would need to take.

Employee attitude surveys

Many of the surveys I've seen from consultants are in this category. The survey questions are checking for overall mood. I think it's probably true that a happy workforce performs better, and it has been proven that customer service reps who feel supported by their management are better at delivering customer service as perceived by customers. But many of the questions asked on employee attitude surveys have no impact on performance because validity and reliability are too often an afterthought.

If you must use such a survey, work to tie it to qualitative data from interviews, or consider conducting a few focus groups with the workforce to help you make sense of the data. Try to tie the survey to factors that you know have an impact on performance like the organizational climate model.

Working with the client's survey

Many clients use annual employee surveys, usually distributed by Human Resources. Many of these have validity and reliability problems, but analyzing them has two advantages.

1. You will have longitudinal data; you can compare year-on-year results and trends.
2. You can ensure a feedback and action planning process to follow your analysis. Many HR departments report survey results to management. A percentage of those surveys are reported back to employees. A much smaller percentage of those surveys show concrete management action as a result. So if you can ensure any feedback and action planning process, it is a quick win for the analysis.

Build your own survey

Survey Monkey, Mail Chimp, Google workspace, Google surveys, Microsoft forms, Qualtrics CoreXM, Survey Sparrow, ZOHO – the list is endless. "Do it yourself" surveys are everywhere and may seem easy. They're not. You'll need to think about how to construct the survey, how to define the sample, how it will be tabulated, what output you will get and how you will feed it back to your client and to the respondents. Asking people to fill out a survey and not giving them feedback and not taking action on their opinions is destructive.

The survey

Think about the validity and reliability issue. If you can find some tested questions online, it will help.

Think about the scale. American psychologist Rensis Likert created a scale that is most frequently used for quantitative data. The scale is based upon the extent of agreement with a statement.

1. Definitely Disagree
2. Inclined to Disagree
3. Neither Agree nor Disagree
4. Inclined to Agree
5. Definitely Agree

Questions should be worded with this scale in mind. For example, "our goals are clear" elicits a clear disagree or agree response. If you mix positive and negative orientation, i.e., "our goals are not clear," then does a 2 rating mean the goals are clear? The answer is ambiguous and can't be compared to other answers.

Be careful with open-ended questions. How much space does the software allow? Some people will write a book. You will need to use content analysis to pull out common responses and quotes. Depending on the size of your sample this can be an onerous task.

The sample

Why don't we just do the whole company? This might seem like a reasonable idea for a quantitative survey that software tabulates. But survey software may charge you by number of respondents. They may also charge you by the number of demographic categories for which you're seeking discrete output.

So for every sample, you must define many variables - how large it should be, number of demographic cuts, etc. This task isn't impossible, and there is a science to answer these questions. But the net is that many people do not know the complexity of the request.

A survey cautionary tale

A large company called "the most innovative company in America" had a morale problem. It was true that there were rumblings of some unhappy customers and rumors that government regulators were nosing around, but people were actually leaving and this was a company that everyone wanted to work for. The CEO wanted to find out "what the hell is going on." He wrote a few open-ended questions, wanted no demographic information, like employee level, job, gender etc. He only wanted to know the division where the respondent worked. He also didn't want word or character limits on responses, stating, "I hate when they do that!"

And so it was done. An impassioned email was sent from the CEO to the entire company, about 29,000 people. He told people they were part of a great company, fallen on hard times. He knew some people were unhappy, but here was the opportunity to "lay it on the line."

People did. Nearly two thirds of employees responded. The company email server blew up. There was no plan to process the data.

Fortunately, a small New York-based consulting firm was opening an office in town and a young principal was on a partner track. He had been calling on people he knew in the company in an effort to see the CEO. He got a meeting and agreed that his firm would process the survey as a demonstration of capability, for free. He promised a report in four days. They gave him the data.

There were fifteen questions, almost twenty thousand responses and some people wrote pages on each question. The young principal panicked and called the New York office. There was too much data to email, but he sent hard copy and flash drives overnight to New York.

I was the given the task of content analysis with a team that started out as two analysts and ended up with ten. We worked from the time we received the data until 3:00 a.m. the first day, from 8:00 a.m. till 5:00 a.m. the second day. By now we had expanded our team to basically everyone in the firm. I asked for more time.

The team was falling apart, not just from the workload and late nights. Reading this material was horrifying. There were reports of the worst kind of leadership behavior, harassment, and criminal activity, including stealing customers' funds. It took a toll on all of us.

I remember a lot of back and forth with my colleagues about my additional time request and conversations with the partners of the firm about "what was taking so long." The third day came and went; we worked all night.

In the middle of the fourth day, with still no response to my request for more time, the news broke that the SEC had announced a fraud probe into Enron and its auditor Arthur Andersen. All of our analyses and the originals of all data were gathered up and sent to our attorney's offices.

Enron declared bankruptcy two months later, Jeff Skilling ultimately went to prison and the former CEO Ken Lay died in prison awaiting appeal.

It was a painful experience for a lot of people, fraught with scandal and tragedy. And while certainly not a central question of Enron's collapse, I remember asking, "Why would anyone do a survey like this with no plan for processing the output?" THAT is a trap not to fall into.

Output, feedback, and action

What will the output look like? How will we feed it back? How will that affect our recommendations?

These are questions you should ask about surveys, people stuff analytics - in fact *all* analytics. Output of analysis stems from hypotheses, but it goes further. It answers the question: If the output shows what I think it will show, what action will the client take? If, however, it shows the opposite of what I expect, what is the recommended action? Then finally there is the question of feedback: How will I feed these data back to the client to facilitate that action? Who else needs the survey data to ensure that results come from that action?

Stephen Covey, in *The Secrets of Highly Effective People*, asserts that "successful people start with the end in mind." That may or may not be true for success in all fields, but it is certainly true for analysts in consulting.

CHAPTER 12

A DAY-IN-THE-LIFE

A Day-in-the Life was the name Gemini Analysis and Design gave to detailed role/process observation and analysis. I saw it used in other firms as well. Katzenbach Partners used it on a sales study where it was called a "ride-along" because the consultant rode along with a delivery truck salesman. The Forum Corporation used it for a bank customer service project where a consultant observed tellers in a branch bank.

On an offshore oil platform, I once observed safety procedures. I even unloaded food supplies and was given a job safety evaluation, which I passed, but had several opportunities for improvement. (Yes, from unloading groceries. It gave me new respect for real process and personal safety in that potentially dangerous environment.)

The day-in-the-life protocol at Gemini consisted of timing actions and noting task durations and interruptions. It also assessed the management of conflicting instructions and objectives and observed interpersonal interactions, communication methodologies, and general ergonomics. There were also variations depending on the role.

One of my early Gemini projects was the post-merger integration of two laboratory chemicals manufacturers in which a value brand acquired a premium brand. It was the view of the acquiring client leadership and the project lead that the one "synergy opportunity" (read that as "cost-savings" area) was to rationalize the sales forces. This translated to the idea of firing most of the premium brand's salespeople who were paid substantially more.

In the initial interviews, several people in the acquired company questioned that strategy and so Sean, the sales stream lead, was assigned to do a day-in-the-life analysis of the two sales jobs, both the value and premium brands. Sean may have been a Newbie consultant like me at the time, but he had eight years of sales experience at GE. The results came back.

The value brand salesperson, who may or may not have a college degree, called upon purchasing managers at laboratories at universities and bulk chemical manufacturers. Each salesperson made eight to ten calls per day of about fifteen minutes in length per call. These calls were mostly orders and reorders of salts and solvents in bulk.

The premium brand salesforce had at least an undergraduate degree and often a graduate degree in chemistry or chemical engineering. They called upon chemists and chemical engineers in laboratories of food manufacturers, pharmaceutical companies or specialized government testing facilities. Each salesperson made one to two calls per day, sold small quantities of high purity salts and solvents and often participated in troubleshooting with the client.

As Sean reported his findings to the Lead Analyst it was clear that these were two very different sales jobs. I was surprised at how difficult it was to convince our team leader that firing all the premium brand salespeople was a bad idea. In the team meeting I supported Sean's assertion, but my nine years of entertainment sales experience seemed to have less credibility than Sean's GE experience.

Fortunately, Pablo, the marketing team stream lead and a Newbie with a marketing PhD, shared his customer perception mapping analysis. There was no overlap between the two brands in customers' minds, indicating the need for a two-brand strategy. Both sets of research convinced our team leader and the client of the wisdom of maintaining both sales-forces and we found cost savings in other areas.

Day-in-the-life analysis is often assigned to onsite Newbies based upon findings from initial interviews. It can be problematic, so it's important to understand <u>why</u> you are conducting this study. Observing someone doing their job can be incredibly threatening. You will need to explain the" why" in your introduction. You should also explain that this is a role evaluation and <u>not</u> an evaluation of the person.

The challenge of pre-existing beliefs that Sean faced isn't uncommon, so it is critical that this analysis is based upon documented observations. The more detail you can capture, the better.

If there is an information system that tracks this work, such as a customer service system or back office payments system, gather these data for the observed period. Also gather performance management data, i.e., goals and objectives, metrics, etc.

Document meetings that occur during the observed period. What was the objective (e.g., announcement, discovery, problem-solving, negotiation/commitment building)? Was the objective clear? Was the objective achieved? How long did the meeting last?

What issues or problems did the worker face with this job? Sometimes this is obvious - for example, a critical computer system goes down during a customer service call and the worker has to say to the caller, "I'm sorry our system is down, I can't get to that information." In other scenarios, you may have to ask the person in the role, "Did you just experience a problem?"

At the end of the observation period, which may range from a few hours to multiple days to get the full picture, I usually discussed with the worker what I observed and reiterated the why and how the data would be used. I found it useful to show the person my report before delivery to "make sure it's accurate" and also to demonstrate that the data was aggregated data and that their name wasn't mentioned.

A Day-in-the-Life uses observation, so it requires detail focus and the willingness to ask why, when you don't understand something. If you get the answer, "it was the way I was trained" or "that's the way we've always done it" that might be a clue of a lack of efficiency or effectiveness.

Also critical are documentation, discussion with others and judgement as to what is important.

INCREASE REVENUE: STRATEGY PROJECTS

C onsultants help people and companies change. Most often they do this in a project - short term work using a methodology they may have used before. No two companies are alike; no two problems are the same, but projects have some similarities.

You may remember the point I made earlier, "everything is people stuff," and that my career focused on people, but I thought it more useful to group projects the way a client might.

- **Increase Revenue: Strategy Projects**
- **Grow Revenue: Acquisition Strategy and Innovation Process**
- **Increase Profit: Continuous Improvement (Operations) Projects**
- **People Stuff Projects**

Missing from this description of work are new technological systems implementation and systems integrations work. These are areas of consulting work that grew very rapidly during my career and have exploded since I retired. Digital transformation and the integration of Artificial Intelligence as well as autonomous, algorithmic, and automatic systems, are learning how to run everything. By all accounts, AI represents an ever-growing percentage of consulting work.

I have not included these projects because I never did this work and as a "late adopter," I am probably the worst person to write about it. I maintain, however, that despite the mind-bending capabilities of new electronic gee-whizzery, business is still about people and companies are still interested in revenue, profit and people stuff. Technology may create huge consulting projects but those will likely facilitate growing revenue or profit.

So this isn't a mutually exclusive, collectively exhaustive list of consulting projects, issues, or methodologies, but it's a start.

Increase Revenue: Strategy Projects

These projects are Newbie nirvana. Everyone wants to set a new direction for companies. Strategy consulting has a golden aura, a glow, a mystique, and definitely prestige for most new entrants to consulting. If we come back to earth for a moment, however, a strategy is a plan:

- What are you going to do and why?
- How are you going to do it?
- Who will do what by when and at what cost?

That's it - just a plan. More specifically, strategy is a plan to grow revenue or profit or both in the face of competition or other uncontrollable variables (like available supply, changing technology, or government regulation).

The word strategy comes from the Greek word *strategos,* which means generalship, and military warfare was the first use of the concept. Most people trace the widespread use of the word to Carl Von Clausewitz, the Prussian general who wrote *On War*, which describes the strategies of Napoleon and Frederick the Great. Von Clausewitz gives some credit for his observations to an ancient Chinese text, Sun Tzu's *The Art of War* written around 500 B.C. While he never uses the word strategy, Sun Tzu is prescient in concepts that easily translate to business. In one of the most engaging strategic planning projects I ever ran, the leadership team compared Sun Tzu's descriptions of battlefields, "Ground... death ground... downhill and uphill... the mud or swamp," to the Michael Porter Five Forces model of industry structure (discussed shortly) and the nature of competition. The group found winning niches where they compete effectively even today.

Is business war? Some like the military model and often elevate strategy accordingly. I like to remind those people of the words of General Dwight David Eisenhower, commander of Allied Forces in western Europe in World War II (and 34th president of the United States):

"In preparing for battle, plans are useless, planning is essential."

CHANGING ENVIRONMENT DRIVES STRATEGY

This quote speaks to the value of thinking in advance of action, but hints that action "on the ground" will need to be adapted to changing circumstances.

The Plan

Strategy is still just a plan - what and why, how, who and when. The thinking behind the plan should prepare the business to adapt as needed.

There are a lot of strategic planning frameworks. Every consulting firm has one, but here is a generic framework to think about.

When a client decides that they need a new strategy it is usually because they missed opportunities in a new or changing environment or they didn't anticipate the competitor response. Sometimes the client doesn't notice until revenue drops substantially.

An expert strategy consulting firm (content consultant) may bring evidence of those changes based upon industry experience, and/or collect and analyze data to show the changes that indicate recommended actions.

A strategy process consultant may have industry experience and opinions about actions, but approaches the task differently. He teaches research and analysis to the leadership and creates processes like environmental scanning so that the client doesn't get caught flat-footed again. The strategy process consultant often works alongside the client to execute the strategy.

Implementation: strategy execution

A McKinsey senior director once said to me, "Implementation is the client's responsibility. We would never usurp our client's job." My other favorite quote is from Brigadier General David Sarnoff, who was on Eisenhower's staff as well as the CEO of RCA:

"A 'B' quality plan executed in an 'A' quality fashion will always beat an 'A' quality plan executed in a 'B' quality fashion."

I believe that process consultants have an advantage in strategy execution, but the content consultant's approach is equally effective when the client is thoroughly engaged.

My first project was a new product feasibility study for a heavy duty truck company in the United Kingdom. The project lead engaged the client in the analysis by conducting weekly updates. By the time the client got the recommendations, "build the eight-wheel truck, stay away from distribution box vans, there's no available premium for heavy duty," he was convinced and implemented everything.

In contrast, my second project with the same project lead was a study of the market for automatic transmissions in buses in nineteen developing countries. The client insisted on a "hands-off approach" and never implemented anything, though there were seven of those markets ripe for his company's transmissions.

Even Newbie content consultants can help the client execute strategy. Ask the project lead if you can gather feedback on the analysis and recommendations from people who would act upon it. Approach this delicately in the spirit of adding richness to the presentation, rather than telling the project lead how to do his or her job. Also if the project lead worries that doing this would "leak" the answer before the big presentation, ensure that input will be confidential and ideas will be given credit. At a minimum, remember to engage the client system when you manage projects.

I have already described how business strategy progressed in the 1970s from the BCG analytical portfolio management matrices to the models of industry structure and the nature of competition of Michael Porter of Harvard. The following chapter "Using a Matrix to Plan Revenue Growth " offers the Ansoff matrix as a simple way to address these issues. The chapter that follows on the strategy process goes into greater detail on strategic frameworks.

CHAPTER 13

USING A MATRIX TO PLAN REVENUE GROWTH

A few years ago I joined an online community of people seeking to become board members or advisory board members for small entrepreneurial businesses.

If this sample of small companies was typical, entrepreneurs seemed to be mostly concerned about growth strategy. How can we get more customers? Should we enter other markets? If so, what markets and when? Should we introduce new products? If so, what products and when? While MBAs would say marketing strategy was the solution, these entrepreneurs weren't necessarily thinking about the 4 Ps of marketing strategy - product, price, promotion, and place (distribution channel) – but rather on <u>more revenue</u> to cover increasing expenses.

Gaining sales in a competitive market requires a plan that everyone in the company understands and buys into. So the idea that a CEO (or a consultant) should go into a room alone and come up with the strategy is ill-conceived. It is group decision-making followed by group implementation. It often starts with a facilitated small group process such as a strategic off-site or an innovation discussion.

There are many strategic frameworks to make this discussion flow easily. Some are more complex than others and some frameworks require more research than others - gathering more data before having a discussion. One framework I used with small companies or divisions of large companies is the product/market matrix.

THE ANSOFF MATRIX*

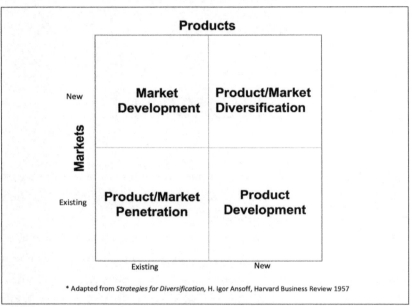

* Adapted from *Strategies for Diversification*, H. Igor Ansoff, Harvard Business Review 1957

Igor Ansoff introduced the product/market matrix in 1957 when he was a professor at the Graduate School of Industrial Administration at the Carnegie Institute of Technology in Pittsburgh, Pennsylvania, now Carnegie Mellon University. Dr. Ansoff first published the product/market matrix in an article entitled "Strategies for Diversification," and it later formed the basis for his book *Corporate Strategy* in 1965. I like the Ansoff product/market matrix because of its simple premise: **"growth is a function of innovation in developing new products or in serving new markets."**

Most business leaders can get behind this premise and with minimal advance reading come to a meeting prepared to discuss their views about how the firm or division could grow. Research and data collection will be a first step following the meeting, but it will be focused research in a chosen direction. We'll look at variations on this matrix, but let's first examine how it works.

Product/market penetration

Who are our existing customers? Why do they buy? If the product is bought multiple times, do they rebuy at the next cycle? If they buy from more than one supplier, what is our product's share of wallet? If it is a one-time sale, do customers recommend the product to others?

Might we attract more customers at a lower price? A higher price? What distribution channels are we ignoring? How might we promote differently (more advertising, more sales people) to increase sales? Which products are profitable? Which customers are profitable?

Some firms never get out of the existing/existing quadrant in their early discussions. The questions cause them to dig deep to find answers. For example, after examining customer and product profitability, some firms adopt a "core-products-core-customers-only" strategy, divesting themselves of money-losing products and customers. This frees up time to expand product/market penetration, the "easiest" form of growth strategy.

The next area of discussion could be products or market. Many firms find it easier to answer the question, "Who else could we sell this same product to?"

Market development

In order to pursue a market development strategy, first describe current customers and their purchase criteria. Then discuss what constitutes a truly new customer and what is just further penetration of an existing customer group. In the end, what box it's in doesn't matter. Whether a prospect is "truly new" is less important than the decision to pursue this customer.

Some questions that might drive this discussion:

- Who else might use this product? (Expectant mothers might use a low-impact yoga class designed for seniors.)
- What new uses might our existing product be put to? (The 3M Post-it note was a failed adhesive that became a page-marking note for church music scores and then a host of other office uses.)
- What new customer segments might we serve? Different regions? Foreign sales?

At first it might be enough to brainstorm possible opportunities for market development. Each market development strategy will need to be analyzed according to clear criteria:

- Is this a **real** opportunity for anyone? (Do customers want/need this product?)
- Can our firm **win**? (Do we know anything about these customers? Is our offering unique among competitors?)
- Will it be **worth** it? (Are there economies of scale in our current production and distribution systems? Will we make any money at this?)

The research, analysis and development of a plan follows, i.e., what are we going to do and why? How will we do it? Who will do what by when? Then the hard part – implementation.

Product development

Some firms tend to venture into product development first, often before maximizing existing product sales to existing markets. A sales-oriented CEO in a service business once said to me, "Look, if I call on a customer today and he doesn't buy from me, why would he buy from me tomorrow unless I bring him something different?" This firm ended up with many different service offerings that were specific to individual customers, and profitability suffered until they rationalized offerings.

Some firms develop products internally while others purchase companies or license products to bring to the market. All should have a disciplined process of product development that looks something like this:

PRODUCT DEVELOPMENT

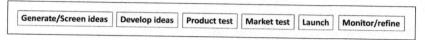

| Generate/Screen ideas | Develop ideas | Product test | Market test | Launch | Monitor/refine |

The question of what constitutes a new product often arises. As with the market development strategy quadrant, where the strategy is placed is less important than agreement on the plan.

When a group had difficulty thinking of product improvements and small innovations, I shared these three components of a product:

Hardware – the physical component

Software – instructions for use

Service – something we do for the customer

THE ANSOFF MATRIX* — RISK

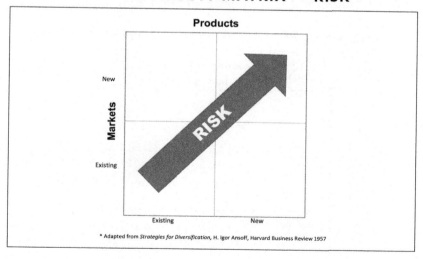

* Adapted from *Strategies for Diversification*, H. Igor Ansoff, Harvard Business Review 1957

Any component can be the "main product," i.e., what the customer actually buys. For example, the iPhone may be the phone itself (hardware),

IOS for iPhone (software), or a technical service plan (service). But a product can be differentiated by increasing a component, decreasing or eliminating another component, or creating new features altogether for a component.

Product/market diversification

Some groups want to pursue both product development and market development simultaneously.

As Dr. Ansoff made clear, product development and market development are diversification strategies. Doing both at the same time is possible but it increases risk dramatically. How large is the change we will make? Do we have the operational resources to pull this off? Do we have the management time to devote to it? Firms diversify all the time. Dr. Ansoff's point was that diversification is a complex strategy to achieve growth. It should be pursued carefully with a hard look at the firm's capabilities and unique strengths, and potential synergies with the existing business. Walk before you run.

THE ANSOFF NINE-BLOCK GROWTH MATRIX

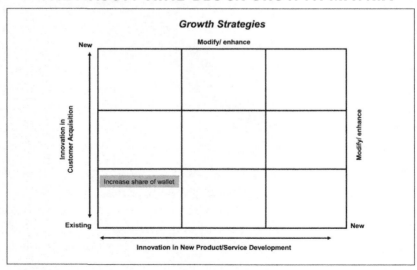

In leadership team discussions, when someone raised the objection, "But it's not <u>that much</u> of a change in the product or market," I suggested this nine-box variant of the Ansoff matrix. This answered the objection, but it added complexity and time discussing the criteria for each box. Sometimes this was beneficial as groups tended to analyze lower left options first when researching options.

Generating strategic options is often the easy part. Many leadership teams even find it to be fun, but in the real work of implementing a growth strategy I advised taking "baby steps first."

I once worked with a group of mid-level leaders at a major international bank's infrastructure and energy finance group. Senior leadership had given them the opportunity to devise the department's growth strategy. In a few hours of brainstorming they came up with multiple strategic options.

ANSOFF NINE-BLOCK EXAMPLE: PROJECT FINANCE

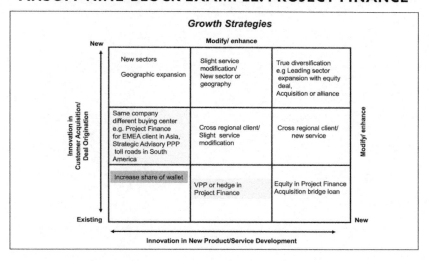

Ultimately, they chose some short-term strategies to increase business from existing clients, and scheduled research and development in some minor new product and market development.

Senior leaders were so impressed by their work and the short-term results they were able to achieve that they engaged the group on research into their identified longer-term opportunities. Several of those mid-term leaders rose to senior positions in the bank.

The Ansoff Product/Market Growth matrix is a good introductory strategic planning framework to start growth discussions. Interested leadership teams can push their analysis further with such tools as Michael Porter's Five Forces Analysis to determine the nature of industry competitiveness and differentiation. Or they might look to avoid competition altogether and discuss Chan Kim and Renée Mauborgne's Blue Ocean innovation/strategy framework.

However, as previously mentioned, 75 percent of people do not naturally structure their thinking using a framework. Introducing multiple frameworks at the same time may benefit those 25 percent who are "framework thinkers" but will only confuse, and probably lose, the majority of people. Keep it simple.

CHAPTER 14

STRATEGY PROCESS

Helping leaders make strategic change
Over my entire consulting career I struggled to describe to others what I did. Sometimes "management consultant" sufficed at a cocktail party, but it came with its own baggage.

"Oh, you work for management to help them screw the workers?" or

"Oh, you describe ordinary business problems as 'life-threatening' so you can rip off companies with obvious ideas stolen from second-level managers?"

I learned people's experience with consultants often depended on where they sat in the organization, and that experience was frequently not positive.

Ultimately, I described myself as a strategy process consultant, or a process consultant focused on strategic leadership and change. In the last ten years of my practice I landed on the tag line "Helping Leaders Make Strategic Change." I thought it spoke to the frustration I had observed among C-suite executives, namely, "I know where we need to go and what has to be done. I just can't get *people* to do it!"

"Helping Leaders Make Strategic Change" said, "I'm going to *help* get you where you want to go and bring *people* (your leadership team, the workforce) along with you."

Truthfully, the tagline was an effective marketing message only some of the time. Often people just saw me as one of the component parts of my practice: a leadership team facilitator or off-site designer, a training designer or materials developer, a stand-up trainer, an organization design consultant or a leadership coach for interpersonal relationships and/or group communications.

Sometimes, though, I found an engagement that allowed me to put all my skills together and live up to the tag line. I was the consultant who understood people and process, and, at the same time, focused on achieving business results.

Understanding that the people were critical came to me far too slowly. I was good at Organization Behavior in business school, but was more interested in strategy.

A strategy professor tried to tell me. "MBAs always look down at OB, but when they come back as senior executives all they want to learn is the 'people stuff.'"

It didn't sink in. When Dr. Derek Pugh, the OB department head, suggested that I major in OB, I said, "Oh, God, Derek, I couldn't do that! No recruiter would take me seriously."

A few years later, I went back to school to study organizational development, where I learned that the Dr. Pugh, who I so imperiously blew off, was quite well known in the field. I worked in training and consulting and gradually became aware that the "people stuff" was pretty important.

As a trainer I realized that changing behavior might start with an insight about how to do something more, less or differently, but it required action and practice to get consistent results.

- Over time I learned that what was true of individual behavior was true of business strategy as well. Individual insight, even "the BIG IDEA," by itself was never enough.
- The insight had to be collectively internalized.
- Individuals and groups then had to take new actions and practice new behaviors.

- Results had to be measured and monitored, and new changes had to maintain or increase the desired result.

THE STRATEGIC CHANGE MODEL

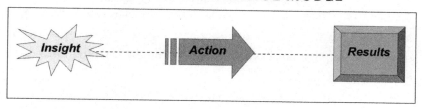

This is the strategic change model that I developed:

On more than one occasion, a prospective client would say, "Hey, wait a minute. We want a *strategy*, not a *change*," or words to that effect. *Strategy* is often seen to be based upon a unique idea, something we hadn't thought of. *Change* is often seen as someone trying to do something <u>to me.</u>

I get the attraction of Insight – the Big Idea. I also get that we often isolate strategy – the plan – as a discipline separate from operations – doing it. But saying that we need a new plan means that what we are doing isn't working, which means we must do something different or *change*.

I worked with a client who was a national radio representative; the company sold national spot advertising on a group of radio stations across the United States. At the time (pre-Internet streaming) radio's share of national advertising was declining. The client came up with a concept called The Radio Store, a one-stop-shop for everything the radio medium could do - local promotions, multiple media tie-ins, events, spot-planning etc.

The company sold the idea to their customers, largely advertising agency account executives and marketing departments. They expected the sales force would just get on board, but their client radio stations expected their "reps" to pitch their individual station in a dog-eat-dog competitive media buying environment that was contributing to the "race to the bottom" of the industry.

Very little change happened. We created a separate sales force to call higher and wider, but reps and stations viewed it as competition. We did expand radio's share for a while, and it was an exciting period for those who bought into the "big idea" and changed their behaviors. However, the failure to bring everyone on board with the plan meant that implementation was not enough to counteract radio's decline. This decline turned around, of course, when Internet radio increased national distribution of what had been a local medium.

Planning seems to have more cache than executing the plan. Few would ever be so crass as to say out loud "brains plan, hands operate," but this sentiment does exist, despite all the research that proves the efficacy of including those who do the work in planning. So this brings me to my first principle of Strategy Process:

"None of us is as smart as all of us."

Strategy is a collaborative process. Everyone must internalize the insight, the reason for the strategy. They must act together, from measuring progress to end results.

So in my view, strategic planning isn't a standalone activity; it is inextricably intertwined with strategy execution. This is why I tend to favor cross-functional strategic planning teams composed of members of the leadership team and operational leaders. This brings us to my second principle of strategy process:

"The only constant is change."

As noted, a strategy is a <u>plan</u> to achieve a desired result in the face of <u>competition</u>.

A plan is a description of:

- What you are going to do and why (context, objectives, and high-level actions)
- How you are going to do it (detailed step-by-step activities)
- Who is going to do what, at what cost and by when (resource

allocation, budget and schedule)

Competition is any entity that might attempt to achieve the same result as you or otherwise impede your ability to achieve that result. This is what makes the strategy process challenging. Not only must we plan our own actions, but also we must anticipate our competitors' response and how the plan will change as a result. For that reason, flexibility and adaptability are key traits of any strategy.

My practice evolved to a process approach to strategy that integrated planning and execution and was both collaborative and adaptable. I applied this process to typical strategic leadership and change projects:

- Engage the client system
- Create insight
- Inspire action
- Measure progress and results
- Refocus, adapt and respond

Engage the client system

No client ever said to me, "I want to rethink how we plan our strategy or who we involve in the process." Instead, the client might blame the strategy saying, "We need a strategy that will work." Sometimes I was hired "to help implement," or to help leadership "get on the same page" about a strategy produced internally or with another consultant. These were frequently symptoms of a strategy process that didn't sufficiently involve key members of the leadership team and I would respond with leadership engagement and facilitation.

Often leadership facilitation projects grew out of a leader's frustration. "Everybody's got an opinion." My favorite description from a client was, "This place is a gaggle of geese on the ground, everybody milling about and honking. What I want is a flock of geese in the air, flying in a tight 'V' formation."

In the first meeting the hiring executive would ask directly for a strategy and would say something about buy-in or, in some cases, a small group would discuss different points of view about where they currently were.

The first phase of the project always involved interviews of the leadership team and opinion leaders in order to engage with those who would implement the new strategy. When I worked at Gemini Consulting doing reengineering projects, these initial interviews served two purposes: diagnosis – framing the issues; and building the relationships needed to succeed. At Katzenbach Partners, interviews were often part of the sales process. Jon Katzenbach would conduct five to six interviews for free to increase his clarity and the client's commitment in order to close the business. I rarely had the luxury of giving away initial diagnosis, but I did underprice initial analysis, at the end of which the client gave a go/no go decision.

Frequently, insights began to emerge during the engagement process. Almost always I was able to identify opinion leaders who could help with the research and form the basis of the client team.

Create insight

A new strategy most always requires new information or a new way of looking at what we already know. This new insight must be shared widely enough to inspire collective action. There is research (e.g., discovering something new about customers or competitors) and internalization (communicating the information in a way that builds acceptance and commitment to act).

To that end, traditional content-driven strategy consultants present industry research, competitive analysis, and client capability analysis to the client before building a strategy for the firm. They do research and expect the client to internalize their information and then act.

A strategy process consultant teaches the client how to do this work. Strategy process consultants often combine research and internalization by working closely with client teams who share the workload. It's messier, but in the end a firm learns a new capability and is less dependent on outside help.

The insight needed can be about changing customer needs, new competition, or a changing industry structure. Insight also may be needed to understand the impact of new technology on existing products and services or how the business has grown beyond the operational processes of earlier stages. Choosing what to research is a critical path activity of initial interviews and other diagnosis.

The research is then organized into a way of thinking about it – an analytical framework.

Making sense of research – frameworks

Frameworks are an organization's logic to structure analysis. They often contain an understood action or actions based upon findings: "If we find such and such then we will do this." A framework is often a picture, a graphical representation of the situation in which the company finds itself. It is a map, complete with a big "You are here" sign, i.e., "if you are here and your competitors are there then do this."

Some consultants fall in love with a particular framework and over-apply it past the point of clarity. Still, frameworks can be helpful in understanding detailed research data.

BOSTON CONSLUTING GROUP'S
GROWTH SHARE MATRIX

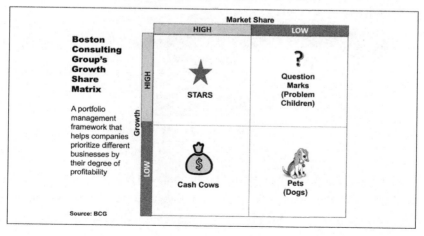

Frameworks have a long history in the strategy field. As discussed earlier, BCG introduced the Growth Share Matrix portfolio model for conglomerate businesses. This framework was more complex than it seemed at first glance because the scale was in logarithmic numbers. BCG consultants could help place the client's businesses, and then the strategy revealed itself:

- Invest in stars
- Milk cash cows
- Improve the share of question marks (or "problem children" as they were first named)
- Divest the pets (or the "dogs" as they were originally called)

As a strategy process consultant, I occasionally used a simplified version of this matrix to frame a leadership discussion if the strategic problem was poor prioritization of businesses and the framework resonated with the client.

MICHAEL PORTERS FIVE FORCES EVALUATION

In the 1980s Dr. Michael Porter of the Harvard Business School began writing about the nature of competition given various forces of industry dynamics. I have used his Five Forces model as a discussion with many leadership teams. This framework did a good job of describing the conditions in the current market. My clients often found that it was helpful to explain the context or the why behind their chosen strategy. For strategy formulation, Porter's generic strategies (low cost, differentiate, or niche) often left the client a bit stumped.

Clients understood low cost strategies, but struggled with aligning all organizational elements to deliver them. Many clients wanted to differentiate, but struggled with the how. They could conceive of the small group of customers that defined a niche, but struggled with how to protect it.

Most often the client came up with particular strategies to deal with the conditions in each of the forces. What should we do to gain advantage with large suppliers? Collaborate with non-competitors to gain scale. How can we protect ourselves from new entrants? Engage an association with quality certification or pursue licensing (like psychologists and electricians) to create barriers to entry. The model was less helpful on innovation and differentiation.

In the 1990s, Michel Treacy and Fred Wiersema wrote *The Discipline of Market Leaders: Choose Your Customers, Narrow Your Focus, Dominate Your Market.* These two management consultants posited the idea that market leaders rigorously define the value that they provide to customers in one of three ways:

Customer Intimacy – companies that are ultimately responsive to customers

Operational Excellence – companies that rigorously reduce costs and often become low-cost producers

Product Leadership – companies that strive for superior innovation especially in new technology

The point of this framework is that success requires focused practice and so I found this framework particularly useful with smaller companies struggling to be all things to all people. Often the leadership team included leaders for whom different disciplines resonated.

"Charley's an efficiency nut and can't see that customizing products for each customer keeps them with you long term."

"Jean has no idea of product unit profit."

Viewing strategy as a *choice* of things you <u>do</u> and things you <u>don't</u> <u>do</u> is often an epiphany.

One framework I liked was Blue Ocean Strategy. W. Chan Kim and Renée Mauborgne, professors at INSEAD, described how companies like Southwest Airlines and Cirque du Soleil manipulated the determinants of value in their industry such that they were truly differentiated. They then had no comparable competitor. The process that Kim and Mauborgne suggest is to first agree the determinants of value or common industry practice – advance seat selection and vast service areas in airlines, animal acts/thrills and danger in circuses – and then decide what they could reduce, eliminate, raise importance of, or create new or different value from. Southwest Airlines is a limited, no-frills market area that competes with driving in a car; Cirque du Soleil is extravagantly designed acrobatic performance art.

CYNEFIN FRAMEWORK

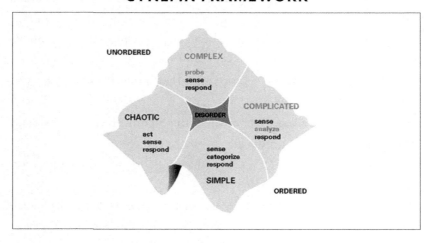

The twenty-first century brought with it lots of uncertainty and risk.

Colleagues responded by using frameworks such as VUCA and Cynefin that are designed to help clients cope. VUCA (Volatility, Uncertainty, Complexity, Ambiguity), as put forth by Nathan Bennett and G. James Lemoine in the *Harvard Business Review* (January-February 2014), describes four types of strategic risk and prescribes actions for each.

Cynefin (a Welsh word meaning habitat or place to make a stand) prescribes similar actions to address the unknown. When things are known and simple you can analyze, categorize and respond. When the situation is complex, complicated or chaotic you must act and experiment. The Cynefin framework was created by David Snowden of IBM Global Services.

BENNETT AND LEMOINE'S VUCA ACTION GUIDE

+	Complexity	Volatility
How well can you predict the results of your actions?	**Characteristics:** The situation has many interconnected parts and variables. Some information is available or can be predicted, but the volume or nature of it can be overwhelming to process **Example:** You are doing business in many different countries, all with unique regulatory environments, tariffs, and cultural issues **Approach:** Restructure, bring on or develop specialists, and build up resources adequate to address complexity	**Characteristics:** The challenge is unexpected or unstable and may be of unknown duration, but it's not necessarily hard to understand; knowledge about it is often available. **Example:** Prices fluctuate after a natural disaster takes a supplier off line **Approach:** Build in and devote resources to preparedness – for instance, stockpile inventory or overbuy talent. These steps are typically expensive; your investment should match the risk.
	Ambiguity	Uncertainty
	Characteristics: Causal relationships are completely unclear. No precedents exist; you face "unknown unknowns." **Example:** You decide to move into immature or emerging markets or launch products outside your core competencies. **Approach:** Experiment. Understanding cause and effect requires generating Hypotheses and testing them. Design your experiments so the lessons learned can be broadly applied.	**Characteristics:** Despite the lack of other information the event's basic cause and effect are known. Change is possible, but not a given. **Example:** A competitor's pending product launch muddies the future of the business and the market. **Approach:** Invest in information – collect, interpret, and share it. This works best in conjunction with structural changes, such as adding information analysis networks, that can reduce uncertainty.
—	**How much do you know about the situation?**	**+**

In my practice, I often used a process of trend analysis and scenario planning to deal with risk and uncertainty. This process worked with a relatively large, extended leadership group (fifteen to twenty-five people) and built a strategic coalition that engendered commitment to a change in strategy. This commitment quickly led to action.

In interviews we determined what leaders saw as the trends affecting their business; we also provided some trends from general and industry research. Trends can be general economic trends like expectation of GDP growth during the period. Or they can be quite industry-specific; for example, the growth of non-union contractors acquiring construction business in New York City. In the first workshop, leaders agreed on the trend having the most impact on their business and what level they expected the trend to reach during the planning period. Between workshops 1 & 2, small groups developed scenarios based upon the intersection of two trends.

Each group discussed the scenario formed by the most likely position of each trend and determined the implications for strategy. The groups then tested the risks of actions if the trends driving the scenario moved more quickly or slowly than anticipated.

SCENARIO: PLANNING WORKSHOPS

In the construction firm example, Group C compared the implications of increasingly sophisticated clients and an increasing war for construction talent. The group then brainstormed strategies to mitigate these trends.

In the second workshop these implications and risks were combined into a strategic framework and first action steps were identified.

Depending upon the degree of uncertainty and risk, additional workshops were sometimes required to resolve conflicting strategies and align actions into a coordinated plan.

SCENARIO C-1:
SOPHISTICATED CLIENTS & TALENT WAR

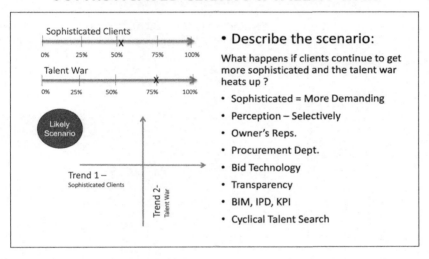

Some caveats about frameworks as a means to create insight:

1. **Pick <u>one.</u>** I am framework-agnostic. In my practice, I chose a framework or let the client choose based upon the circumstances and what resonated with him or her. What I am rigid about is working with one framework at a time. Some consultants and even some clients want to combine multiple frameworks. I learned that this combination only leads to confusion for most of the audience. Simplicity and focus are the watchwords of good strategy.

2. **Not everyone thinks in frameworks.** In initial interviews I often showed key members of the leadership team an example or

two of frameworks and discussed them. If all went well I could see what types of framework resonated. But if they stared blankly and didn't make the leap to the words and pictures on the page I would back up and let them describe the business and the factors for success or failure in their own words.

CHANGING THE SCALE CHANGES THE OUTCOME

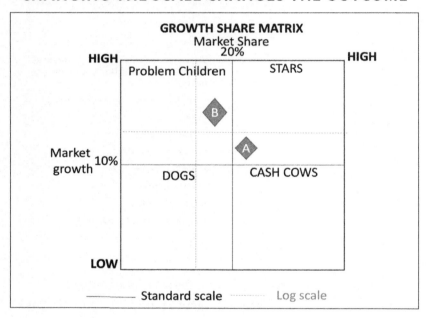

3. **Real differences of opinion often masquerade as a "lack of understanding" of the framework.** Early in my career, two executives in a component chemical business were heatedly debating the Growth Share Matrix. Brian, the manager of a new agricultural chemical in a high growth market where he had a small share, (Business B) insisted we should use a logarithmic scale as the instrument was designed. Arthur, the manager of generic acetylsalicylic acid, the pre-tableting component of aspirin, who had a relatively dominant position in a low growth

market (Business A) maintained that a linear scale was much simpler. The meeting adjourned and I met with the two executives individually. Each began with his justification for and against using more complicated computations of growth and relative market share. I asked each of them to sketch the matrix based upon what they thought the new calculations might show. The Business B executive who argued for changing the calculations showed his business moving to a "star" from a problem child. Star businesses (high market share and market growth) get maximum investment whereas the leaders in problem children business are often replaced because they are deemed to be the cause of low share in a high-growth market. The Business A executive thought the change would mean his star would become a cash cow, a low-growth business with a high share and thus would be "milked," i.e., receive minimal investment because it could expect neither market nor share growth. This quickly demonstrated that the discussion wasn't about the scale and led to a discussion of investment, risk, and leadership that enhanced the strategy. In this case the relationships I formed with these executives during initial interviews and follow-up meetings built the trust to surface such differences productively.

4. **A strategy is just a plan**. What you are going to do (and not do) based upon assumptions about customers, competitors, economic conditions, government regulation, etc. Any insight that comes from a framework needs to be validated in the realworld and amended if necessary.

Inspire action

As a strategy process consultant I felt my clients had an advantage over the content-driven approach. More people engaged in the planning process meant smoother transition to action.

STRATEGY PILOTS

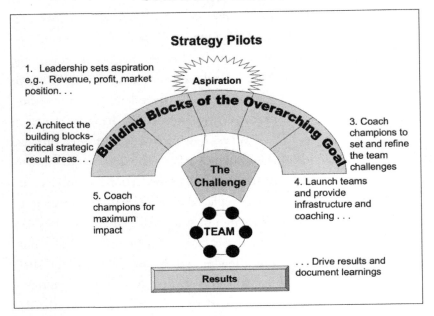

A new strategy requires change; someone must do more of something, less of something, or do something differently. Without that, new strategic results aren't likely. Sometimes strategic action may be experimentation and data gathering. In my practice, I often followed a strategy process intervention with a strategy pilot process, like the one above. We empowered several teams to try out various strategies to see which worked quickly. Senior leaders gave each team an aspiration – e.g., a revenue or profit goal, new customers or increased share of existing customers spend.

They planned what could be achieved in a short period of time, usually three to six months. Clear measures of success and regular data gathering and review were also important.

What was most amazing to me was how much could be accomplished in a short time. The process was also a leadership cauldron. In some cases the team leaders for these strategy pilot projects ended up running new divisions for the company.

Measure progress and results

"You get what you measure" is an old saying in business. There are two types of measurement: results and process.

Results measurements for strategy tell you how you know if your strategy is successful. Results can be measured, for example, as the number of new customers or an increase in revenue or profit, either as a figure or percentage. You are answering the question "How do we know we have achieved what we set out to achieve?" This implies a goal at the beginning of the project, e.g., revenue increased, customers added, with the same or greater gross margins.

Process measurements tell you how you know you are on track to achieve those results. Processes can be measured in the components that will build to the final goal, e.g., first new customer, new customers per month, an increase in revenue month to month, or a change in product unit profit over time. You are answering the question, "How do we know we are on track to achieve our goal?"

Metrics are feedback. They should lead you to action to change or maintain performance variables. How you measure - consistently, rigorously, honestly - will affect your client's trust in those metrics.

Refocus, adapt and respond

My advice to clients: "A strategy is a living document. If you haven't reviewed it and your results against plan in a month, how do you know you are on track?" It is useful, however, to outline in advance what would cause a change in course. There is a fine line between pivoting to a new strategy when required and being impatient and giving up too early.

Why strategy process again?

Some consultants sell new strategy projects to the same clients every few years. Perhaps that is useful, but it always seemed to me that business leaders should know how to plan their own growth and so I began teaching the strategy process. I often provided more questions than answers, but by helping leaders make strategic change - creating insight, inspiring action, instilling the need for measurement and adaptive behavior - I helped my clients achieve results and ultimately run their businesses themselves.

ACQUISITION STRATEGY AND INNOVATION PROCESS

Client executives often think that growing revenue through acquisition is easier than growing revenue organically, by innovating. In my experience this is rarely true. Changing one firm to develop new products is hard; changing two firms, each with its own history and culture, to develop new products or attract new clients is damn near impossible. Consultants are hired at many stages of the M&A process, due diligence to post-merger integration. These are often tough jobs that require more Journeymen and Pros than Newbies.

Where do mergers come from?

There is a business cycle typical of many industries. This cycle usually begin with a single startup company followed by many others selling similar products with no one firm dominating the industry. Some industries reach a kind of equilibrium with many firms competing.

Then something changes. A new firm enters with a radical change in technology, or the business cycle slows down, or a firm locks up a supplier. Organic growth becomes difficult. Firms start to lose business and a consolidation cycle, mergers and acquisitions, begins.

MERGER CYCLE

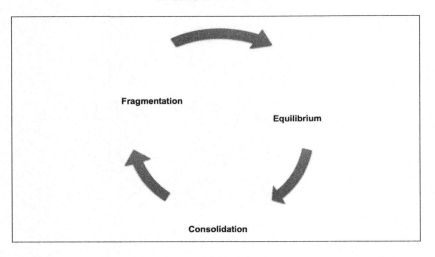

Fragmentation

Equilibrium

Consolidation

For some industries, like management consulting, this goes on perpetually. For other industries there are longer periods of stabilization. The length of what passes for equilibrium has something to do with the degree of firm differentiation through proprietary products or technology, and consequent barriers to entry or intensity of competition, but consolidation comes to most industries. Once merger activity begins it tends to accelerate. Once one merger happens others follow.

Investment bankers sell the idea, and then finance and manage the transaction. Accounting firms do due diligence. Attorneys close the contracts. Management consultants often help create acquisition strategies and sometimes help with post-merger integration. Pros, the most senior people in consulting, often get the calls for help with what is the toughest type of change.

With all these professionals involved one might think that mergers would be successful. Unfortunately most mergers fail to create a company that exceeds the value of the antecedent firms.

It's the people stuff that gets blamed. "Our cultures clashed." But really it is a lack of planning and a failure to act when signs of difficulty surface.

As a consultant I was around fourteen mergers. In most I was onsite doing other work and stuck as an observer while the companies disintegrated around me. Twice, I worked for a consulting firm that was acquired. I moaned along with everyone else and couldn't get these consulting firms who sold post-merger integration to take our own medicine.

There are a lot of consulting projects around mergers, and far too many are ill-conceived cost- reduction projects. I think that the complexity of mergers requires the level heads and experience of Pros, hopefully to get things started right, but if necessary to restart integration when things have gone very wrong.

Chapter 15 "Acquisition Strategy" addresses how to think about growing revenue through mergers and acquisition including how to think about integrating the two firms <u>before</u> you begin.

Then in Chapter 16 we turn to the innovation process. Blame *Inc.* and *Fast Company* magazines for the golden sheen that innovation projects have with consultants. Year after year they publish the "Most Innovative Companies" list. There are myriad articles about disruption, breathless features on Ideo, the Palo Alto design consultancy. The rest of the business press is on the bandwagon now, but *Inc.* and *Fast Company* definitely started it

Innovation always seems like it will be exciting, creative and fun work driven by the Big Idea:

- A brand new product – Walkman, iPod, Smartphone
- A brand new grouping of customers to be served – people who want music portability, people who want to combine learning seminars and cruise vacations, gadget-freaks and late adopters
- A brand new way of operating - getting cash from a machine, ordering books online

But as one might imagine the idea is only a part of it. Each idea has to be evaluated and tested multiple times, prototyped for proof of concept, production tested for feasibility and market tested for customer response. Then it has to be launched and tracked. At any stage, a company can find itself going "back to the drawing board."

I still think innovation is easier than acquisitions, but neither are simple.

ACQUISITION STRATEGY

I 've just had a call from Dewey, Selham, and Howe. Amalgamated is going on the block. We have until Monday to let DSH know if we are interested in making a bid."

Unfortunately, this is often a CEO's first introduction to acquisition strategy. Many acquisitions are opportunistic, serendipitous, or event-driven: two CEOs meet on the golf course, a trade conference rumor provokes an off-hand inquiry with a surprisingly receptive response, or an unsolicited call comes in from an investment banker.

It is perhaps not unrelated that most acquisitions fail. In a study, almost 60 percent failed to increase combined shareholder returns compared to industry averages (Mercer Management Consulting Study of 300 mergers over ten years).

Consultants are sometimes engaged to do due diligence, meaning "Is this worth what they are asking?" All too frequently consultants are called when a big acquisition goes horribly wrong. The service offering is usually called "Post-Merger Integration" but could be called "Fix This." Sometimes consultants are engaged early enough in the process to shape the question, "Should we acquire a company or just grow organically?" This chapter will discuss the acquisition process starting from there.

Acquisitive growth vs. organic growth

Acquisitive growth is a difficult management competency to master, perhaps even more difficult than organic growth.

In order to grow organically, a company either has to acquire more customers (sell to more people in your market, expand geographically, sell to different people) or the organization must gain more revenue from each customer (sell more volume, raise prices, cross-sell new products or services). Organic growth isn't easy. It is difficult to determine what customers value and then improve your business to deliver more of that. And competitors will try to thwart whatever change you make. But at least you are working within one value chain*, business model and organizational framework.

Acquisitive growth means mastering someone else's value chain, business model, and organizational framework and understanding how to combine them with your own to yield new value for a combined group of customers. Acquisitions can produce a one-time step-change in scale or scope, but not without the daunting task of creating a brand new organization from two old organizations who each believe "our way is better."

*A value chain is the unique combination of business elements - purchasing, production, technology, finance, marketing, people, etc.- designed and organized to deliver the value that your customers buy from you. A business model is the financial representation of the value chain showing how the business generates revenue at what cost to generate what profit. An organization framework includes organizational structure, systems, management practice, process and procedures, and cultural norms that align and organize people to deliver that value to customers.

If an organization succeeds at acquisition, the challenges of organic growth remain. Competitors become much more aggressive because you have upped the ante. They know that some of the combined firm's customers and employees are likely to be unhappy and willing to "jump ship." (This expression comes from eighteenth-century naval battles when sailors would join the enemy by literally jumping from one ship to the other, an apt analogy for what happens in many mergers.)

Acquisitions do offer a substantial opportunity. You are suddenly exposed to an entirely new group of people who define their business differently, with different knowledge and skills, and, perhaps, more effective processes and technologies. Imagine the opportunity for both groups to learn new capabilities. This opportunity is lost, however, when acquirers act like conquerors. "If you're so great, how come we **bought** you?"

Yet there are companies that succeed at acquisitions. In general this is because they plan what they are looking for, under what circumstances they are willing to acquire, how much they'll pay, and when and why they'll walk away. They may still take advantage of serendipitous unsolicited calls from managing directors of investment banks, but they are prepared for them. They have an acquisition strategy.

Here are a few important thoughts gleaned from these companies:

Be clear about what you are looking for

Cisco Systems, Silicon Valley's networking giant, has acquired more than 120 companies since 1993. They acquire smaller companies often in the post-startup, mezzanine financing phase. They begin by identifying and analyzing market trends. They state on their website that they acquire businesses that will allow them to enter new markets or those with products that will accelerate or expand an existing Cisco market. Cisco is extremely rigorous in evaluating potential acquisition targets. John Chambers, the founder and former CEO, articulated the Cisco acquisition success criteria:

- "We share a vision – of the market, the technology and how to make money in it.
- We are clear about what we are buying – (technology, business model, products, and people). We like products with substantial differentiation and market shares over 40 percent.
- Our corporate cultures are a match.

- The target is relatively close to Cisco geographically. (No one manages companies at a distance well.)
- Our existing customers think highly of the firm."

Chambers says that Cisco frequently walks from deals where two or more of these criteria aren't met and can't be resolved.

Symantec, the security firm, provides another example. They look for companies that "fit with Symantec strategy, have scalability to grow sustainably, and provide risk-adjusted returns to shareholders."

ACQUISITION TYPES

All Mergers And Acquisitions Are Not Alike: Value Chain Position

VALUE CHAIN POSITION	PLAYERS	PURPOSE	ISSUES
The horizontal merger	Two competitors	Scale Access to customers, product, capacity, technology Eliminate a rival	Two brands? Cross selling Distribution Redundancies Continuing competition
The vertical merger	Customer/ supplier	Lock in supply Guarantee market	Where to account for profit Transfer pricing External customers/other sources of supply
The diversification	Industry to industry	Access to different value chain Risk balance (counter cyclicality) Access to capital/ access to value	Redundancies Staff roles and corp. policies How much autonomy?/synergy? Profit hurdles/Control systems
The transformation	New industry, or value chain	Innovation changes the game / sets new standards	How much is the new industry like either old one?

What kind of acquisition?

The two examples above are essentially big companies buying much smaller ones. The big company gets new technology, products, and smart people. The smaller company gets access to financing, customers, and leverage with suppliers.

Some companies vertically integrate by buying suppliers in order to decrease their cost base. The automotive industry has both acquired and divested suppliers for years. Some companies buy competitors to increase market share – more customers or greater share of wallet. Think Marriott's acquisition of Starwood. Sometimes they just want to take them out of the market, like Scholastic's acquisition of *Weekly Reader*. Some companies look to diversify, to enter an entirely different industry (like Google acquiring Android and Motorola) or to radically transform an industry by combining two dissimilar industries (like Facebook acquiring Oculus Virtual Reality).

Each type of acquisition brings its own marketplace issues and integration challenges.

MERGER INTEGRATION STRATEGY

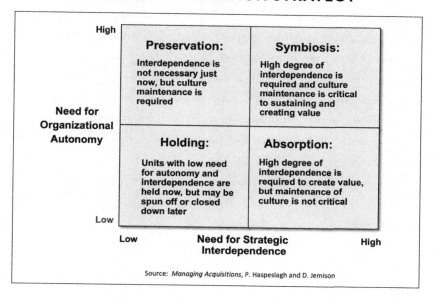

Source: *Managing Acquisitions*, P. Haspeslagh and D. Jemison

Anticipate competitive response

Acquisitions are aggressive competitive acts; competitors will respond. In 1995, I was part of a post-merger integration team. Mallinckrodt

Laboratory and Specialty Chemicals, the fourth largest producer, acquired JT Baker, the third largest producer. Just as integration got underway the number two competitor bought a large distributor, which eliminated 40 percent of distribution for both integrating businesses. The combined company ultimately replaced its distribution, but there was some scrambling for the next year.

Think about integration issues early and often.

Suffice it to say that serial acquirers think about integrations issues <u>before</u> the deal. As the deal is considered they may use an integration decision framework like the one Professors David Jemison and Philippe Haspeslagh proposed in their 1995 book *Managing Acquisitions* displayed at the left.

Within a given approach, managers must decide how to manage the integration of different business segments, functions, and capabilities.

Serial acquirers usually have an integration roadmap. Many start with applying the acquiring company's financial and human resource systems.

Lots can go wrong in integration. Cisco's Chambers admits that even though they are very diligent in integration planning, "one in three of our integrations fails." The soft issues usually get the most press:

> "They never understood our culture." "We weren't treated with respect." "They really had no idea about this industry." "They weren't business-like at all."

But the problems often come down to poor analysis and planning, to jumping when an opportunity arises and then putting in an ill-conceived bid.

CHAPTER 16

INNOVATION PROCESS

"Innovation? Disruption? Give me a break!"

Many of my clients were frustrated by the media attention to innovative companies like Apple and Google. Group discussions on social media sites were not much help.

For example, consider some LinkedIn responses to the question, "How do you implement innovation in a conservative organization?" "You don't." "The culture won't let you." "It's all about the appetite for risk." "You can't change people's thinking." "Hire a bunch of young people and keep them – if you can." "It's hopeless – look at Kodak, Blockbuster, Borders bookstores."

Clients want to grow revenue and that requires innovating new products or changes in the way the client goes to market. Consultants are often asked to run an initiative to increase innovation.

So how do you make a company more innovative? What processes are needed?

What is innovation?

For something to be an innovation it has to be new and it has to work. If it is a product or service, an innovation is different than any other product: it "works," fills a need, does something I want, and I'd be willing to pay for it. If it is a way of operating, a process or procedure, it's different than what we are currently doing and gets better results.

So the process of innovation produces a result – a new product, service, method, or business model (method of making money from the value provided to customers). Now we are getting somewhere because a result can be measured.

The process of innovation also produces something useful that solves a problem. Who would judge whether the innovation was useful or solved the problem? The customer would, and we'd know that by measuring the extent to which it was adopted, i.e., bought and used.

The idea of newness is central to a discussion of innovation. Newness seems to produce excitement in some people, who simply must be the first to have the latest electronic gadget. I am a self-described late-adopter, so newness is less important to me than functionality, which means that an innovation has to work much better than what I am currently using. This is why my smartphone is always several versions behind.

Newness is often a matter of scale. A jet engine, enlarged and turned vertically, becomes a rocket that will take us into space. Or a Walkman shrinks and becomes an iPod Nano. Or vacuum tubes shrink to transistors and then to integrated circuits carved into a silicon chip.

Newness can also be an entirely new concept: the *idea* of portable music, the *idea* of light produced by electricity flowing through a filament rather than a flame of some kind. Or it can be something produced in such a new way that it makes it difficult for traditional competitors to duplicate, a prime example being digital transformation. But we'll talk more about that when we discuss business model innovation.

What is innovation process?

A process is composed of required inputs, activities and decisions that produce predicted outputs. Understanding the outputs we seek is a great first step. What a company needs to do to achieve a moderate innovation differs from business reinvention. Creating a line extension, a slightly different service to achieve an incremental gain in market share, will be different from starting a new industry. However the underlying process is the same.

One caveat before I share a process model framework for innovation: There are many innovation process frameworks to use. The important thing is to pick **one** that resonates for your organization and stick with it. Here is a model I used:

MODEL FRAMEWORK FOR INNOVATION

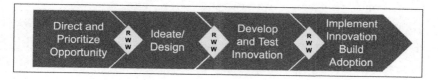

This model has several elements I like:

- It begins with defining the problem you are trying to solve or the opportunity you wish to capitalize upon.
- It ends with adoption, which to me is the measure of success.
- The model differentiates between idea generation and testing of ideas or designs. In practice there is often no clear bright line between these steps, but I find that showing them separately ensures that ample attention is given to each activity.
- The model shows evaluation decisions between steps (gray diamonds). I believe that evaluation must happen at multiple stages in the process. Innovation is as much a matter of "killing" unpromising ideas as it is investing in perceived winners. The core elements of R-W-W are three questions:
  - **R - Is it real?** (Is there an opportunity for this idea with these customers? For anyone?)
  - **W - Can we win?** (Competitiveness of the product and company)

- **W - Is it worth it?** (Reward – profit vs. risk)

R-W-W is a simple evaluation that gets more detailed as investment grows. The Define and Prioritize step makes sure that there is a "problem we are trying to solve." The inputs to this process can be regular competitive analysis, environment scans for new technology, and changing customer needs. Sometimes Define and Prioritize bleeds into Ideation. Sometimes we find a technology that could completely eliminate some of our core processes and so we begin to examine how we'd utilize it. Sometimes we examine the "underlying functionality" or "job to be done" and challenge the existing paradigm. For example, someone at Sony looked at the "job to be done" of listening to music and asked, "How could we make it portable?" That question gave birth to the Walkman. Steve Jobs asked, "How could I carry more of my music?" He introduced the iPod, with the tagline "1000 songs in your pocket."

Similarly, Ideation sometimes bleeds into Testing. Rapid prototyping to test and learn from failure quickly greatly hastens the process, assuming risks are low and there is a clear process for learning. Without a learning process, innovation groups are unnecessarily chaotic and tend to reinvent the wheel. One good learning process is the US Army's After Action Review:

- What was intended?
- What actually happened?
- If it's different, why? How do we know the cause? (use observable data vs. opinion)
- What action should be taken now? By whom?
- Who should we inform to avoid similar outcomes in the future? Who will share this?

The Implementation step can include testing. Many of us have had the experience of a using a new software release that we say is just a "buggy beta version" where we're expected to find the "bugs." It is faster, but may not produce a beautiful customer experience.

Adoption is not just a matter of customer adoption. Integrating a new product, service or methodology into the operations of the innovating organization can be extraordinarily tough. The degree of difficulty is related to the size of the change, but sometimes the seemingly smallest change can produce phenomenal resistance.

When resistance occurs it is a sign that you have undermanaged stakeholders' expectations or involvement in the process. Once resistance occurs, listen and summarize what is said before responding. Then clear up misunderstandings, acknowledge shortcomings and be supportive in emotional and political issues.

How does a company implement innovation?

Implementing innovation is simply planned change, and like other types of planned change it follows a process:

- **Establish the why of change**. What evolving customer needs are we trying to meet, or what competitive threat or disruptive technology are we trying to respond to?
- **Establish the how of change.** What are the expected results, and by when? Gain commitment to your version of the process described above, plus organization, roles and responsibilities, funding, decision structures, metrics and rewards.
- **Monitor results and improve the process.**

Now that sounds really easy, doesn't it? It's not. Here are a few issues to think about:

Organization: There is always a debate whether to insulate innovation in its own organizational unit - the Lockheed "skunk works" or Macintosh Pirates - or to hold everyone accountable, like 3M or Google's mandate that employees spend 20 percent of their time on "new stuff." The separate organizational unit creates focus, but also creates an integration problem later. The "everyone innovates" model is inclusive and can produce some surprising results, but requires massive infrastructure to manage.

Funding: Whose project gets money and whose doesn't can be a huge issue. I've seen several organizations that set up an internal venture capital structure to manage this quite successfully. The most important success factor seems to be transparency –communicating **why** one project got funded and another didn't.

Metrics and Rewards: Measuring the percentage of new products as part of the mix is good, but backing up to each stage gate, e.g., how many ideas, how many working prototypes, how many successful market tests, is better. My favorite metric and reward is the "W. L. Gore annual award for the idea that looked the best on paper, but was the most spectacular failure." My friends at Cowden and Associates, a Pittsburgh-based health and welfare consulting firm, had some fun with this approach and ultimately added ideas as well as more discipline to their planning.

Business Model Innovation: Friends with more recent MBAs than mine can't believe that "business model" is a relatively new term. I think it came into use in the late 1990s and early 2000s with the Internet boom, and is used by entrepreneurs and venture capitalists alike.

The term simply means a succinct definition of how you make money. There are many ways to break it down using Business Concept, Revenue Model, Cost Model and Profit Model as the component parts.

Business models today are usually discussed in the context of "disruption" because of a new technology. Kodak had its business model disrupted by digital cameras that enabled sending pictures by email. Blockbuster's business model was disrupted by Netflix that first mailed DVDs and later sold streaming so customers didn't have to leave home to watch a movie. Borders was the first big bookstore to fall to Amazon's online bookstore business model.

Business model innovation is a special case process. It relies on scanning technology, understanding future customer desires, challenging assumptions in the existing paradigm, and experimenting a great deal.

Changing to an Innovating Culture: I have now lived so long that the people who used to deny the existence of corporate culture have graduated to the view that culture is obstructive and unchangeable. ("Our culture won't support that.")

Culture change isn't impossible, but companies that succeed in changing culture over time do it by changing behaviors and the organizational support (like rewards and recognition) for different behaviors.

Innovation cultures continually scan for the new - technologies, processes, products that might be used. Controlling the process is important as there are pitfalls.

Two such pitfalls to the innovation process are:

The cult of creativity: Loving ideas so much that you are not paying enough attention to delivering results. I worked for a CEO who was a font of new ideas. When turning his ideas into a plan he'd say "that's just a detail." He adopted every divergent thinking technique that had been invented and was always buying new books on creativity. He made brainstorming a firm religion.

Unfortunately, many projects got started but few delivered results. There was little cultural support for winnowing down ideas, evaluation, testing and building adoption. Most people agreed that it was a fun and exciting place to work, but the firm eventually went bankrupt.

The corporate crunch: Setting unrealistic hurdle rates and holding nascent projects to the same standards as established businesses. This often happens in multidivisional companies that have been in business for a long time. Divisions are held to rigorous performance standards on their day-to-day businesses and the Capital Budgeting Process is run by the controller. "Why should we invest money in a business that does not promise rewards that compare to our best businesses today?"

As any entrepreneur will tell you, new businesses frequently lose money until people manage their way down the experience curve, reducing costs as they learn. Holding new businesses to the returns of long-established businesses is unrealistic and means that the company won't innovate or that innovators will learn to be extraordinarily optimistic in revenue projection in order to garner investment. Innovators are an overly optimistic lot to begin with, and encouraging them to stretch their optimism is a recipe for loss.

CONTINUOUS IMPROVEMENT PROJECTS

"Not Again."

"Yes, again."

"How many times?"

"Until we get it right."

I probably worked on Continuous Improvement projects more in my career than any other type of project. These projects were called by many different names: Quality Circles, Focus on Productivity, Total Productive Maintenance, Total Quality, Reengineering, Business Process Improvement, Six Sigma, LEAN, Lean Six Sigma, Agile, etc. The list goes on. I became methodology agnostic. "Pick one." I'd tell clients. "Then stick to it. It's not about the framework. It's about the discipline."

I did quite a lot of Continuous Improvement training in its different forms. Regardless of the methodology, I would start the training by saying:

"This stuff isn't rocket science. It boils down to 'Measure where you are -Improve something-Measure where you got to - Repeat. That's it. Dead simple."

I'd then add, "Oh yeah. We do want to be consistent in what and how you measure. And we expect you to put some root cause analysis rigor into what you improve, but in simple terms this is it:

Measure where you are- Improve something-Measure where you got to –Repeat."

"This isn't new!"

Right. I could go through the history - Frederic Taylor's *Scientific Management,* the Gilbreths, Walter Shewart, Dr. Demming. To refresh, just reread Chapter 1, "Investigating the Consulting Industry."

However, Continuous Improvement's roots are even older - the scientific method:

- Observe (collect data on a process and/or an outcome - **Measure**)
- Question why (root-cause analysis)
- Form a hypothesis or testable explanation (cause)
- Predict based on the hypothesis
- Test the prediction through experimentation - **Improve**
- Draw conclusions - **Measure**
- **Iterate**: use the results to make new hypotheses or predictions

This aligns with most CI problem-solving models such as Six Sigma's Define –Measure – Analyze – Improve- Control.

"This is just cost cutting, right?"

I was asked this question in the early 1980s by a Heinz union worker in a Quality Circle.

I was young; I answered tentatively, talking about "productivity and better ways of doing things." The initiative I was asked to facilitate was called Focus on Productivity. The big FOP signs were all over the plant.

It didn't help that the *Pittsburgh Post-Gazette* front-page story that day was about the CEO, Anthony O'Reilly, who had just been paid $37 million in bonuses and stock options.

"FOP" my union friend bellowed. "Fatten O'Reilly's Paycheck!"

When the laughter died down, I said, "OK, so you don't want to work on costs. What do you want to work on?"

"Safety!" Came the answer. "You want to improve things? Improve the time lost in accidents."

We did and we made some improvements. But the name stuck. The FOP program was ever after called "Fatten O'Reilly's Paycheck," and the initiative was shorter lived than it might have been.

Continuous Improvement methodologies have been most often used to eliminate waste from operational process. It has a reputation in some quarters as cost-cutting and headcount reduction. But, CI was used to improve process safety at BP after the Texas City and Deep Water Horizon accidents. I have also used it to increase sales revenue by taking waste and errors out of sales and delivery processes and to generate new successful ideas coming from research and development.

R&D? But that's Innovation, right?

Innovation and Continuous Improvement have a lot in common, not the least of which are "Methodology Zealots," true believers in a particular methodology as the one true way.

I encountered these "true believers" preaching Lean Six Sigma, Human Centered Design, Rapid-Results, Rapid Application Development, Agile, and Total Quality Management, to name a few innovation or improvement methodologies.

In one organization where there was an innovation initiative running concurrently with an improvement initiative, conflict over resources got a bit ugly.

"You are just rearranging the deck chairs on the Titanic," shouted innovation teammates.

"You are working where the rubber meets the sky," the improvement teams shouted back.

I was asked to facilitate conflict resolution meetings, while the real issue was solved by resource allocation compromises. Both groups came away with an understanding of the similarities and differences in innovation and improvement processes.

Both innovation and improvement are fundamentally **team processes** that rely on a rigorous adherence to a **structured process**. Both start with **problem definition and measurement**, and both have challenges transferring solutions to the implementing organization. Both use divergent and convergent thinking to first generate then evaluate ideas, and share many of the same tools.

There are differences, however. Often innovation projects have a longer time horizon, a greater degree of newness and change and therefore require more upfront investment. Improvement projects by contrast can often pay back investment in a shorter period, leading some to say "CI is free."

"OK, but why do so many companies do CI initiatives over and over again?"

Consultants and academics bear some responsibility here. We create the bright shiny new methodologies that managers who are susceptible to "latest fad syndrome" use to play "methodology bingo." Some initiatives aren't well planned. Other times so much energy is spent on methodology training that there is little left for actually improving things. Sometimes there is little rigor in defining projects, measuring or finding root cause. Often people declare victory too soon, missing final measurements or the continuous part of CI. Most frequently, it is because leaders don't engage with the process and changes don't get integrated into the day-to-day. In short, there is a breakdown in one of the four simple requirements:

1. **Measure where you are**   2. **Improve something**
2. **Measure where you got to**   3. **Repeat.**

The chapters that follow address what could go wrong with Continuous Improvement initiatives. Could these concepts be applied to other types of consulting projects? Yes. Could the lessons be applied to how you improve as a consultant? You bet.

"Practice makes better. Nobody's perfect."

CHAPTER 17

A CONTINUOUS IMPROVEMENT INITIATIVE ROADMAP

The Measure-Improve-Measure CI mindset is easy to understand conceptually, but it is a discipline that requires consistent practice much like martial arts or learning to play the piano. There is a CI mindset that starts with thinking about numbers as trends, e.g., *it took three minutes of cycle time to complete today, which is down from three-and-a-half minutes yesterday.* Or the cycle time could be compared to a similar process or a competitive benchmark.

CI is most often used to improve business and operational processes. A process is simply a set of activities with inputs and outputs of each activity step.

The second part of the CI mindset is process focus. Process focus is different from a focus on completing tasks. It involves seeing work as a flow of activities or process steps, each with inputs and outputs. These can be placed in an optimum order. Fair warning: once you begin to see the world this way you will never be the same. You will view every customer experience as a process flow and see how it can be made faster, better, or cheaper.

A PROCESS FLOW

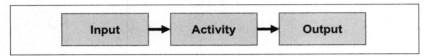

Implementing Continuous Improvement across the organization requires leadership focus and commitment; one consistent methodology; measuring inputs, activities, and outputs for each step; and, of course, overall results.

A CI initiative has a startup expense, but can become self-funding (paid for by revenue increases and cost savings) in a year. That doesn't happen automatically. It takes practice.

What does a CI initiative look like?

As I mentioned, a CI initiative can come in many forms, each with its own language and framework. However, they all have an underlying DNA: teams, a rigorous problem-solving model, and control.

CI initiatives employ teams because generating new ways of doing things benefits from multiple viewpoints. A CI project can be done individually, but for larger projects, teams will spread the work and members will reinforce each other's learning and discipline.

They use a structured methodology to ensure problem-solving rigor and consistency and control to make improvement sustainable. Continuous Improvement methodologies tend to define themselves by the problem-solving model they use. Some feel strongly that one model is better than another. This is the source of the "methodology bingo" I described earlier. "What we really need is [insert methodology here]."

As noted, I counsel an organization to use one and only one methodology, but it doesn't really matter which one. Improvement is about overcoming the "but we've always done it this way" inertia. Confusion about how to solve the problem slows everything down. Combining and refining models is an advanced concept. Help them get some results first. Here is an overview of a few methodologies:

PROBLEM SOLVING MODELS

Scientific Method	Characterize	Hypothesize	Predict	Experiment	Conclude

PDCA	Plan		Do	Check	Act

Six Sigma	Define	Measure	Analyze	Improve	Control

5 Step Problem Solving Method	Define the problem	Identify Root Causes	Develop Solution / Implement Solution	Evaluate & Follow-up

Design for Lean Six Sigma New processes 12 steps	Define	Measure	Analyze	Design	Verify
	1. Define the problem	4. Current state	7. Prioritize Design Inputs	10. Confirm Plan/Build
	2. Specifications metrics	5. Goal	8. Quantify Design Inputs	11. Control Inputs /Monitor outputs
	3. Quantify measurability	6. Design Inputs	9. Plan Implementation	12. Sustain/ Translate

Most of these have four to five basic categories; some have up to twenty-five steps. My colleagues and I even designed custom models for clients who felt their "uniqueness" required their own problem-solving model. What's important is that your organization agrees on a single model. It makes communication much easier.

The last step of most of these models addresses the question: Is the change sustainable? Once an improvement is in place, it is important that people don't go back to the old process or any improvement will revert to previous levels. This takes hard tools like control charts and response plans as well as soft change management skills.

Getting started: begin with leaders

When I worked at GE the story told on the origins of GE's Six Sigma initiative was that Larry Bossidy of Allied Signal said to Jack Welch, "Do you really want your legacy to be Neutron Jack?" Up until then GE's

CEO Welch had been divesting all businesses that weren't number one or two in their markets. There were many reductions in force and the black humor at GE likened Welch to a neutron bomb: "the buildings are still here, but the people are **_gone_**."

As the story went, Bossidy, Welch's friend, who had left GE for Allied Signal, was impressed with Motorola's extraordinary quality improvements with the Six Sigma methodology they invented. He had instituted it at Allied Signal with strong results and introduced it to Jack Welch. The origin story may be apocryphal, but Welch was one hundred percent committed to Six Sigma. He led projects himself and insisted that all his senior leaders become a black belt, the strenuously certified project leaders of the methodology.

I told this story a lot to leaders who wanted to hire me to help with CI initiatives. Many became similarly committed; many did not. It is important that leaders agree what should be improved and why, and communicate clear connections to strategic priorities. As a consultant, ensure that leaders are aligned on chosen methodology, expected outcomes, setup and infrastructure funding, roles, responsibilities and rewards.

Train resources

Some companies get stuck in the training start. Some train everyone in the company, doing small "training projects" e.g., a spaghetti chart to lower traffic by the water cooler, which shows no relevant results. Then they wonder why people, staff and managers burn out before getting to work that might make a difference.

CI embodies skills that ultimately everyone can and should learn, but start small. Some good roles to start with are:
- CI specialists to lead and staff projects
- Senior CI process experts who help leaders pick the right projects, troubleshoot projects and coach teams
- The ideal is to have a team solve a big problem and achieve great results so that everyone wants to be involved.

Build infrastructure

You need to have a process for identifying improvement projects, deploying teams and tracking results. You will need to have training materials, and a toolkit and job aids. There needs to be a process in place to help teams that get stuck.

Initiatives like this must have supporting systems and processes like databases that track a project, metrics, and a control plan so that over time teams can translate previous work rather than reinvent the wheel each time. You'll need to have a system that tracks the benefits, without double counting. And you should think about rewards and celebrations for big improvements.

Get project selection right

The objective on any CI initiative is to actually improve something in a measurable, noticeable way. Motorola invented Six Sigma in the 1990s because their Bandit pager, the star of their line, had a 50 percent failure rate. The Bandit had one thousand components, and in order to get to their target failure rate each component had to have a near perfect, or 0.00034%, failure rate or Six Sigma. So they built a highly statistical measurement process and an improvement process to go with it. The goal was clear. Many said it was impossible, but first the Bandit and then all of Motorola's products achieved Six Sigma quality.

Contrast this with companies that "Do CI" because it's the right thing to do. There's no overall goal, and employees are allowed to select whatever they want to work on. Then everyone is surprised that "all this money we've spent hasn't been anything but expense."

Deciding what you want to improve is critical and project selection starts at the top.

My friend and colleague the late Dr. Richard Taylor was fond of saying, "There are a limited number of Continuous Improvement projects. It's less than ten. Once you've done those, it's all about translation – doing the same project in slightly different circumstances or with different inputs."

One day I challenged Ric: "So what are the less than ten projects?" It was a fascinating discussion. We agreed to talk about projects not in terms of solutions, but rather the problem being solved, which is appropriate because problem definition is the beginning of any improvement effort. We came up with the following seven projects:

1. **Not Good Enough - not meeting an external quality standard.** The external standard could be a customer specification - for example, a specific micrometer-measured, two-sided, tolerance of a physical part (not lower than 2.1mm, but not to exceed 2.8mm), or guaranteed "not-to-exceed" parts-per-million of harmful chemicals in a solution (one-sided ppm standard). The standard could be a regulatory requirement like average lending as percentage of capital on hand or the immediate shutdown of a cybersecurity breach. It could be a competitive benchmark like Amazon Prime's "free" delivery cost (average delivery cost times average number of annual deliveries divided by annual Prime membership fee). The project originates from data that show a shortfall in meeting the external quality standard; the analysis determines why it is failing. Is it meeting the standard on average but failing because of a wide distribution of performance – lack of precision? Or is it failing because the mean performance is outside of the standard? The solution may require shifting the mean or reducing the variability, or both. It will also depend on the particular inputs that drive that performance and how we can control them, but the problem is the same. We are not meeting the standard. Regardless of this solution strategy, it still involves manipulating process inputs, whether they are electrons, paper, or nails, in a more advantageous and controllable manner.

2. **Not Fast Enough – cycle times that are too long.** We have all become accustomed to thinking about delivery cycle time in the instant-gratification-internet-age, but cycle times have life or death consequences in healthcare and disaster recovery.

Time to market drives success in any innovation-driven industry, like software development or financial services technology. The Lean methodology aids analysis for this project category. Removal of the waste, elimination of rework, moving non-value-added but required work out of the customer line and optimizing value-added steps are standard solutions to increase speed. This group may well have more Continuous Improvement projects than any of the other six categories.

3. **Not Cheap Enough or not meeting an internal cost requirement.** While there are external standards like customer specs and regulatory requirements as discussed in Group 1, there are also many internal standards driven by the business. The most obvious internal standard is profit, which is product price minus fully-loaded product cost. Neither the customer nor the regulator cares if a product makes an internal profit hurdle rate, but executives and ultimately shareholders certainly do. There are also other internal standards including many human resource standards like diversity and pay equity, which can be rolled up to a cost. Additional examples are employee satisfaction and attrition rates, which also affect internal costs. Even community involvement of the business will ultimately result in an internal cost/reward. Remember that cost and profit are always a function of something else: labor hours, supplier order lead time, scrap and rework, degree of automation, etc. The analysis of cost is dependent on how it is tracked across inputs and process activities, how indirect costs are allocated, and what items are included. A useful guide for analysis is the concept of value: What does the customer actually pay for? What does the customer not care about but regulators deem essential? What must the business do despite a lack of interest on the part of either customers or regulators?

4. **Projects that prevent bad stuff from happening.** Safety (pre-

venting incidents), Risk (avoiding process safety; financial, marketplace, political and other types of risk), and Attrition (retaining the people we have invested in) are the most rewarding Continuous Improvement projects. They are often the most difficult projects in which to ensure sustainability because new risks emerge all the time. People will find new ways to get around a safe procedure; competitors will adopt a new disrupting technology; and governments will find new ways to make it difficult to compete. **Note:** For companies that like to track results metrics like dollars saved or revenue generated, risk avoidance projects are problematic because you can't track what doesn't happen. Even if you could, how can you be sure it is enough? You never totally eliminate residual risk. On the other hand, the delta, e.g., days away from work this year vs. last, represents fewer people getting hurt and is a good indicator of safety improvement. Tools like Failure Modes Effects Analysis (FMEA), Quality Function Deployment (QFD or Houses of Quality), and Kano Analysis will help anticipate future risks. Scenario planning helps anticipate marketplace risk and the Blue Ocean strategy methods (combine, eliminate, increase, decrease) prescribe action to mitigate marketplace risk. A mistake-proofing methodology precludes the operational errors we want to avoid.

5. **Baseline – where are we now?** If there is a place where readers would like to jump in and disagree, here comes your chance. This is not really a group in itself because establishing current performance should be part of any CI project; otherwise, how would you know you have improved? In many situations, establishing the current state is not easy. Sometimes people say, "We have no process for that." What that usually means is that there are as many processes as there are process users. Then the project is about documenting and measuring what is being done, perhaps agreeing on the "one best way" and standardizing.

Sometimes standardizing is complicated by local regulation or cultural norms. Other times there is no value to standardizing because different process users never interact and don't report performance data to the same place. However, documentation and shared learning still can improve overall performance. One might say, "A baseline project is not a true CI project – it's just a first step." Maybe, but establishing baseline performance can involve creating a metric and gaining organizational agreement. Baselining is critical and often such a difficult first step that it may be a project on its own, and one which might spawn additional projects.

6. **Measurement projects – would we even know if we improved?** Measurement projects, like a baseline project, could be considered as just a part or phase of a complete CI project. However, the measurement project proffered here goes to a new or modified way of applying a measurement system to multiple outputs, and hence across multiple projects. Consider Net Promoter Score (NPS), which was first derived as an indicator of loyalty in the rental car industry. NPS is the answer to the question, "How likely are you to recommend [the company] to others?" The refinement of NPS has made it a valuable tool for multiple industries today. Often technology provides new measurement tools, but they must be vetted and validated. In other cases, researchers look for better leading metrics to foretell conditions – these too are appropriate as measurement projects. This category is too often overlooked, and it is a critical group.

7. **Design projects – we can't get there from here.** For a brand new product or service we may not have a process. Or we might discover that our existing process cannot reach the customer requirement or internal goal or may cause other unintended consequences. In these cases we may have to design a process. I have written elsewhere that many people think that process

design is innovation and therefore fundamentally different from improvement. However, innovation and improvement utilize many of the same tools – divergent thinking tools like brainstorming and evaluative convergent thinking tools like filtering matrices. Both use structured methodologies to produce measured results and both use teams and focus on sustained change. What is different is that process design often has a longer planning time horizon. New products are often planned for five years and improvements are measured quarter by quarter. Design projects often require a greater investment and therefore are expected to have a greater payoff. For me the similarities outweigh the differences and so I include them here.

These are the seven types of projects that Ric and I came up with. We were not sure if these categories are MECE (mutually exclusive and collectively exhaustive). But we believed that they cover the CI landscape and that a team discussion at the beginning of a CI project as to which category your team is working on might simplify things enough to be worth the time.

Roadblocks - what can go wrong?

Unfortunately, many CI initiatives fail, and by fail I mean fail to achieve results and are ultimately abandoned, despite large investment. Common pitfalls include:

A lack of leadership engagement

Like any change, CI must be led. Leaders must demonstrate that they have "skin in the game" by learning the language and leading by example, doing projects. There are a lot of reasons that leaders don't engage - nobody asks them or they think CI is operational.

Sometime leaders think CI is for people below their level. They delegate the initiative, but you can't delegate change. If leaders aren't engaged, the wrong projects get picked, infrastructure doesn't get built, some people become obsessive looking for perfection, others try to game the system. *"Things fall apart. The center does not hold. . . ."* Well, you get the idea. Leadership is critical.

The great becomes the enemy of the good

Sometimes CI practitioners forget the continuous and iterative nature of CI. They hold out for the big score and ignore the small quick improvements that can be instantly available. CI results come from many small changes; making it about only BIG projects is destructive. The net effect is that results are too slow in coming and the CI effort is abandoned.

Too much training

Most CI initiatives train practitioners and project managers and some train leaders. Sometimes there is so much training that there is little opportunity to do actual improvement work. CI should be about improved results. Sometimes there is three weeks of residential training with no allowance for doing one's "day job." Sometimes training isn't coordinated with project selection.

Worse is the "real training project" corollary. CI practitioners are asked to bring a project to practice CI during the training. If these projects are HUGE – usually suggested by a manager who doesn't understand CI – the practitioner gets overwhelmed and never achieves results or attempts a second project.

Or the "moving the watercooler" corollary -working on the wrong stuff. If the practitioner chooses an easy project - "Moving the water cooler to a more central location" or "cleaning up my desktop" – there is no quantifiable result. Managers are unimpressed; practitioners are demoralized and CI withers on the vine.

The "Certification Cotillion"

CI specialists are generally a good idea, but sometimes they go overboard.

They view themselves as a special class of people differentiated by their training and more by their certification. "I'm the Master Black Belt." People in these roles should be teachers, not the anointed. Ultimately CI is everyone's responsibility.

Methodology bingo

Sometimes when results are slow in coming, a practitioner or a manager reaches into the methodology bag and pulls out another methodology. "[Lean, Agile, Six Sigma, or whatever] is something we should use!" Everyone stops, reorients themselves, retrains, still fails to achieve results, and abandons CI until the next "silver bullet" comes along.

Cheating and celebrated mediocrity

If you want real improvement then the results must be trusted. Anything that undermines trust in the process results is death to CI, e.g.
- Declaring victory with a big celebration and articles in the employee newsletter before you have completed enough cycles to be certain the process is controlled and the results sustainable
- Not reviewing claimed results such that "fudging" or double counting with other projects happens
- Rewarding numbers of projects, or training weeks completed, vs. real results that drop to the bottom line.

We just got tired

Change fatigue is a real thing. Most organizations deal with this by creating new initiatives when the bloom is off the rose of the last initiative. This management theory is "Give them a new 'bright shiny thing' and they'll forget." In actuality managers get tired too and need to work on something new. Change fatigue presents as:
- Arguments about the methodology, i.e., "What we really need is Lean (or Agile, Work Out, etc.), not Six Sigma."
- Leaders move to their next job and the new boss wants to start

with a clean slate.

- Entropy – the half-life of each initiative gets shorter and shorter and people begin to talk about the "flavor of the month."

The secret is to make CI a common process, the way we work, but also to watch for burn-out. If Continuous Improvement becomes continuous change everyone loses.

CI isn't theoretical physics, but it does take some methodological rigor and disciplined practice. If an organization sticks with the discipline, revenue increases, cost reductions or improvements in quality or safety of 30 percent are not uncommon.

CHAPTER 18

WHAT PROBLEM ARE WE TRYING TO SOLVE?

Many people describe themselves as "problem-solvers." But what most of us mean is that we are "solution-finders"; we barely hear the problem before jumping to a solution we saw applied at some other time and place.

When training Continuous Improvement (CI) my favorite starter question was, "Why do I say that Problem Definition is the most important phase of CI? Why would I say such a thing?"

It was an obvious question that always generated the predictable answer: "Because if you don't define the problem correctly the rest of the project is worthless and you get no improvement."

"Then why do so many Continuous Improvement projects have to circle back and redefine the problem?" I would ask. This produced the sheepish answer, "We aren't thorough enough in defining the problem." I would then tell class participants honestly that they weren't alone, that even with over thirty years at this CI stuff I still fell prey to jumping to a solution. Then I proceeded to give them a process which, if followed, will help:

- Determine the customer

- Focus on the problem area
- Define the problem
- Frame the problem
- Gain stakeholder agreement on the problem

Nothing improves until you say what needs to be improved, how and for whom. Problem definition isn't always easy, but it is the most important step.

Determine the customer

Many CI practitioners are operationally focused. They know the process and can see the problems as they occur. Therefore it is useful to define the problem from the customer's point of view. I always started with the end customer, the one who pays money for a product or service, because the end customer (even if a long way from the problem) is why we are in business. I then worked my way backward to the person who receives the output from the step of the process we are describing. Along the way there may be many intermediate customers: external groups like regulators and internal groups such as accounting, who count the outputs or use them in some way. Understanding the problem from the customer's viewpoint helps to define it and adds urgency to its solution.

Focus on the problem area

Sometimes a problem presents itself with a simple or obvious solution. A credit union failed to notify a customer that his mortgage was declined. The customer, a long-time credit union member, learned about the decline from the seller – how embarrassing! This happened because of unclear internal responsibilities. The solution was to change the process in order to set the mortgage officer as the single point of contact (with backup designation) and a deadline for notification of twenty-four hours after a failed credit check.

However, some problems come up over and over again. These "chronic problems" are often more complex. The process for these problems may cross functional lines, or have multiple or diverse inputs or different responses in different operating conditions. A complex problem like a missed mortgage delivery date might have its roots upstream of operations with a supplier or with the design of specifications. A SIPOC diagram, shown here, will help to focus problem solving. As the diagram details, the team saw that the problem was with the front end of the mortgage approval process and this insight led them to do a more complete process analysis later.

SIPOC BANK MORTGAGE

Suppliers	Inputs	Process	Outputs	Customers
First contact qualification	Initial data collection	Credit qualification	Property qualification	Mortgage approval
• Bank phone processor • MX - Online Mortgage • Senior exec • Member's accountant • Credit agency • 3rd party appraiser • RE agent	• Initial data collection (IDC) packet • IDC instructions • Information to request credit report • Credit report	• First contact qualification • Initial data collection • Credit qualification • Property qualification • Mortgage approval	• Complete IDC • Credit report • Property appraisal • Mortgage approval/ non-approval decision	• Member's wife • Member • RE agent • Senior exec

Define the problem

Writing a simple problem statement for a complex problem is one of the most difficult tasks in Continuous Improvement. People want to put in their solution "Design a new process that. . ." However, there is a single question that helps focus the definition:

"What is wrong with what, and so what?"

What is wrong defines the defect. **With what** defines the object area of focus. And **so what** defines the impact of the problem on cost, customer satisfaction, and a host of other quantifiable areas and builds the business case for solving the problem. Put the answers on a simple worksheet with tiny spaces for each to encourage single phrases. Writing a simple problem statement then becomes a matter of stringing these elements into a single sentence:

PS WORKSHEET

What Is wrong?	With What?	And So What?

Components:

Defect	Object	Impact
Delayed past due date	Mortgage requests	Lost sales, reputation damage, customer loss

Problem Statement:

Mortgage requests are delayed past due dates leading to lost sales, reputational damage and customer loss

"Mortgage requests (object) are delayed (defect), leading to lost sales, reputational damage, and customer loss (impacts)."

This statement doesn't quantify the number of mortgages delayed or by amount of time they are delayed. That can be done in analysis. Nor does the problem statement suggest root cause or dictate a solution, though defining the problem in this way is a big step toward solving it. The problem is clearly a process problem; if we were to look back at the SIPOC diagram of the high-level process, we might investigate step-cycle times and inter-step handoffs.

Frame the problem

Perhaps the biggest difficulty that CI practitioners face is that the problems they try to solve are TOO BIG. The vernacular for this challenge is "trying to solve world hunger."

The tool that is useful to break down a larger problem is the scoping tree. By asking the questions *what type*, *who*, *where*, and *when* we can reduce the problem into bite-sized pieces that can be solved in microcosm. Then the solution is applied in different places, which may require some adaptation but will be considerably faster. (We ask what, who, where, and when, but <u>not</u> why because we do that later for root cause analysis.)

Another way to scope the problem is to set boundaries by determining what is in the problem definition and what is out of scope. Process maps and the Is/Should Matrix (discussed in the next chapter) are also tools to limit scope.

FRAME THE PROBLEM

Scoping Tree Example

Member complaints about slow home Insurance claims payments leading to x policy cancellations		
Primary residence	Second Home	Renters Insurance
Weather Related: Damage	Fire	Theft	Liability
Claim Center 1	Claim Center 2	Claim Center 3	Claim Center 4
Dec-Feb	Mar-May	Jun-Aug	Sep-Nov

Stakeholder agreement on the problem

Once you have a definition of the problem and the scope you will address, take it to everyone who touches the problem. This builds urgency to solve the problem and eagerness for the solution. It also surfaces objections before you start work, e.g., anyone saying, "Wait, that's not the problem as I see it." Sometimes stakeholders say, "You know, as long as you're looking at receivables, could you look at payables too?" The great advantage of a scoping tree, or another scoping tool like the in-scope/out-of-scope matrix, is that it identifies the area of focus. At this point you want agreement on "what problem we trying to solve" so you can get agreement on the solution later.

Be prepared though. The one sign of a well-written problem statement is that everyone wants to jump in and offer a solution.

CHAPTER 19

THE IS/SHOULD MATRIX

The Is/Should Matrix is a Continuous Improvement (CI) tool that helps increase clarity in defining the problem by asking: What is actually happening?
- What IS happening that SHOULD be happening?
- What IS happening that SHOULD NOT be happening?

What is not happening?
- What IS NOT happening that SHOULD NOT be happening?
- What IS NOT happening that SHOULD BE happening?

What is actually happening?

The answers to these questions are entered into the simple matrix at left.

This matrix makes visible different interrelated problems and different aspects of the same problem.

When and why to use the tool

The Is/Should Matrix is primarily used in defining the problem - to clarify an unspecific, vague or poorly-defined problem. The focus is on writing down the observable facts of the problem, rather than noting frustration or other emotions that may cloud the issue or any speculation about possible root causes or potential solutions.

WHAT IS ACTUALLY HAPPENING?

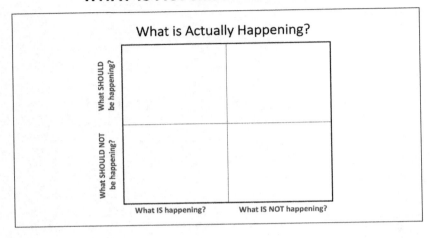

Many times a problem surfaces as an ill-defined "headache," a knowledge that something is not working well, without knowing what specifically leads us to that conclusion. That is exactly the type of situation for using the Is/Should Matrix.

START WITH THE POSITIVES

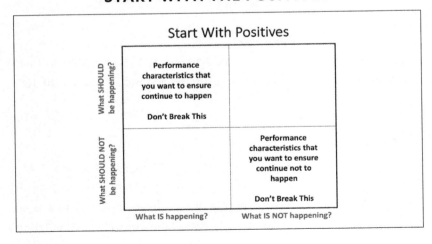

The output of the Is/Should Matrix analysis is often that there is not one problem, but multiple problems. Therefore, this matrix can be most helpful when problem solvers are too close to the problem and/or can't differentiate the multiple problems.

MOVE ON TO POTENTIAL IMPROVEMENTS

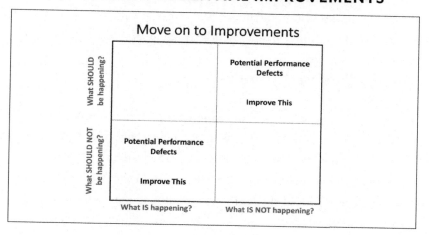

How to use the tool

Start by drawing the basic matrix.

Fill out the matrix with what is happening that should be happening. Starting with the positives ensures focus on what is working.

Fill out the things that are not happening that should not be happening. These two quadrants of the matrix are constraints to problem solving, things that our improvement shouldn't "break."

Next fill out the other two quadrants:

- What is happening that should not be happening?
- What is not happening that should be happening?

These entries are what need to be improved. They may be separate improvement opportunities, each of which might be written into a problem statement, or they may be different aspects of a problem.

The example below comes from a large process industry company. In this environment, Control of Work (CoW) policies are intended to reduce personal and process safety risks. CoW policies often include guidelines for working at heights, breaking containment of flammable or toxic substances, or welding or other "hot work" in the presence of flammable substances. This example shows the original description of the problem and the completed Is/Should matrix and problem statement that the team ultimately chose from the many in the original "headache statement."

Original "headache" statement
Example:

"Our control of work process isn't compliant with the company standard.

Actually, we don't have one CoW standard; we have four depending on the legacy of the site. Some are close, but others aren't.

Last week I was focused on someone with improper tie-off working at heights when I noticed that there was welding going on right next door and this technician was pulling a valve that could have been live and he didn't even have a permit for the work.

I want to use CI, but writing the problem statement is hard."

COMPLETE WITH PROBLEM STATEMENT

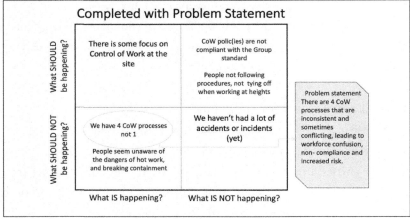

192

Completed Is/Should matrix and problem statement

After listing many of the separate problems that they were seeing, this CI team decided to focus on the different CoW standards first. They found that a single standard that was compliant with the Group standard allowed them to address the risk they were seeing.

Using the Is/Should Matrix can simplify the CI process by allowing focus on one problem at a time. This matrix is also a versatile tool that can be used in the framing of any consulting project. The tool highlights where there are multiple problems that might be interrelated but are separate problems to be solved.

Other uses for the Is/Should Matrix

This tool can be used anytime a problem is unclear. It can be used to troubleshoot a process, program, or equipment that isn't working, and is especially useful if there may be multiple problems. I've used it in a first meeting with a client having difficulty determining just what needed to be solved. It is based in facts and useful when multiple problems are smooshed together, inhibiting clarity.

CHAPTER 20

FOR GOOD MEASURE

There is an oft-repeated saying, "What cannot be measured, cannot be managed." While I might quibble with the lack of attention to emotion in the cliché, measurement is critical to improvement. Otherwise how would you know you improved?

CI involves:

Metrics: measures, metrics, indicators, key performance indicators (KPIs) either in numbers (continuous data) or attributes (discrete data like pass/fail, on/off, yes/no, etc.)

Measurement: the process of how we measure with precision and accuracy every time

Issues with metrics and measurement are often where CI projects go off the rails.

Metrics

Continuous Improvement is usually about improving a process. Any process, therefore, has three areas of metrics - inputs, activities, and outputs or results.

Inputs might be labor or materials, but they are often outputs of a previous process, e.g., the invoicing process produces an invoice, which, if not paid in 90 days, becomes input for the collections process. An output metric for the invoicing process, number of invoices outstanding after 90 days, is an input metric for collections.

Metrics usually fall into three categories:

- **Quantity** – counts, percentages or other ratios
- **Quality** – performance against specifications or other internal or external standards
- **Timeliness** – cycle times, and deadlines

Cost or profit is often a focus but it's usually a subordinate metric of one of these three categories. For example, producing too little with the same labor raises unit costs and reduces unit profit. Rework and scrap raise overall process cost, and missing delivery deadlines may incur penalties that reduce profit.

Selecting metrics for Continuous Improvement is fraught with the same issues that afflict business.

Issues with metrics

There are often issues with the numbers themselves - too many metrics, conflicting metrics, not the right metrics, and leading vs. lagging indicators, to name a few.

- **Too Many Metrics** – People have measured performance since pre-history. (There are cuneiform tablets from the Sumerian city of Ur with what appears to be worker-task cycle times dating from around 5000 BCE.) The phrase Key Performance Indicator (KPI) entered the lexicon with the work of Art Schneiderman at Analog Devices in 1987 and Robert Kaplan and David Norton's work on the Balanced Scorecard in the 1990s. The idea was that a few critical metrics - one or two in each of four domains (Finance, Marketing, Operations, and Human Resources) - determined the entire performance of a corporation. Alas, the word "key" in KPIs has been lost in many organizations. Sometimes managing the people and the process has been lost. Tom Johnson points this out in *Profit Beyond Measure: Extraordinary Results through Attention to Work and People* by using the performance of Toyota vs. the "manage by the numbers" US automakers. Toyota focused on giving authority and autonomy to line workers. They managed the process and improvement, and results went up substantially over their US counterparts. Now, in the era of Big Data, it seems that because we can measure and analyze something we must. In CI initiatives, we often create new metrics and that can overwhelm an already over-measured workforce. **Use what you have and rationalize metrics wherever possible.**

- **The Wrong Metrics** – In CI we often find that, despite everything we are measuring, we aren't measuring what matters. For instance, we may collect data on total sales by region and not by customers that buy across multiple regions, leading us to misjudge who our top customers are. Or we may track inventory turn, but fail to count work-in-process in inventory and backlog, leading us to over-order from suppliers.

In addition to not measuring critical metrics we make two fallacious assumptions:

- **You can't measure that!** This is usually said about qualitative data – for example, data strongly influenced by human emotion. Customers who are satisfied will continue to buy from you, but customers who are surprised and delighted will tell their friends and help you grow your business. How do you measure delight? In 2003, Fredrick Reichheld created the Net Promoter Score based upon the answer to the question, "How likely are you to recommend?" This is a "proxy measure" for customer delight. Proxy measures are often based upon correlation analysis, but can be based upon simple observation. "When this happens, I also notice that this happens."

I have seen proxy measures for risk reduction based on the percentage of procedures signed off in a log. I also have seen proxy measures for Continuous Improvement progress based on collective enthusiasm, average time between a first CI project and the second and third by the same person. Proxy measures take some thinking, but then so does improvement.

- **Results are all that matter!** This is often said by executives whose bonuses are tied to the bottom line. We should definitely track and monitor results, but these are lagging metrics. "Accounting numbers are always looking in the rearview mirror." "Last month's sales are a fact; this month's calls per week and close ratio - you can do something about those." Or in the words of my late Results-Alliance CI colleague Ric Taylor, "Monitor outputs; control inputs." You have to get upstream of leading metrics to control a process, e.g., material supplier cost drives overall cost; share of wallet drives customer profitability. Ask what inputs drive the output. Then test the impact and control the variation.

- **Conflicting metrics** – If you want to uncover conflicting metrics, ask your people, the process users, "Are there any areas where we ask you to do one thing, but reward you for doing something else?" At one call center I worked with, a CSR's answer was shocking. "I'm told we want to increase customer satisfaction, but I'm measured and paid bonus based upon average call handle time. They've even put the current call clock on my screen along with the week's average handle time. So if I get an unhappy customer who's going to take a while, I disconnect while I'm talking. Then I pick up the next call in the queue." **Identify conflict and resolve it.**

How to measure

If we are tracking improvement, we want to know we can measure precisely and accurately. There may be a natural variation to the results achieved at any stage of the process. We can understand those variations by understanding the mean and standard deviation of those numbers.

Our concern with the measurement process is to understand how much of the variation in our results is due to variation in the process (equipment and people), and how to measure it.

Imagine that I want to lose weight. First, I need a **measurement device**, a bathroom scale. I can choose a scale according to many criteria, but I want a scale that is **precise.** I want a scale that can differentiate weight within a half a pound or so; a weigh station truck scale wouldn't likely meet the test. I settle on a digital scale that records increments of 0.2 pounds, even though a weight change of half a pound is my concern.

Next, I need a **consistent** (precise) **measurement process**. I weigh myself every morning before getting dressed and having breakfast, with the scale in the same place, and on a level surface. Even though I've learned that if I stand on my toes toward the front of the scale my weight is less, I stand flat-footed in the center. I need to be assured that I can repeat the same process precisely so I am comparing apples to apples, or in this case relatively precise pounds.

Repeatability is one measure of precision. **Reproducibility** is another. Repeatability determines whether the same person can use the same measurement device and get the same result, or if there is variation in the measurement device. Reproducibility of a measurement process determines whether different people can use the process and the equipment to get the same result, or if there is variation caused by different people measuring slightly differently. I would need to have a clear and reproducible measurement process if I were running a weight loss competition, for example.

I also want the scale to be **accurate,** that is, the pounds measured should bear some consistent relationship to an external standard. In my case, the external standard is my doctor's scale, which consistently weighs three pounds heavier than mine, but then I'm seldom on the doctor's scale completely undressed or before breakfast.

The difference between precision and accuracy is often shown by an illustration of a target:

A random pattern across the entire target is neither precise nor accurate. A tight cluster of bullet holes in the outer ring is precise, but not accurate. A widely spaced grouping, around the bullseye is accurate, but not precise. A tight group in the center is both precise and accurate.

Precision is the absence of variation in the results. Accuracy is closeness to the intended true value. (I accept my doctor's scale as truth. In business, truth might be set by the customer.)

ACCURACY AND PRECISION

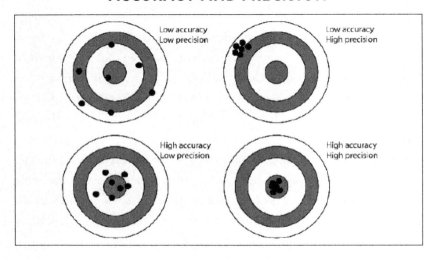

Metrics, measurement and improvement

Improving a business process may require reducing the process cycle time or scrap materials, eliminating rework or increasing the process yield (increased outputs for the same inputs). CI practitioners often reduce waste and/or reduce variation in the process. If you are a CI practitioner you know that a Measurement Systems Analysis (MSA) analyzes repeatability and reproducibility to determine how much of the variation in your process is due to variation in the measurement. If you can't trust the scale or you are using it differently each time, how would you know you actually lost weight?

CHAPTER 21

SOLUTIONS, NOT SYMPTOMS

"But we just redid our comp ratios."

"Look, I don't care <u>when</u> you did them, I'm telling you your comp ratios are <u>wrong</u>! My mortgage processors are leaving in droves and the reason they give in exit interviews is <u>compensation.</u> They can make more money doing the same work at other banks. Hell, apparently they can even make more money here processing credit card apps."

The manager of mortgage processing at a diversified financial services firm was frustrated with her Human Resources rep, whom she felt was "just not listening." Fortunately, a Continuous Improvement coach (CIC) who had worked with both managers stepped in. "Let's field a Rapid Results Team on this, collect some data and work together toward a resolution," she said. Both managers grudgingly agreed.

This firm had been working with Continuous Improvement for three years and the CIC's rapid results process had a good reputation for solving problems quickly. The five-person Rapid Results Team included finance people as well as HR and mortgage processors. The team scoped the problem and discovered that the forty-six-person department had lost fourteen people in the past eight months, most of them experienced processors, a 30 percent attrition rate! They, too, now understood why this was such a hot issue.

The team read though the exit interviews. It was true that the number one reason for leaving was "better compensation at my new job." The HR rep on the team confirmed that one processor had just transferred to the credit card group for a 20 percent salary increase, but that person had six years of credit card experience at another bank and had been promoted to a team leader grade level.

In the interviews, people described an accelerating pace of work. "We're used to picking up the slack with the new hires, but this is getting ridiculous. People are cutting their breaks, not taking lunches and I don't remember the last time I took PTO." (This was personal time off, including vacation, sick days and personal days.) Statistical analysis confirmed that the department was taking 20 percent less PTO than the rest of the firm.

The team investigated to see if volumes really were heavier and, if so, why. Three items became immediately apparent. First, the average processor experience level in the department had dropped from eight years to four years because of staff turnover.

Second, they learned that there was a housing boom in several of the firm's markets. A marketing program increased mortgage volume by almost 30 percent over the previous year. The department had hired ten new processors, which may have been too few people. This helped satisfy the immediate demand but also put a drain on the experienced processors' time.

Historically, new hires were given three days of training their first week and then trained "as-needed" by more experienced processors for the first year on the job. With the influx of new hires and increased volume, the experienced processors found the part-time on-the-job-training to be more and more difficult.

Finally, management announced the introduction of new mortgage products, which increased the complexity of the work and created even more demand on people's time. The department was already missing performance targets and now processors new and old were becoming very dispirited.

The team quickly determined that the escalating workload from increased volume and hiring was contributing more to the problem than misalignment with market salaries. And it would only get worse as more experienced people left. The traditional practice of having experienced processors "pick up the slack" and coach the Newbies was fine in a low-volume steady-state environment, but wouldn't work with increasing volume and decreasing experience. They created the following illustration to demonstrate the point.

MORGAGE PROCESSING VICIOUS CYCLE

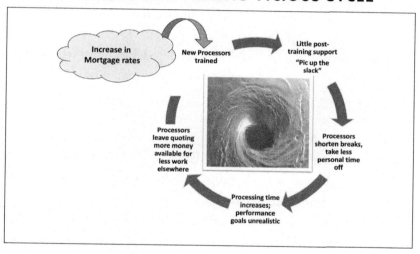

The increase in mortgage sales and number of new hires put pressure on the experienced processors to help the trainees. They took the additional workload out of their own time (shorter breaks, decreased PTO, etc.). Processing time went up; goals weren't met. People started to burn out; then they missed performance bonuses.

Experienced processors started to look for other jobs. It didn't matter if the other jobs didn't have as much vacation or performance bonuses, elements that go into compensation ratios. The processors weren't getting those benefits anyway. The problem compounded as more people left.

"It's a vicious cycle," said the coach, referring to the magnifying negative elements making it worse and worse. "It's like a whirlpool."

The "vicious cycle whirlpool" in the drawing drew the attention of the mortgage processing manager and Human Resources.

The solutions were to:

1. Change the hiring profile to hire more experienced mortgage processors in the short term to alleviate the workload.
2. Create a formal process for coaching new hires that was accounted for in workflow planning.
3. Adjust the salaries of some experienced processors and make the benefits component of compensation more visible.

With all of the data, the team's conclusion was clear: just raising everyone's pay wouldn't have worked because compensation was a symptom, not a root cause of the attrition.

In helping companies improve, I saw many people try to fix a symptom rather than look for the root cause. This error often occurred when someone assumed that a single piece of data told the whole story. In this instance, that datum was that exiting processors said they were leaving because of inadequate compensation.

It was true that a few people's salary hadn't kept pace with what they could earn elsewhere, but their total benefits package was still competitive. The bigger problem was that what they were being asked to do for that money had become unreasonable. They were set up for failure. The presenting symptom was compensation; that wasn't wrong, but it wasn't the root cause of the attrition. Understanding that more volume of work and increased training responsibility were escalating workloads suggested the successful solutions.

Symptom or root cause?

Assuming that a symptom is a root cause is a common failing of experienced people who remember a time when it <u>was</u> the root cause. "I have seen this before: Our comp ratios are out of whack." Inexperienced people don't have that history so they are more likely to investigate, which is why you should always have some Newbies in root cause analysis sessions.

Root cause tools like 5 Whys, fault trees, and process analysis are all small-group facilitated processes and therefore susceptible to the assumptions and biases of those in the room. These tools help identify a range of possible causes. But a cause identified with brainstorming tools like these should always be investigated and examined with data analysis.

FILTER FAILURES IN AGGREGATE

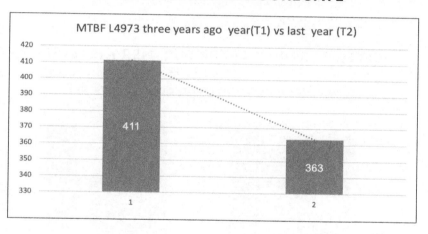

A chief maintenance technician in a chemical plant "hated these big companies shipping their manufacturing overseas." Then a fluid filter that was used throughout his plant started to have performance problems. The supplier had recently moved production to Thailand, and the chief tech instantly said, "**That** is the problem. We need to dump this supplier!" He even produced data. The mean time between failures (MTBF) of this filter had declined from an average of 411 days with a standard deviation of twenty-four days to an average of 363 days with a standard deviation of eighty days dating from the time of the off-shoring three years prior.

The graph was damning.

Then an operations technician showed him the same data broken out by plant section. What was apparent was that nearly the entire MTBF decline was from one area of the plant. That area had added new input lines and was operating beyond the pressure specs of this particular filter.

Rather than scrapping a Tier 1 supplier of many plant parts, the solution turned out to be buying six filters with more robust pressure specifications for a single unit of the plant. (As it turned out the same manufacturer supplied the new filters.) The increase in variability was primarily caused by the 200-day drop in MTBF but also by an unclear definition of when to change out filters. In all units technicians were simply changing the filters at inconsistent times.

FILTER FAILURES AFTER FURTHER ANALYSIS

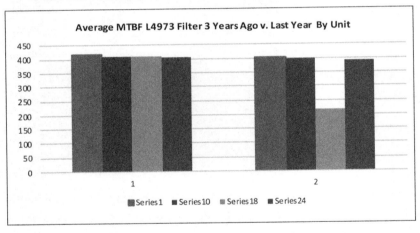

You have to dig deep into the data. Otherwise you may simply find what you are looking for.

Once you think you've discovered the root cause and have devised a solution that will solve it, then test it. Design an experiment and gather new data to test your hypothesis about root cause and another to confirm the solution.

Solving symptoms rather than root causes is common in business. It is an understandable downside of how the experienced brain works. However, Continuous Improvement professionals repeat this simple mantra: *Solutions not Symptoms, Solutions not Symptoms. . . .*

The process that follows from the mantra is:

- **Identify potential root causes** (Hint: slow it down, test your assumptions, ask, "How do you know that?")
- **Investigate** (Hint: gather data, form hypotheses about root cause)
- **Analyze data** (Hint: confirm hypotheses, create solution)
- **Test solution** (Hint: ask, "Did it eliminate root cause? Did it solve the problem?")

Attempting to solve a symptom may be human nature, but solving the root cause ensures that the problem is truly addressed and stays completely solved.

CHAPTER 22

RESISTANCE TO CONTINUOUS IMPROVEMENT*

ontinuous Improvement practitioners often meet resistance in implementation. Sometimes individuals push back because learning a new discipline is hard, but other times the resistance is a symptom of poor organizational implementation. Here are some excuses and remedies:

RESISTANCE AND REMEDIES

THINGS INDIVIDUALS SAY	REMEDY OR APPROACH
"We don't have time." "This just slows us down."	CI can save time – if you measure end-to-end time and focus on "time thieves" (bottlenecks people complain about).
"This feels like extra work."	Address the improvements that are central to the work.
"We do this already." "Not new."	True – CI ensures consistency and controlled results.

"Great! <u>More change.</u>"	Think of improvement, not change for change sake.
THINGS INDIVIDUALS SAY	**REMEDY OR APPROACH**
"This process is too structured."	Use it as a guideline of steps, not a rigid prescriptive model.
"We already know the answer."	Then show it with data - it helps convince others.
"I don't have any problems."	Usually a reaction to the word "problem" - try "opportunity."
"This takes a lot of commitment."	Most good habits do. Are you improving critical work?
WHEN STUCK IN THE PROCESS	**REMEDY OR APPROACH**
"Problem statements are hard."	Practice makes it easier; use words Object, Defect, Impact.
Scheduling of team -"I can't get people to work on this."	Find impassioned, interested team members. Often a symptom of a poorly defined project or unknown impact.
"There's no passion for this."	Need to find hidden metrics – connect to the business.
Project loses steam after identifying causes or solutions.	Often a symptom that project was scoped too large – pare back to milestones or rethink interim metrics.
"Ninety days is way too short." "This problem is too big."	The project was scoped too large. Use a scoping tree to break down – measure defect, not impact.
"Value comes too late."	Are there other metrics being delivered earlier?
IMPLEMENTATION SYMPTOMS	**REMEDY OR APPROACH**
"Those guys up there don't care." No sustained leadership	Valid – it is hard to make CI work without support. Connect with business leaders about critical business improvements needed and demonstrate results.

IMPLEMENTATION SYMPTOMS	REMEDY OR APPROACH
"If we did this we'd shut down operations."	This is related to individual time and resistance to difficulty, but if true, it is a symptom of out-of-control operations and poor scheduling. Start small and eliminate the constraints that cause poor quality, rework and frustration.
"Flavor of the month" "People are just checking off boxes."	Some organizations follow fads. The cure is demonstrating value with a results metrics dashboard and sticking with CI.
"CI projects don't deliver."	Perhaps we chose the wrong projects or gave up too soon.
"CI projects spiral outward."	Important to use a scoping tree to keep project focus.
"We're picking the wrong projects." Poor prioritization	Need to find other underlying metrics that have business impact. What are the drivers for this project?
"People are just documenting old projects."	May be okay for teaching the process, but a symptom of measuring number of projects and non-value-added.
"Low cost-benefit projects."	May be okay for teaching the process, but look for other metrics being satisfied (defining measurement, baseline etc.).
"Process isn't valued by our culture."	Process is defined as "bureaucracy" in organizations where "process people" add too much complexity. Start small, simplify everything, and build a track record. In a paraphrase of Alice's Restaurant: "One person is crazy; two are harmony; three or more are a movement."

Thanks to the late Dr. Richard W. Taylor for his substantial contribution to this chart

CHAPTER 23

MATURITY AND CONTINUOUS IMPROVEMENT

"You are only young once, Alan, but you can be immature forever." I'm not sure who first said this to me, probably some elementary school teacher upset by my constant "cutting up" in class. I've heard it from several managers over the years, who recognized that my humor was a thinly disguised problem with authority. Now, in my relative dotage, I've taken it as a guiding principle for my life.

While helpful for me, this adage is definitely NOT true for Continuous Improvement initiatives.

Implementing Continuous Improvement (CI), like all change in organizations, is a race against entropy, loosely defined as gradual deterioration and decline. CI is a discipline, a mindset, and a set of tools that take a while to learn, but fall into disuse quickly.

Organizations are composed of people, and people are forgetful and easily distracted. So a set of competencies that are hard to learn and difficult to practice can become a burden, then the subject of mockery and displaced by some other concept, and finally ancient history to which most are indifferent. So quickly building the self-reinforcing CI habit with a critical mass of the organization is essential to maturity in Continuous Improvement.

What is CI maturity?

As discussed, CI is a structured methodology for performing better. Fundamentally it's:

"Measure where you are – analyze why – improve – measure where you are then."

Then repeat that process - continuously.

A CI initiative is mature when it is self-sustaining, and the CI implementation process is "systematic and in control," i.e., the improvement process is:

- Targeted strategically
- Documented, well understood, and practiced
- Clear as to accountabilities for who does what (including monitoring and responding to deviations to the improvement process) with demonstrated competencies for each accountability
- Founded on organizational policies, procedures, systems and structures that ensure results and improvement

In short, the organization is improving in its targeted metrics and it is likely to continue to do so.

To CI practitioners, it will be obvious that this is maturity from a process point of view.

LOOK WE GOT THE ARROW CHART SAME NAME?

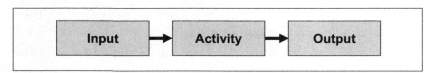

The inputs are strategic direction, CI competency (knowledge and skill), improvement opportunities (defects, problems, gaps, targeted projects), and supporting infrastructure (policies, procedures systems and structures).

The activities change over time as people learn this process and evolve toward maturity. CI isn't "one-and-done" learning; it is a staged learning model. One gets better with practice.

The outputs are the improvements: strategically directed (the "right improvements") and measurable, i.e., sustainable and improving over time. There are other staged learning models. The building trades have apprentice, journeyman, master; some religious orders are divided into novitiate, postulant, nun or monk; and Six Sigma has the belt system of Asian martial arts (Yellow Belt, Green Belt, Black Belt, Master Black Belt). The progression is one of learning:

- Introduction – often learning from a teacher
- Application – learning from practice
- Mastery – learning by teaching others

In many disciplines master or *sensei* is a student's designation of respect for the teacher. It is not a title assumed by the master, whose state is one of continually learning. Humility is fundamental to mastery.

Let's think about the activities of implementing CI in these three learning stages. The table below illustrates ideas for progressing from Introduction to Application to Mastery, without intending absolutes or hard lines between learning phases.

BUILDING CI MASTERY

ACTIVITIES			
INPUTS	INTRODUCTION	APPLICATION	MASTERY
Strategic Direction	Align leaders and staff on strategic priorities: "Why CI? Why now?" Talk about results metrics in threes -where we were, where we are, where we are going.	Continually communicate the "why" and results achieved. Target new opportunities. Rotate senior leaders with CI Coaches. Create a strategy process that differentiates CI-amenable priorities from tasks or step-change.	Balance alignment and standardization with breakthrough innovation.
Compe-tency	Train leaders, CI coaches for senior leaders, and some high-level practitioners.	Train the next level of practitioners. Use those who completed projects including senior leaders to share experience at training. Set up forums to share improvement projects. Expand competence to innovation and process design.	Provide ongoing development for senior CI coaches in initiative-wide control and in technology-enabled transformation.

CI oppor-tunities	Pick a few high-visibility, translat-able "projects" to start with	Translate first projects, start new projects, begin asking everyone for improvement ideas.	Search for external op-portunities; systematically research other companies for improvement ideas.
Infra-structure	Aggressively document process-es, project prog-ress (with all its warts and lessons learned), benefits achieved, other processes this im-provement might apply to, control plans and sustain-ability measures.	Build a search-able database of improve-ment projects; build a data-base of critical input metrics and their effect on critical out-puts. Standardize and automate as appropriate.	The "self-im-proving system" –rigorously controlled processes with documented procedures with CI "baked in" and includ-ing periodic system rede-sign.

Here are a few takeaways from this table:

1. **Start with strategic direction**. Far too many CI implementa-tions start with training and a few projects. They then try to "loop the leaders in" later. This causes wheel-spinning and ac-tually may cause the workforce to wait and see if management buys in.

2. **Start small.** Ensure that you get improvement in the areas you target.

3. **Pick replicable projects.** Working on the accounts receivable process for one product line can be copied easily for another product line. I frequently told training classes that the real mon-ey in CI isn't in the first project, but in the second, third, or fourth project in the same area. It gets easier, less resource-inten-sive, and the results accumulate.

4. **The key to sustainability is documentation.** Keep records of processes, projects, key inputs and their impact, your successes and most especially your failures. Continuous Improvement is about continuous learning.

5. **Mastery is about teaching others.** CI specialists are not enough. Leaders must become teachers. That is the way CI gets integrated into the culture of the organization.

I was often asked, "How long does it take to implement CI?" The answer is "it depends."

How long it takes to implement CI depends upon where the organization is today. (This is a partial list.)

- Are we process-focused OR activity-focused? Do we look at the big picture or do we manage the organization from a to-do list?
- Is there a real hunger for learning OR are we stuck in "the way we've always done it"?
- Have we had success at making large scale change OR do we constantly gravitate to the latest management fad?

Each of these questions presents two different current states. The latter state lengthens the time it will take to become mature at Continuous Improvement.

I saw organizations get to consistent application in a relatively short period of time of three to five years. I also saw organizations struggle for ten years or more to get to the same place. By then, these organizations were fighting a continuous battle against deterioration. Many gave up or moved on to the next fad.

Getting to mastery takes longer. Toyota started developing the Toyota Production System (TPS) in the 1930s, called it TPS beginning in 1948, and we've been talking about it since 1975. Still I'm not sure that Toyota would say they've reached mastery.

It is a continuous journey, but as Lao Tzu said, "Even a journey of a thousand miles begins with a single step."

EMERGING IMPORTANCE

O ver my consulting career I came to understand the importance of "people stuff." My development paralleled a growing understanding in business publications and consulting.

Earlier I shared how an LBS professor laughed at my MBA disdain for the organizational behavior courses where I excelled. "In senior executive programs," he said, "all they want is the people stuff." I didn't get why. "Surely if you have a new strategy people just do it, right? What leader would hire a consultant and not act on the recommendations?"

Obviously, I hadn't yet formed the bias described in the introduction, "business is about people... customers, staff, suppliers, and community." I defined consulting then as providing needed expertise and not as facilitating change. I had no idea that helping leaders engage in change, that helping people change, would be my life's work. I got the first inklings of this a year after I graduated.

The CEO in the ERF project had engaged directly with his team of LBS student consultants, meeting with us several times. The final "presentation" was a discussion. The second project our team did was a "desk study" of the market for automatic transmissions in the bus market in nineteen markets in the developing world. We discovered seven markets that were ready for entry according to detailed criteria and analysis. The client took a hands-off approach, never engaged with the consulting team, and cut the partner's final presentation short.

One year later, the ERF client had implemented our recommendations; the second client had done nothing but let the report gather dust.

"Oh," I thought, "leadership engagement might be important in change?"

In 1981, after business school, I started selling training and consulting for the Forum Corporation. I met executives who complained about uncooperative people. But even at Forum, which had leading lights in Organization Development on staff, people laughed at the "fuzzy-headed OD geezers." (They were in their fifties.) Then, in 1982 Tom Peters and Bob Waterman wrote *In Search of Excellence*, which highlighted cultural values like "Close to the Customer" and "Productivity through People." The book sold three million copies in four years. Finally the "soft stuff" had started to gain traction.

My first big change effort was the wildly successful British Airways privatization in 1984-1987. At the time, I had no idea of its import; I saw it as a custom training project. But I watched Chief Executive Colin Marshall change and grow during the project. He attended almost every final day of Managing People First, the leadership development and change management session for the top two thousand people, to hear the presentations of change team plans. At the first session he was aloof and arrogant. "Get us a cuppa tea, won't you, Paddy," he sneered at his training manager. By the last sessions, he'd arrive, remove his jacket, loosen his tie, roll up his sleeves and say, "Good morning ladies and gentlemen. What do you have for me?" I also witnessed the challenge of keeping the entire leadership team "on the same page," what some called "aligned."

Shortly thereafter I was part of a team General Motors engaged to conduct a leadership development change effort like British Airways. This was in the wake of a large-scale McKinsey reorganization project that broke up the Chevrolet, Pontiac, Buick, Oldsmobile, and Cadillac organization designed by Alfred Sloan, CEO in the 1940s. GM had had

850,000 people, and the new organization reduced headcount by eliminating duplication of the brand-based structure. Unfortunately, the new organization of vertical boxes and wires also destroyed the horizontal organization, networks and peer forums that ran the company.

We designed and delivered Leadership Now for the top one thousand executives, except for the top leadership team. There was little top team engagement, no change teams, and few results.

Around this time, I took courses in organization development and became an independent consultant for the first time. Lights began to turn on. Senior executives asked me for people stuff, beginning with intergroup conflict management. "Stop sales from lighting engineering's waste baskets on fire." (Yes, really.) Or I was asked to "get my leadership team on the same page about this change." Or I was asked to "structure this company, so we actually get stuff done." These executives wanted help with difficult situations or change efforts, but they didn't frame the issue like that. People were getting in the way of what the executive wanted to do.

What consultants offered at the time

When I joined Gemini in the mid-1990s, I was surprised by the lack of sophistication in organization development (OD). I was given organization charts and told to count the levels and spans of control, or number of workers reporting to a supervisor of manager. Gemini reengineering projects routinely reduced levels from the front line to the CEO to three or four regardless of international reach. They believed that the ideal span of control (number of workers to a manager) was twelve, regardless of the experience of the workers, complexity of the work, or risk involved. Risk, complexity, and inexperience require closer management oversight, i.e., a lower span of control. Spans of twelve are appropriate for routine work with experienced workers, but complex technical process safety work with few managers and inexperienced workers creates accidents.

At Katzenbach, I analyzed job descriptions and performance appraisals to ensure that people performed according to objectives. I analyzed communication patterns during mergers, turnover vs. promotion records, and exit interviews for content. The exit interviews were funny because of the euphemisms leavers used to avoid the truth and depressing when people were honest.

People stuff is more recognized today

During the last ten years of my career I ran Continuous Improvement initiatives in large companies, many in the oil and gas industry. Earlier the word "culture" evoked jokes like "you mean those little white plastic containers my wife keeps in the fridge?"

By the end of my career, however, tough oil workers were describing climate and culture and some even understood horizontal organization design. Of course, using words like "process" and "culture" were sometimes excuses for inaction as in "Our culture won't support that." But it seemed that my bias - business is about people - was no longer such an outlier.

LARGE SCALE CHANGE PROCESS

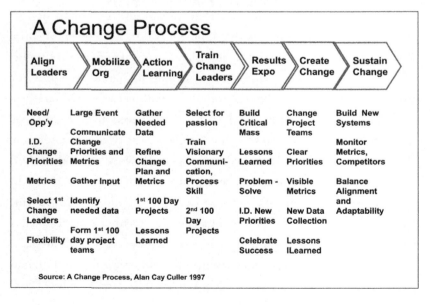

Source: A Change Process, Alan Cay Culler 1997

Consulting firms also learned to speak about change. All the majors have built or acquired large organizational practices, e.g., Accenture bought Kates Kesler, the premier organization design firm. Digital transformation includes change and a technology content.

I went through many iterations thinking about change. I wrote the article "Renewal: Principles Practices and Techniques" that was published in the 1994 *Journal of Business Strategy*. I learned Kurt Lewin's "Unfreeze-Change-Freeze" change model, but added critical capabilities (Leadership, Teams, Communications and Education). John Kotter of Harvard researched and built his change capability model around this time, but I didn't know that then. Soon after, I joined Gemini Consulting, a firm known for big reengineering projects. I was drawn to Gemini by its recruiting and "Business Transformation." I later learned that Business Transformation was a nascent service offering based around a four-stage change model: Reframing – Restructuring – Revitalization – Renewal.

LARGE SCALE CHANGE MANAGEMENT STRUCTURE

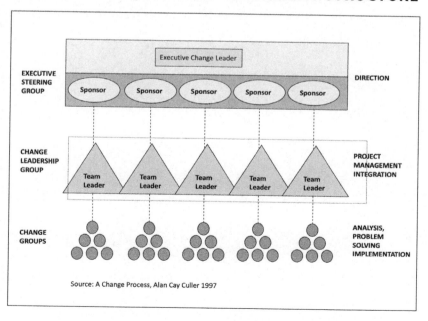

Source: A Change Process, Alan Cay Culler 1997

My work at Gemini led me to an all-inclusive idea about change. In 1997 I wrote a draft article for Gemini's *Transformation Magazine* called "A Change Process," which included a comprehensive model and a change management structure to manage large projects like we did at Gemini. Gemini enhanced and developed my process view of business. My own practice evolved to help leaders with three critical organizational capabilities of change:

- **Integration** – alignment, getting everyone on the same page
- **Innovation** - creating new products, markets, and ways of operating
- **Improvement** - getting measurably better each day, week, month, and year

People are always inventing new words for change. Flexibility, agility, reengineering, and renewal all denote continuous improvement. Step change, reinvention, large-scale change, and transformation are words for innovation, which these days is assumed to come only from digital technology. But no matter what you call it, whether change is incremental improvement or transformative innovation, it is still the "people stuff" - aligning people, leading people, developing people, organizing people, helping people change.

CHAPTER 24

WHAT ARE CHANGE MODELS AND ARE THEY HELPFUL?

"**I** don't get it."

I cringed as this six-four, balding engineer challenged my presentation to the leadership team. He ran the company's most profitable division and we always had difficulty communicating.

"Your boxes and arrows are very pretty and I'm sure you think they mean something, but I have no idea what you are trying to say."

What I had flashed on the screen was a rather innocuous PowerPoint slide: "Change is a process – it has three stages."

Insight---Action---Results

First, figure out why you need to change. Then take some strategic actions to make that happen. Finally, measure your results – repeat and revise as needed as you go along. OK sure, there were boxes and arrows and I was building to the input requirements for successful change, so maybe there were more boxes and arrows than absolutely necessary, but it's an accepted framework. What could be simpler?

A framework - therein lay my folly. People absorb information differently. They also use information differently when they make decisions. One way I came to understand this is through the Myers-Briggs Type Indicator, MBTI – another framework.

Myers-Briggs has many flaws and should never be used for selection or management, but it is a good personal awareness instrument and a team conversation-starter about the differences between people. What I learned from Myers-Briggs is that I take in information intuitively. I'm perfectly comfortable skipping around and letting connections and sequence emerge. I also have no problem processing information and making decisions based upon data that is out of order and has holes. My brain just reorders and fills in, but communicating to people who like ordered, complete, sequential information is a challenge.

Myers – Briggs calls my profile intuitive thinkers, or NTs. NTs love frameworks, models, and pictures that they believe make a story clear. NTs are 26% of the millions of people who have taken the instrument since the 1950s. MBTI also collects demographic data including employment. Interestingly, well over 50 percent of those who identify themselves as management consultants are NTs. This means management consultants may have trouble communicating in frameworks with three quarters of the general population.

So that is the first point about a framework like a change model. A graphic change model will probably require more detailed explanation than the consultant thinks it will.

What I did in this meeting when Paul the engineer didn't get it (and it turned out several others who were less vocal) was to take the slide off the screen and use examples instead.

"I stepped on the scale this morning. I've gained five pounds. What should I do?"

We walked through the weight example, followed by an example in their business in which it was clear that they were thinking about taking action but didn't have the data (insight) to move to action.

The first learning about change models: **most people don't think in**

frameworks. Those that create change models are different from those who act on them. **More explanation is required.**

Change inside an organization can be overwhelming. Those of us who build change models sincerely want to make it understandable, but our abstract conceptual models don't always do that. Putting the change in real terms with examples from the business in question is critical. Still a change model may help consultants think through the change.

Change is a process – it has inputs, activities, and outputs. Like any process it has phases, certain requirements necessary for success, and things that can go wrong along the way. Further, while change can be planned, remember that planning is of more value than an actual plan, which may have to be altered down the road.

There are three distinct types of change models:

1. **Phase models** that outline the phases of change
2. **Requirements models** that outline what is required overall or by phase
3. **Change plans** that show plans across multiple dimensions

Phase models

The first change model I learned was Kurt Lewin's:

Unfreeze – Change – Freeze

In the 1940s Kurt Lewin founded what became known as social psychology and organization development (OD). He created such frequently used tools as action research and force-field analysis. He coined such OD terms as organizational or leadership climate, and group dynamics. Interestingly, Lewin suggested this change model in only one of his writings. He did no empirical research into it and yet it became an accepted model of change.

> Unfreeze – overcome inertia, dismantle the existing mindset, legitimize change
>
> Change – typically a period of confusion as old ways are replaced with new

Freeze – crystallize the new mindset, habituate new behaviors, create support systems

In 1947, this concept of change as a process and not an event must have been revolutionary. OD professionals adopted this language, as did line management. However, some described the Lewin model as "unfreeze-change-refreeze," as if one could use the old support systems to support a new process and outputs.

MY FAVORITE CHANGE MODEL

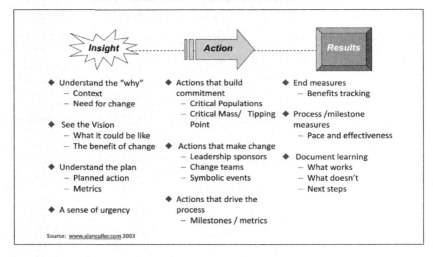

The change process has three distinct phases:

- An awareness of the need for change and a growing urgency to act
- Concrete actions that are often experimental and evolving in nature
- Reinforcement through mindset, behavior, measurement and discourse

People have been renaming these phases ever since.

William Bridges: Endings – Transition/ Neutral Zone – New Beginnings

Noel Tichy and Mary Anne Devanna: The Gathering Storm, Vision and Commitment, Institutionalization

Jeff Hiatt of Prosci: Preparing for change, Managing change, Reinforcing change

A model that I have used is **Insight-Action-Results.**

The impetus behind all three-phase models is to create a picture of a process with a beginning, middle, and end. The process is comforting: "Just get through these three phases and it'll all be over soon." It implies that change can be analyzed, planned and scheduled and that planned change is more likely to be successful.

GLEICHER-BECKHARD CHANGE FORMULA

For Change to get going: C = D x V x F > R
C = Change (desired for the organization)
-D = Dissatisfaction with "now"
V = Vision of what the change will look like
F = First steps
R = Resistance

Requirements Models

In the model above I combined the phases (insight, actions, results) with change requirements, (vision, urgency, and specific kinds of actions). While Kurt Lewin's three-stage model showed that inputs were necessary, others began to focus on overcoming resistance to change. David Gleicher at Arthur D. Little was the first to include requirements such as a vision for the future and dissatisfaction with the past. Gleicher balanced these requirements with a formula for overcoming resistance. The dissatisfaction with the past - "we can't go on the same way" - is the compelling case for change, or "burning platform." Margaret Thatcher was the burning platform at British Airways: "I will sell you. I can sell you in little pieces or I can sell you as a functioning profitable business in a public offering. It's your choice."

Gleicher's formula was subsequently published by Richard Beckhard in his 1977 book *Organizational Transitions*. For change to happen, dissatisfaction with the current state, a vision for the future and successful first steps must be greater than the fear of loss and the unknown, which cause people to resist. People don't fear change but rather fear loss of job, political power, and autonomy. Many people are quite comfortable with making earth-shattering changes to their own life (like selling everything I owned and moving wife and family to London) but they just don't like it imposed on them. They don't fear change; they fear <u>your</u> change.

As I mentioned earlier, I began studying change models, puzzling through what makes change work or not work based upon the successful British Airways privatization experience and the dismal failure of Leadership Now at turning around General Motors. In my article "Renewal: Principles, Process and Techniques" I added the critical capabilities of leadership, teams, communications and education.

MARY LIPPITT'S
'MANAGING COMPLEX CHANGE' MODEL

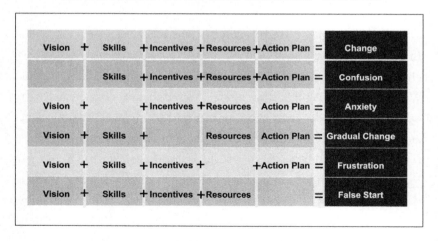

There are several models detailing capabilities, or requirements. Perhaps the best known is John Kotter's model shown here from the 1990 book

The Heart of Change. I like several things about Dr. Kotter's model, but the "Guiding Coalition" is my favorite. Stakeholder management is a critical capability. It is very actionable, but often forgotten.

Another of my favorite models was created by Dr. Mary Lippitt of Enterprise Management. It explains requirements in terms of what it feels like when a required element is missing. Frustration, anxiety, and confusion are not the desired results and actually inhibit the intended change; they also suggest where the problems lie.

Requirements models make good checklists for leaders or change management practitioners. Phase models can be "we are here now" communication tools for practitioners and perhaps the general population, with one caveat: when communicating with the general population use <u>only</u> one model and explain it step-by-step in words with examples.

JOHN KOTTER'S 8 STEPS OF SUCCESSFUL CHANGE

John Kotter's 8 Steps of Successful Change

Step	Action	Observed Behavior
1	Increase Urgency	People start telling each other "Let's go! We need to change things!"
2	Build the Guiding Coalition	A group powerful enough to guide the change starts working together well.
3	Get the Vision Right	People are talking about the vision.
4	Communicate for Buy-in	Fewer 'What' and 'Why' questions; More 'How' Questions
5	Empower Action	People act to improve without asking for permission.
6	Create Short Term Wins	People feel a sense of success and talk about the quick wins.
7	Don't Let Up	Improvements come in waves.
8	Make Change Stick	New behaviors stay when leaders change.

Source: John Kotter, *The Heart of Change*, 2002

Planning models

Where phase models are descriptive and requirements models are an inputs checklist, planning models are active, meant to engage the client in planning. As such they can be especially tricky. Remember that not everyone thinks in frameworks, so planning in a framework (change model) with other people requires a lot of explaining with examples.

When I was at Gemini Consulting we used a transformation map as described by Francis Gouillart and John Kelly in their book *Transforming the Organization.* This tool allowed teams to plan actions on a variety of variables or disciplines. The challenge was always that the discussion and metrics of where we are and where we want to be often were a source of significant disagreement.

Both requirement and phase models can take a somewhat static view of change. Transformation mapping and instrumentation models can be more action oriented, but they often assume a linear path that will not change.

A transformation map begins with describing the outcome, the vision, and then agreeing on the elements that must change to achieve the vision. (It's also important to identify what won't change.) Then for each element the leadership team identifies where they currently are and walks through phases, milestones and interim metrics (the lines radiating toward the vision). This forms a picture of the overall change plan.

TRANSFORMATION MAP CHANGE PLAN

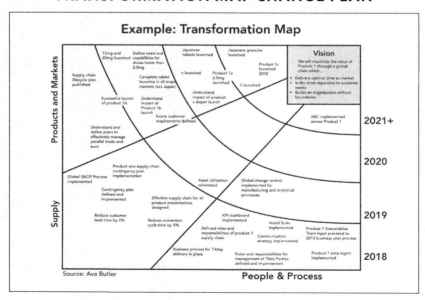

Why not just use Microsoft Project or similar project planning software? A fair question. Depending upon the group, I might use planning software that participants were comfortable with. The advantage of a transformation map for a large scale change, however, is that the total plan is visible on one graphic that can be hung on a wall. The disadvantage is that it is very complex and unintelligible to someone not involved in building it. I have seen transformation map software that combines with an individual stream planning software (like MS Project). Thankfully I never had to use it because the overall map was too detailed to see on a projected screen and the individual plans made MS project look easy. I also think that the downside of any computer planning software is that the **plan becomes paramount and hard to change**.

In many organizations these days, change has become *continuous change.* By this I don't mean continuous improvement but rather change heaped upon change, never finishing one before embarking on another. Change models don't help with that and may make things more difficult. Rationalizing change efforts might be a good first step, i.e., listing all initiatives and change requirements and the resources to support them before proceeding with change.

Which brings me back to my original question, ***Are change models helpful?*** My answer is provisionally yes, sometimes better for consultants than clients. But useful with clients if we…

- Remember that those who use models to visualize thinking <u>are in the minority</u>. The majority of people will need some explanation and the opportunity to process the thinking and give feedback.
- Understand the purpose (for phase models -you are here; for requirements models –checklist; or for planning models - participative planning) and use judiciously.
- Remember that *the map is not the territory.* Even detailed "transformation maps" that allow planning milestones across multiple

domains are just analogies for what is and what might make a difference. Change is a lot less predictable than we think.

CHAPTER 25

HERDING CATS: THE ULTIMATE CONSULTING SKILL

"This place is a Goat Rodeo. Everybody is running this way and that and nothing is getting done."

My client, Fred, an engineer who had risen to CEO of a small specialty chemicals company that just acquired a competitor, grabbed me on my way to my work area first thing Monday morning. He was frustrated.

"Look, I am <u>trying</u> to listen to people like you said, but <u>everyone</u> has an opinion on <u>absolutely everything.</u> This merger is going to close next week and we've got to meet with the JTB leadership team and we can't even get our own act together. How in the world will we do this when they get on-board?"

I did my best to calm Fred down and got his assistant to schedule a meeting of his entire team for Wednesday afternoon. Then I talked to every member of the team and came back to Fred with an agenda for the meeting.

From my interviews I identified seven critical issues, things that were either unclear or that there was disagreement about.

The resulting meeting agenda was something like this:

- Objectives of the meeting: "Get on the same page" – Fred
- Agenda and Ground Rules review - Alan
- Opening statements: each person describes desired outcome and hot buttons (key issues to him or her - two minutes each)
- Key issues: feedback from Alan from interviews
- Clarifications - group discussion
- Points of Agreement - group discussion and action planning
- Points to be Resolved - group discussion and action planning
- Actions and Commitments review

I used to call this process "Leadership Alignment." Over my years as a change consultant I helped many leadership teams come to public agreement about contentious issues and commit to strategies and change actions with which they might have privately disagreed. Another client, Scott, called this *"herding cats,"* and told many people that it was my core skill. *"Alan is the cat-herder-in-chief."*

While humorous, I think that *"herding cats"* is a consulting capability that every leader should learn in order to ensure clarity and unity in his or her organization. Even as "cat-herder in chief, I tried to teach this skill to my clients.

Under what circumstances might a leader be called upon to herd cats?

In any change. Change is accomplished when people in a group come to *collective insight* about the need for the change and agree to take *collective action* to achieve a *collectively agreed envisioned result.* Clarity and unity around the need for the change, the agreed action and the envisioned results are critical.

In any complex task. The project in which Scott first encountered my cat-herding skills was a simple task of writing a Continuous Improvement toolkit. The problem was that there were multiple practitioners with backgrounds in various CI methodologies and they disagreed about what tools to include and how they were described. Clarity and unity once again.

Building customer supplier partnerships. A U.S. automobile manufacturer was changing its supply management strategy to mimic the
Japanese *keiretsu,* i.e., fewer suppliers and a partnership relationship, as
opposed to its years of adversarial dealings based on "beating them into
the price we wanted." It took several meetings, but we were able to clarify
goals and roles, unify about shared objectives and rebuild trust.

To change not only the organization, but the leaders' own style.
Short Brothers of Belfast, Northern Ireland built the first planes for the
Wright Brothers. In the late 1980s, Mrs. Thatcher privatized Short Brothers and sold it to the Canadian firm Bombardier, who built two commuter
prop planes, the Shorts 330 and 360. These were simple sheet metal
construction, wings over the fuselage, thirty- and sixty-passenger aircraft.
They'd been designed in the 1950s and had changed very little since. (I
flew them on US Air from Pittsburgh to Cincinnati and always feared
they would disintegrate during the noisy rattle-prone take-off.) Bombardier planned to stop building them and have Shorts build the fuselage
for the Canadair Regional Jet.

The commercial aircraft division CEO, let's call him Alex, was the
personification of the division. Alex had been the production manager
and prime salesperson. He still flew around the world negotiating with
airlines and national governments to sell these planes. Alex had been
vocally opposed to this merger, and to retiring the 330 and 360. Alex also
had an explosive personality. He lost his temper easily and unpredictably,
but never lost his verbal sharpness in the process. He could slice and dice
you in a sentence. During the interviews so many people described him
as "Genghis Khan" that I was petrified of the feedback session with him.

It turned out that Alex took the feedback well. "I know that about
myself. I'm not proud of it and I can see that it will not work to get these
guys to buy into this." (He'd also already made his peace with the new
strategy, unbeknownst to me or his team.) "What do we know about
Genghis Khan anyway? I bet his soldiers thought better of him than
his enemies did."

Between us we hatched a plan. I researched Genghis Khan and it turned out he was quite prolific about writing rules that held his team together. I wrote a whitepaper *Bilik and Yasa, the Laws and Leadership Maxims of Genghis Khan* and we used it as a model to decide how we would work as a team to implement Bombardier's strategy. Alex used his old persona as a foil to describe how he would behave in the future and his team joined in enthusiastically. Sometimes the courage to publicly admit one's faults is extremely powerful. Shorts is still building the parts for the Canadair Regional Jet, but Bombardier sold Shorts to Spirit Aerospace in 2019.

So "herding cats" is a core leadership skill that can build clarity of direction, unity of purpose, and commitment to make things happen. It can also build the trust that comes from transparency and fair process. There is no magic to it. It just takes practice. There are some critical success factors:

- **Openness** – if you are a leader and you're going to practice this with your team, do it first with a topic you don't already have strong feelings about. Listening without judgment is critical to the initial data collection and to the facilitation.
- **Facilitation** -You can use a third-party facilitator, a colleague, an internal person from Organization Development or Human Resources, or an external consultant. You can do it yourself, rotate the roles of facilitator and scribe among the team, with good process and ground rules.
- **Make agreements visible** – I use flipcharts rather than a whiteboard because it makes it easier to tear them off and post them. Whiteboards and projected computer screens eventually run out of space and so move out of sight and out of mind.
- **Make discussion points (disagreements to be resolved) visible**.
- **Make action items visible** – save the deadlines and final accountabilities until last to avoid overloading any individuals.
- **Agree ground rules** – e.g., speak your mind, be open to con-

structive challenge, listen with respect, and be prepared to change your mind and compromise. Avoid unproductive discussion (use a "parking lot" for off-topic discussions). Have the group agree to self-regulate according to the ground rules.

- **Document discussions and actions** - it is a sign of ownership if someone other than the leader or facilitator takes responsibility for getting the meeting notes typed and distributed.

Some leaders will try to delegate this process completely, either to an internal staff person or to a consultant. In my experience, delegating clarity and unity leads to a lack of both. So tell your clients "saddle up and prepare to herd cats."

CHAPTER 26

LEADERSHIP DEVELOPMENT AND CHANGE

" **I** now realize that change in this huge corporation comes down to me changing my behavior."

The fifty-year-old manager looked genuinely perplexed. He went on, "I get that I can't do it by myself; we all have to change. But we can't do it without me either."

As a change consultant I often heard participants in leadership development workshops make this type of statement. These workshops were conducted to communicate both the need for change and the new culture and leadership behaviors that would be required. I heard the epiphany that "change isn't just about 'those guys up there,' it's about all of us" at the British Airways' Managing People First (MPF), which was the workshop in BA's successful change. I also heard it at General Motors' Leadership Now, the workshop in GM's unsuccessful change.

I heard leaders come to this realization at a host of other companies. While some change efforts were more successful than others, I have no doubt of the impact of leadership development on those individuals. They changed, whether or not their companies did.

Leadership workshops and leadership training

In 1984 British Prime Minister Margaret Thatcher announced that she would privatize the nationalize airline. The airline had lost a billion dollars the previous year and had the worst customer service of any airline in the world. It was the first large change project I did and arguable the most successful. At privatization in 1987 the airline was the most profitable in the world and had the best customer service as rated by J.D. Powers. The British Airways change project included multiple leadership training programs, change teams and leadership coaching, but also involved changes to performance management and executive compensation, as well as facilities and equipment. GM, on the other hand, tried to copy the project but just ran the training, with predictably unsuccessful results.

Leadership development by itself won't make a corporation change, but it certainly helps. After all, if people have been doing things one way for years and now you want them to do something differently, you have to, at least, tell them. They may also need new competencies (knowledge and skills) and the individual and organizational support systems to turn them into capabilities.

The objectives of many of these workshops were alignment and com-mitment, getting leaders to understand the why of the change and then to commit to lead it. Knowledge and skill development was import-ant but secondary.

At the British Airways MPF program for the top two thousand people, we presented a case analysis of a fictitious cruise line that was unprofitable with poor service. The entire development team wrote the case and, as the only recent MBA grad, it was my job to create the pro forma balance sheets and profit and loss statements. (One of the side findings from the workshop was that very few of the top two thousand could read or analyze financial statements, which created a need for further training.)

The discussion that followed the reading of this case identified what BA's leaders needed to do to be a profitable private company with a rep-utation for excellent service with customers. Facilitators recorded the group's reflections on flipcharts:

LEADERSHIP WORKSHOP DISCUSSION OF CULTURE CHANGE

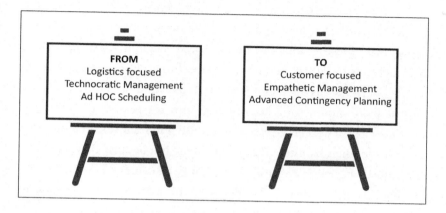

FROM
Logistics focused
Technocratic Management
Ad HOC Scheduling

TO
Customer focused
Empathetic Management
Advanced Contingency Planning

This kind of from-to discussion was a feature of many of these workshops. The lists on these flipcharts weren't the point; the discussion was.

Aside from content, there are many logistical design parameters to consider in planning such workshops. Onsite or offsite? Should participants stay at a hotel (residential) or go home at night? Should people come to the workshop in intact work teams or random collections of levels, geographies and function?

Most organizations I worked with put a great deal of energy into selecting groups for these workshops, especially the first ones. They tended to schedule largely heterogeneous groups, being careful not to have bosses and subordinates in the same group and not to mix the senior with the very junior. They also were careful not to isolate a single individual from a crucial function, division, or other subgroup.

These programs offered different opportunities to commit to lead. At BA there were change teams, small groups that chose to work together to plan particular changes. Each group presented its plan to the Chief Executive Colin Marshall at the end of the week. Other programs featured individual planning. At Continuous Improvement and innovation work-shops there were projects using the relevant methodology. In the best implementations these projects and the results they achieved and learning they provided were tracked and included in performance evaluations.

We often included a creative or fun exercise. BA's MPF program was residential and ran from Sunday afternoon until Friday, closing after the action team presentations and lunch. Days were long. Participants had personal time at 7:00 a.m. and 5:00 p.m., but evening large-group and small-group sessions often ran until 11:00 p.m. and sometimes later. On Thursday afternoon, we asked small groups to spend ninety minutes creating a vision of their view of the new BA and their role in it. We told them to "let their hair down" and have some fun because they would be spending that evening preparing their change team presentation for Colin Marshall the next morning. We designed this exercise to relieve tension and to allow participants to have fun using the teamwork built over the week.

At one of the early sessions a small group composed entirely of aircraft maintenance managers had been difficult all week. These men were fifty-to sixty-five-year-olds and had all come up through the ranks. During the week they had been cynical and sarcastic, and when we explained this exercise, two actually snorted. They disappeared.

The facilitators resigned themselves to the possibility that the team had left the training early and were planning how to explain this to the rest of the class. But when it was time to present visions these gentlemen rushed in and asked to present last. Given their attitude over the week the facilitators were wary, but reluctantly agreed. When the maintenance crew's turn came it was 5:00 p.m. and dark outside. The crew turned out the lights.

As the facilitators quietly panicked, they heard strains of an Abba tune: *"I have a dream, a fantasy. To help me with reality…"*

One by one these grizzled guys walked in, each carrying a lit candle. While the music played they got the entire group to join them in the front of the classroom.

"I believe in angels, something good in everything I see."
They handed out lit candles and soon everyone was humming along.

As the song came to a crescendo, they somehow led everyone to act together.

"I've crossed the stream." The entire group took a step together over an imaginary stream.

"I have a dream." The entire class all sang in unison. Still gives me shivers.

Apparently, the old guys had first laughed derisively at the exercise and then someone said, "If not us, then who?" They were missing because they had driven thirty miles to get the tape and boom box from someone's house, and planned the whole thing in the car on the way there and back. In the end they demonstrated their commitment and brought others along.

Coaching programs

Some companies develop the leaders necessary for a change through executive and other leadership coaching. I've seen this work particularly well in innovation and Continuous Improvement initiatives. An internal or external consultant who really understands the methodology helps participants over the rough spots. What *doesn't* work is if that "coach" does all the work, especially the tough math or analytical solution testing. A good coach helps only when asked and then "teaches" rather than doing the work. The best coaches use Socratic questioning to draw out what the coached already know.

Where this approach is unlikely to work is in the wake of remedial coaching. On occasion, I was hired to coach "problem employees," and once I was the "problem child" who was assigned a coach. I admit to being lousy at being coached. My coach was a competent external consultant, but I was given no notice and no choice and didn't respond well. I think my coach realized that what she had been hired to correct was a fundamental disagreement about a business approach. She offered to facilitate a discussion between me and my non-confrontational manager. He declined. She worked with me for another month. I learned to behave "more like I did with clients," i.e., more diplomatic and less defensive. Ultimately I found the coaching helpful.

Any perceived lack of choice is almost always an obstacle to be overcome. When I coached, I was sometimes able to create an atmosphere of trust that allowed me to be helpful. My own coach was able to do that with me when she assured me that I, not my boss, could choose what we worked on and I could decide what would be shared with my manager. But this remedial type of coaching isn't suited to building commitment to a large scale change

In my change work, I was sometimes the coach to the presiding executive. This was a sobering responsibility. The challenge was to be helpful, but, as much as possible, invisible.

Mike Levin was an American consultant who had worked with Colin Marshall at Avis, and served as Marshall's coach during the British Airways transformation. Levin was a Vietnam era Green Beret who had worked at the Office of Strategic Services, the predecessor to the CIA. He frequently told people that he was an expert in psy-ops, or psychological warfare. Levin's office at Heathrow headquarters adjoined Colin's.

Many of my senior colleagues on this project - John Bray, Dr. George Litwin, Dr. Warner Burke - give Mike Levin a lot of credit for the design and the disciplined execution of the BA project. They also credit him for shaping Colin Marshall into the kind of leader he became during that period. But Colin's leadership team and especially the rank and file were afraid of Levin. Mike had Colin's ear and it seemed that Colin always did what Mike suggested. They called him Svengali and Rasputin. It did not surprise me when Levin was blamed for the "dirty tricks" campaign against Richard Branson's Virgin Atlantic in the early 1990s, despite the fact that Levin had died in 1989.

Opinion leaders

Opinion leaders make change happen. These are people to whom others listen, and they "get it." They understand the need and the requirements, and commit to the change. This group often comes from outside the existing power structure. Sometimes these opinion leaders are first to volunteer for a change team or speak passionately at training. Other times they are the most vocal resistors, whose passion is redirected to make the change more effective. What sets them apart? They are enthusiastic and people listen when they speak.

As a change consultant I learned to watch for such people. Change almost always needs what Harvard professor John Kotter calls a "guiding coalition" in his book *The Heart of Change*. Sometimes even those who most oppose the change have good ideas about overcoming obstacles or potential unintended consequences. I have seen the passionate learn skills to coach others in the change. And not infrequently, these opinion leaders get promoted in the new organization.

New leaders

Will previous leaders lead the new organization? Often not. Sometimes new leaders have more passion for the vision, or different skills and knowledge. For example, as one insurance firm's service model moved more and more online a leader emerged who could easily talk with the innovators in her technical departments.

I worked with Jon Katzenbach, a former McKinsey senior director and author of several books on teams, on an organization design project for a family-owned private equity firm. Mike, the founder, along with two plant experts, bought small manufacturing businesses, improved and held them, and brought in increased profits for many years. The whole business model had been dependent on Mike and his ops gurus who were nearing retirement age. The family was stepping back, taking board positions, and the CFO was in line to become CEO.

The organization boxes and wires were relatively easy, but what was clear was they didn't have the leadership "bench" to pick what to buy or to improve the companies. We created networks by loose industry group-ings so that operational efficiencies could be shared. Jon recommended two executive forums from an extended leadership team. The Strategy Forum decided what to buy, and when to divest (a new concept for this firm). The Leadership Development Forum predicted leaders needed for the evolving portfolio; its membership included junior opinion leaders nominated by their peers. The Leadership Development Forum was to create a "bench," leaders who could step up as the firm expanded. This forum identified opinion leaders and created a program of training and experiences to ensure their readiness for the next level of change. More than twenty years later one investment committee managing director and two division heads came from the first Leadership Development Forum, and the firm is roughly four times larger.

Change always requires leaders who can be clear about direction and attract followers. Consultants can encourage clients to invest in developing leaders for not only this change, but also for transformations that may not yet be visible. Further, understanding how to innovate, integrate and continuously improve may be the most critical leadership skills of the foreseeable future.

CHAPTER 27

"WE NEED A NEW ORGANIZATION"

In disruptive times a harried executive is likely to ask for one of two things - a new strategy or a new organization - and they often hire an "expert" to do it. Like most change consultants I did my share of drawing "boxes and wires."

When I was a booking agent, I booked a speaker for an IBM sales meeting, where I saw Frank Carey, then IBM's CEO, speak. There was a reorganization going on at the time and Carey's opening line was, "If my secretary calls. . . get her name." The room erupted in laughter.

He went on to say, "Really though, IBM <u>never</u> reorganizes without a very good reason. ... of course, at IBM, a very good reason is that we haven't reorganized in a year or so." More hilarity. I remember thinking at the time, "Isn't he the guy doing the reorganizing?"

My view of the role of organization in a company evolved over time based on two fundamental beliefs:

- **An organization is a strategy implementation mechanism** People implement strategy. How groups of people are formed and who reports to whom communicates a great deal about the strategy.
- **The job of the organization is to impart clarity of purpose and**

accountability. Changing the formal organization produces two things:

- It communicates priorities - what's important around here now.
- It clarifies accountabilities for those priorities.

That's it. That's all a new organization does. Clarity of purpose is not nothing; in fact, it's critical to change. But a new organization is not the only tool a leader has to create clarity of purpose. Accountabilities are also important, but structure is only one of several available performance management tools.

As a consultant I came to the view that companies reorganize too much. When asked to help design a new organization I always asked why it's necessary. There are real reasons to reorganize, e.g., changes in business model, post-merger integration, or a new market or product line expansion. But not all reasons are good ones.

My approach to organization design was to teach leaders how to do it. Why? Because if an organization implements strategy, its design is too important to be left entirely to consultants and human resource professionals. **Organization design is a critical leadership capability.**

Here are some things you should get right as a consultant:

Don't do it by yourself. This is something you should do hand-in-hand with the client, if not the leadership team.

Don't get sucked into personality-based organizing. This translates to "Since we outsourced payroll, Maureen in accounting won't have enough to do, so let's give her the customer call center, too." It's like a giant game of pickup sticks. Better to design the jobs first, set the hiring specs, and then put the people in roles based upon agreed specifications. Then come back to individual capability fit.

Don't participate in "red-lining." Red-lining is cost-driven organization design, so named for a phenomenon I observed dozens of times. The consultant and CFO go in a room with an organization chart and draw red lines through people's names. Then they calculate salary and benefits costs of those who are left. If the total figure doesn't meet a preset number, they draw more red lines. If it does they cobble together what's left into an org chart and present it.

An organization should be designed rationally so you can explain it. How else would you achieve clarity of purpose?

High level design

At a high level, there are two different elements to designing an organization:

- **Vertical** – This is the accountability structure – the "boxes and wires" – that details who reports to whom. The objective is clarity of purpose and performance accountability for the day-to-day, routine work.

- **Horizontal** – This is the integration structure, sometimes called the "informal organization." It includes shared services and functions like finance and accounting and human resources, processes and systems, networks and forums, and growth capabilities like systematic innovation and improvement. The objective of the horizontal organization is unity or alignment – how people can work together.

Vertical structure

The major types of vertical organization - functional, product-based, and customer-based - are aligned to strategic business drivers. For businesses driven by:

- **Low cost - a functional organization** reduces duplication and staff costs.

- **Product innovation – product organization,** an organization based on platform, technology or a product allows people with similar expertise to innovate together.

- **Customer loyalty –customer organization,** an organization based on industry, geography, or key accounts allows a company to get close to the customer.

This type of pure-form organization often creates a lack of integration, a scenario popularly described as "silos." In silos, people within one function, product or customer group have difficulty communicating across the organization, perhaps because they spend most of their time with others like themselves or because the "my team" mindset is heightened by competition for resources. I spent much of my career in "silo-busting."

The silo-busting solution is cross-department communication. This can be achieved by discussion forums and networks and by shared processes, such as strategic portfolio management, investment, operational budgeting, leadership development, procurement and sourcing policy, etc.

Since the 1970s, most large companies have been structured in some form of matrix organization that juxtaposes two or more drivers. Matrix organizations attempt integration structurally. They create dual (or in some cases, multiple) reporting relationships, and the accountabilities for each must be agreed or negotiated. Matrix organizations often compromise the clarity of the "pure" forms and require that everyone have higher level skills of influence and negotiation.

All vertical structures, and especially the matrix, can get very complex when you add in multiple lines of business across international borders. In these environments carefully planning the horizontal structure is imperative.

Horizontal structure

When I started my career as a change consultant, the vertical structure was the only thing talked about, even by consultants. In the mid-1980s, General Motors had almost 49 percent of US car and truck sales, 850,000 employees, and the eighth-largest budget in the world, including countries. But the company was cost-challenged because Japanese competition was gaining share with lower-priced vehicles. GM engaged a large consulting firm to reorganize GM in a million-dollar project - a rare, if not unprecedented, figure at the time.

Previously GM was organized into five car divisions and two truck divisions. This organization was created by CEO Alfred Sloan in the 1930s to have "a car for every pocketbook." Car buyers were meant to start out with a Chevrolet, graduate to a Pontiac, Oldsmobile, or Buick and finally end up with a Cadillac. Low-end truck buyers bought Chevrolet trucks, and business buyers bought GMC. Each division had its own design, manufacturing, marketing, and functional services. There was a lot of expensive duplication. Also, over time every marque had expanded offerings; the original differentiation had long been lost.

The consulting firm created a new organization with two divisions, BOC (Buick, Oldsmobile, Cadillac) and CPC (Chevrolet, Pontiac, Commercial - trucks). The divisions shared design, manufacturing, marketing and functional services. The new organization allowed plant closures and saved lots of money. It also facilitated the look-alike GM cars of the 1980s, widely credited with the further decline of GM market share.

What the consulting firm apparently failed to consider was interdivisional integration. Previously, the sprawling GM organization worked because the guys at the Chevy design and technical center knew their counterparts at the other marques, and they picked up the phone to solve problems together. The reorganization blew up the informal organization that made the place run, and it took several years to straighten out and rebuild.

These days, most organization design models are alignment models, i.e., the McKinsey 7S, the Galbraith Star, and the Burke-Litwin Model of Organization Dynamics. They all make the point that organization structures, systems, and processes should be aligned around purpose and strategy. Now, many consultants understand the importance of integration between organizational groups. I should add that while planning the horizontal organization, some organizational designers seem stuck on hard structural solutions and are locked on the matrix as a solution. I have seen four- and five-way matrices that no one understands. Some practitioners emphasize more flexibility, e.g., R&D networks and leadership development forums. Many organization designers rely on formal constructs like information systems and formal processes to enable information sharing and joint decision making, e.g., strategic planning and capital budgeting processes. (Two processes that are often overlooked are how the organization innovates and how it improves.)

RACI: ACTION RESPONSIBILITY CHARTING

RACI — Example: Building the Toolkit								
Activity	Person							
	Nick	Karen	Ben	Stephanie	Consultants	Mark	Kendra	Doug
Design the Basic Structure of the Toolkit	A	R		C		I		
Design the Prototype	A	C		R				C
Write the Tools	R, C		A		R			
Collect Input From Consultants	I		A, R					
Program the Prototype	I	C		A, R				C
Screen the Tools	A, R				C			
Test the Toolkit	A	C	R	R	C	C	I	C
Promote and Celebrate Launch of Toolkit	A	R	R	C	C	C	C	C

R = Responsible person   A = Accountable person
C = Consulted person   I = Informed person

Detailed organization design

The reason many reorganizations fail to achieve the intended results is that the work stops too soon. High-level job "boxes" and integrative processes are necessary, but not sufficient. Ultimately, leadership must prepare detailed job specifications, and then assess, assign and, if necessary, train candidates. Leaders must clearly define roles and responsibilities in their job specifications, and then teams need to agree roles and responsibilities. One option is to use facilitated responsibility charting – RACI – to determine who is Responsible, who is Accountable, who must be Consulted before the fact and who must be Informed after the fact.

Decision rights also need to be agreed. A good tool here is the facilitated decision rights tool RAPID.

RAPID: DECISION RIGHTS CHARTING

Key decisions: RAPID methodology

- There is only one D
- Locate the D at the level of organization where you would expect the decision to be made...
- ...but recognize that the line can always intervene (note: there is a single line of 'command and control' for any decision; "people can have two bosses, decisions can't")
- If D belongs to a group, clarify how the decision gets made (e.g. majority vote)

- There is only one R, who should be the individual who does 80% of the work to develop the recommendation
- R has broad visibility and access to information for relevant inputs
- R has credibility with both Is and D
- At times, R and D are same person

- Can be multiple Is
- Assigned only to those with valuable, relevant information that could potentially change the decision
- Avoid I proliferation – more people will want to be involved than need to be

Recommend

Input **Decide** **Agree**

- May be multiple Ps
- In some cases P should also be an Input to ensure good upfront planning

Perform

- A's should be assigned sparingly
- Usually for extraordinary circumstances relating to regulatory or legal issues
- A is on the R – if the A and R can't agree, the D breaks the deadlock

RAPIDs should reflect what will work in 90% of situations –
Design for the rule, not the exception

RAPID was originally designed at Bain & Company. RAPID works like RACI, but is applied to decision roles as opposed to actions. The acronym stands for R, the person who recommends; A is a person at a different function or level who must agree with the decision; P is for the performer who must carry out the decision; I provides input; and D is the person accountable for the decision.

RACI clarifies action roles, RAPID clarifies decision roles. Because they are so similar I rarely used both frameworks with the same client at the same time. If the issue was not getting stuff done (and in my experience this was more often the issue), I used RACI. If the issue was who made what decision, I used RAPID. If the client was already familiar with one or the other, and there wasn't an issue clash, I used the familiar tool.

Further, like all change efforts you have to over-communicate about it. You are changing some people's jobs, and you must re-contract with the entire organization.

And that is just a start at organization design. You may be thinking, *"sheesh – organization design is a lot of work; it's enough to make my head hurt."* Yup. So you can see why I think reorganizing because "we-haven't-done-it-in-a-while" isn't a good idea.

Clients may hire you to do it for them. You should teach them the basics. Say something like "You may hire an architect to help design a building, but you have to be clear about what you need, want and like." As Bauhaus architect Mies Van Der Rohe said, "God is in the details."

Organization design is no different. It is a critical leadership change capability.

CHAPTER 28

FORMING AN INTERNAL CONSULTING FIRM

"Why on earth would you help a client take the work inside?" The year was 2006, and I had just received my first consulting engagement helping a client form an internal consulting firm. A partner in a small consulting firm was incredulous that I would agree to such an assignment. Like a lot of "expert" consultants he wanted to protect the dollar value of his expertise.

When we worked together previously, the firm had lost business when a service offering commoditized, i.e., clients either hired our people directly or took our presentation materials and trained their staff to replace us. Our answer was to rewrite our consulting contract to specify that the client could not hire our people or use our materials internally during the project and for two years after it ended. This never worked. Now I was abetting a trend to eliminate consultants.

"You're poisoning the well!" he said, perhaps a bit louder than necessary.

Now all these years later, the clients that I've helped do this might use fewer consultants overall, but they also don't use consultants the same way. Most especially, these firms don't use consultants over and over for exactly the same type of work. They developed internal capability as they improved performance. Consultants help with things the client hasn't yet learned to do themselves.

Why develop an internal consulting firm?

To get the work done

I helped my clients start an internal firm because the work was extensive and the firm needed to develop the capability internally. I never sold it as a way to decrease consulting spend, just a way to ensure that the work continued. Most of this work was Continuous Improvement and hiring consultants to do this long term was prohibitively expensive and would have doomed the client to giving up on CI.

Most of the clients I worked with in this regard were medium-sized firms and larger, over $200 million in annual sales and one thousand people or more. But I have seen smaller firms hire a single consulting manager who screened and managed independent consultants and small firms as if they were building an internal department.

To create a functioning staff organization

Staff organizations often perform an expert and a regulatory role. Human Resources or Engineering, or Accounting become practiced at telling businesses what they can't do because of legal exposure or other kinds of risk. These staff departments become bureaucracies that are not seen as "helping," or being of service to the business.

Over my career, I reorganized Human Resource departments to segregate day-to-day transactional work like employee relations, compensation and benefits, and performance management from longer time horizon strategic work like workforce planning, leadership development, and succession planning. I also reorganized staff groups in a service center concept that mimicked outside consulting in the relevant industries, including a pay-for-service model that replaced staff cost allocations.

This work is essentially the same as creating a consulting firm. Internal consulting firms are a new staff organization structure within an existing organization, but they are built upon a client relationship model of staff service.

To embed a competency

What united all these models is that the firm wanted to grow a critical competency that they foresaw using repeatedly such as Reengineering, Continuous Improvement, or Innovation. Serial acquirers often hire strategy consultants to develop due diligence and manage integration. Some holding companies or private equity groups set up internal operational assistance staff.

Some of these groups have a unique specialized skill; others are staffed with extra junior "pairs of hands." Still others staff a combination of permanent hires and contractors much like a big body-shop temp agency. But many of these units are set up like consulting firms, with client development models, content and consulting skills training, and the infrastructure to develop and build firm capability while achieving results for clients. These "internal consulting firms" seem to be successful and worthy of a closer look.

To develop leaders

One of the advantages of developing an internal consulting firm is that the "consultants" develop knowledge of different parts of the organization and serve as service providers or "servant leaders." I worked with one firm that used the internal operations improvement firm as a training ground for high-potential leaders. A side benefit of this work for me was that I developed relationships with leaders who sometimes hired me later as they rose to lead large organizations.

What kind of consulting firm?

I hope I have made the case for the differences between types of firms, by discipline, by service offering and between process and content. While some of the internal firms I have seen are content based, the firms I installed were process firms.

Purpose: doing vs. teaching

In all likelihood the client will choose the type of consultant that they are used to. If the client is stuck on this decision, ask, "Why do you want to form an internal firm?" If the answer is that he or she wants staff specialists to do technical work for the line, then you are most likely building a content-oriented firm. If the answer is to teach or to build capability, then a process-oriented firm is a better fit.

Don't try to combine process and content

I worked for three firms that sought to combine content and process consulting, strategy development with strategy implementation, or the analytical with the behavioral. It always sounded like such a great idea to combine these two streams of consulting, but it never worked. Content people have "answers" and process people have "questions" and the only thing they seem to have in common is little use for each other.

Service offering

The large generalist consulting firms pride themselves on being able to solve every problem using every known methodology or framework. However, most successful internal firms start with a single service offering and often a single methodology or framework.

For example, if members of a company group are forming a strategic assistance firm, not only do they avoid operational improvement work, but they work with a single strategic methodology, such as Michael Porter's industry and competitive analysis (5 Forces), or Chan Kim's Blue Ocean Strategy (Innovation focused), or Michael Treacy and Fred Wiersema's Value Disciplines (Customer Intimacy, Product Innovation, Operational Excellence).

Similarly, Continuous Improvement groups pick Lean or Six Sigma while innovation groups select Human Centered Design, Agile, TRIZ, etc. Flexibility as to service offering and methodology is an advanced concept, kind of like "spin" in tennis. ("First, learn to get the ball over the net, then you can try to slice.") Just as external firms may graduate to new methodologies (different ways to solve the same problem) or add service offerings (different problems to solve) AFTER they build an "identity" for solving a particular kind of problem in a particular way, internal firms should start simply.

THE MAISTER CONSULTING PYRAMID

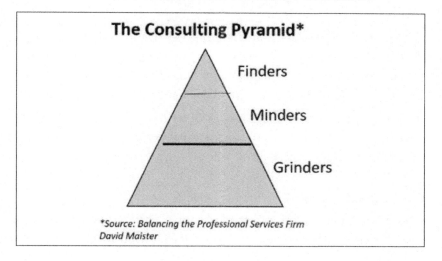

Structure

Earlier I mentioned the consulting pyramid described in David Maister's article "Balancing the Professional Services Firm" and his book *Managing the Professional Services Firm*. This structure is divided among those who sell the work (Finders), those who manage projects and the daily interface with clients (Minders), and the often junior consultants who do the work (Grinders). Maister notes that established methodologies can be taught more easily to juniors and so pyramids are broader at the base.

In internal firms Minders and Finders are often in short supply. For example, some Six Sigma implementations have only "Black Belts," whereas successful Six Sigma structures have:

- Yellow Belts (often in the business) who work on large projects
- Green Belts who work on small projects and coach Yellow Belts
- Black Belts who work on more complex projects and coach Green Belts and Yellow Belts, and
- Master Black Belts, who "find the work" and structure improvement efforts with the business leaders according to strategic need

There should also be a Six Sigma Program Manager who reports directly to a C-Suite executive and who ensures that improvements focus on the C-suite's strategic priorities.

So a wide-base pyramid structure comprised mostly of individuals who do the work ("Grinders" in Maister's terminology) can be problematic for an internal firm. In a Six Sigma initiative Black Belts may get some projects done, but there is no one to ensure these are the right projects (i.e., tied to business priorities) and that may waste money. Without the "Finder" or Pro who develops clients the internal firm may just dry up and blow away.

Client development

A pitfall for an internal consulting firm is the "Field of Dreams" assumption: "If you build it they will come." People who form an internal consulting firm assume that the "businesses" will just see their expertise and automatically use them. Nothing could be further from the truth.

A business leader must recognize the need for help and that the internal consulting firm can provide it. As the American psychologist Carl Rogers once said, "Help that isn't asked for is seldom perceived as help. Rather, it is looked at as interference at best."

Also the "because Papa said so" model – a single CEO directive in the form of an email announcement - doesn't work either.

The most successful firms have people who meet with potential "clients" and frame needs in a "statement of work" with clear objectives, expected outcomes, measures, and a timeline. They also agree on a process for managing changes as new data arise. This is equivalent to the partner role in an external firm.

Hiring and training

Who is hired to work on projects depends on the service offering and structure. Some successful firms have hired consultants from external firms; some have hired and trained internal people. Others have a combination of internal and external people who work on a full-time, part-time and/or contractor basis. Clearly whom you hire dictates training needs.

Everyone must understand not only the service offering, but also the consulting model with its requisite consulting skills, staff and client management. And classroom training by itself does not a consulting firm make. Planning the learning infrastructure, as well as creating and documenting the toolkit, project history, and databases with search capability, all make learning easier.

From my experience, the best internal consulting firms rotate line people in and out of the "firm" to distribute expertise throughout the business. General Electric CEO Jack Welch demanded that all his leaders above a certain level become a Six Sigma Black Belt. Many went on to become Master Black Belts who trained as well as coached. This made for an integrated approach.

Owning results and funding the firm

Perhaps the trickiest issues around internal consulting firms are who owns the outcomes and who pays for the work. This also depends on whether the firm's approach is content or process consulting.

If a client buys a recommendation but fails to implement, he or she may blame the consultant. When a Black Belt turns the improvement over to the process owner and the process owner doesn't maintain the control plan, who is responsible?

These issues must be discussed and worked out prior to starting the firm and reinforced in the client contracting process.

Who pays and how? Over the years, I saw multiple payment schemes. Some companies hold the consulting firm costs centrally below the contribution line for which the businesses are held accountable. Some allocate costs to everyone whether they use the services of the internal consulting department or not. Some have service level agreements between the firm and the client with cross-charges based upon either time used or the results delivered. I also saw benefit- or gain-sharing agreements, i.e., "I saved you $x, $.3x accrues to my budget, $.7x accrues to yours."

These are all "brown dollar" funding arrangements (internal allocations vs. real money exchanges) but they still can have a huge impact on the bottom line for which businesses are held accountable. It is imperative that the implications of funding decisions be discussed with "customer" business leaders. The American colonial war cry is a good guideline: **"No taxation without representation!"**

Think about the infrastructure and expertise needed to <u>manage</u> the operation. There can be huge benefits, but they don't drop automatically to the bottom line. Someone must ensure that the business uses the service and that the customer is satisfied.

LATER CAREER CHOICES

I started my consulting career blissfully ignorant of the field and what might occur as I progressed. I gave little thought to "up or out" but I left several firms, effectively making that decision for the firm. The transition to selling was less painful for me because I had spent many years as a salesperson, and when I worked for myself and if I didn't sell, I didn't eat.

Research, writing, service offering development, and thought leadership were just things I did as a consultant. Maybe if I had stayed with a single firm, I would have published on leadership or post-merger integration, two service offerings I worked on at Gemini. There I was a discipline head in a firm where direct selling was organized into client industry verticals and disciplines were tasked with service offering development.

The Journeyman transition from doing the work to managing the work happened so early at Harbridge House that I didn't notice. Some of my team members noticed. I remember a couple "Alan, stop 'managing' me!" reactions when I was learning how to track project progress and timesheets.

I remember chasing timesheets from people very much senior to me on the British Airways project. I also remember moving a production team out of the office to a private residence with a generator during Hurricane Gloria so we wouldn't risk missing deadlines on a leadership workshop. I also arranged for back up rental cars and a U-Haul van so the team could drive from Boston to Montreal if planes weren't flying. We did lose power, but only briefly, and the airport never shut down. Seniors made fun of me, but I got the reputation of a "belt-and-braces" project manager that left nothing to chance.

But I never had the "promo-or-no-go" angst that I watched Newbies go through later. "Will I make engagement manager this review cycle? Or have I been too long in the senior associate role?" For this book I talked to some who experienced these transitions.

And so suddenly I was the senior guy.

I remember when I realized that I wasn't "the kid" anymore, when I was older than my colleagues, older than many of the leadership team I was facilitating. I was perhaps not older than "<u>the</u> client," but I was the second oldest person in the room. And then I got even older.

I've discussed the selling or thought leader choice that arises as you become senior in a firm. I mentioned how some mid-career consultants switch firms at this time to get a shot at partner somewhere else when they feel they are denied partner where they are. Perhaps they don't want to sell or be a thought leader, and so find a firm that wants a Pro to just "do the work." I ended up specializing in change and found work outside full-time employment at a consulting firm.

Senior people in consulting, thought leaders who may not publish, may have a lot of mentees who rise in the firm and keep pulling them into projects. Sometimes Pros are active developers of leadership talent among the client opinion leaders and those people rise to levels where they hire consultants. (That, by the way, is the single best strategy for having clients who are younger than you. Having clients who are all older than you means at some point they retire or die and you are left without work.)

Pros often choose to move outside the firm, perhaps to be an executive in industry as we have discussed. But not infrequently senior people choose to start their own firm or to become an independent consultant. These often seem like lucrative choices that "keep the multiplier," the gross profit margin on their own time and the time of others. There are chapters in this section on these two options, which are not as simple as they might appear.

Also included in this section are what I learned about getting paid as an independent and consultant dreams of getting off the road.

CHAPTER 29

MID-CAREER TRANSITIONS

Up or out? Grow or go? Really?

Up or out? Grow or go? Really? The larger firms - McKinsey, BCG, Bain, Deloitte, E&Y, PwC, KPMG, Accenture, Capgemini, AT Kearney, Booz Allen Hamilton, etc. - are fairly explicit about either the "up or out" or "grow or go" promotion model. Even the boutique firms may be explicit depending on the history of the firm. I have talked with some people at even the largest firms for whom the reality of approaching this milestone was a shock. "Me? Really?"

For others, it came as a relief. "Wow, you mean I can finally have a normal life, go out during the week and get to know my neighbors? Awesome!"

Sometimes, analysts who join from an undergraduate university are sponsored for business degrees, usually with a contract to spend several years with the sponsoring firm. In my experience, however, these sponsorships are few enough to be considered non-existent. But if you are an analyst with a recommendation from a Big 3 firm, you can probably get into the business or law school of your choice and may even qualify for financial aid. I observed career paths from undergraduate analyst to MBA to Big 3 firm and up and up. I have also seen such careers end in the "out" choice at a later level.

Entrants with a graduate degree face the same decisions at the "up or out" juncture, but they are less likely to hear, "It's time for you to get another degree." Of course, some graduate "leavers" do go back for other graduate degrees and move into technical or academic careers.

If you are promoted to the next level, my advice is to not be a jerk about it. Keep up your relationships with your friends inside the firm and those who leave. Don't talk endlessly about your new job, or other people. And especially don't offer unsolicited advice.

Keeping in touch with leavers and being active in the alumni network is a common trait of successful partners. They seem to maintain connections with potential high flyers for ten to twenty years until they become clients. Keeping in touch with connections should be easier now with social media, but this kind of relationship requires more than the random "like" to a Facebook or LinkedIn post.

If you are among those asked to leave, still keep in touch with your friends. And remember that most consulting firms are "good places to be from" early in your career.

Often, people who have worked for five years at one consultancy but discover that they aren't progressing, switch firms. Smaller firms often hire engagement managers and project managers from larger firms. Some of these people trade around from firm to firm and end up becoming an independent consultant or they start a smaller firm themselves. (Later chapters address both of those situations.)

If you find yourself moving from one consulting firm to another, it may not be as easy a transition as you imagine. As we've discussed, every firm is different. There will likely be a different language (panels to charts to slides) and there may be different approaches (e.g., process or content) and different service offerings (e.g., technology-enabled process improvement and automation may sound the same, but may be radically different).

Culture in consulting firms is insular. There is often one right way to do things and everything else is wrong. Look at the general profile of people at the level you will be joining. If there is no one who has ever worked anywhere else except this firm, prepare yourself for an assimilation challenge. If everyone comes from a different place, ask how they arrive at consistent methodologies. If they have no answer to this question, it may be that every partner defines his or her own methodologies, and it will be like joining several loosely related firms rather than one integrated one.

The "grow or go" path at some firms seems like a gentler model perhaps because it allows for a little more time in lower-level roles. At middle to upper levels I have seen it apply mostly to senior people who do not do well at direct sales. Most are people who would rather spend their time and energy in research and in developing service offerings. Consulting firms liberally throw around the term "thought leader," but, where it exists, this path often allows consultants to progress to senior levels without the requirement to bring in large clients and "whale-sized" projects.

These promotion patterns are more prevalent in content consulting because content consultants sell new ideas, answers. "Up or out" is a way to have "A" players at every level while making room for "new blood." Process consultants execute ideas, but they still must have effective management and new clients, so aggressive promotion/outplacement strategies exist in process firms as well.

Industry to consulting: Coming in and moving out

Coming in

I did not come into consulting from a career in industry so I asked those in my network about their experience after working five to ten years outside of consulting.

Here is what they told me:

S ____ joined a firm after eight years in sales and marketing at a Fortune 100 company and was staffed on a large project as a stream lead the first day.

"There was an entirely different time horizon and pace to the work. I went straight from the airport to the client site. I …was greeted by the project manager and the lead analyst. 'Let's have a look at your workplan,' they said. 'Workplan? What's a workplan?' I asked."

C ____ was an experienced chemical plant manager who was recruited to manage large reengineering projects in the chemicals industry.

"I had managed two chemical plants before I came in. On my first project I took the team for a plant walk through. They all had their brand new yellow steel-toed work boots and shiny white hardhats, but I had to tell them not to step in the puddles because this is a chemical plant!"

B ____ came to Gemini from the oil and gas industry and remembered his first contact with an Analysis and Design VP.

"The guy described *himself* as 'a mile wide and an inch deep' and then proceeded to discount everything I had learned in ten years in the business."

R ____ came from corporate banking. She had worked in corporate development on some M&A projects and was staffed on a post-merger integration project.

"Where I used to work the hierarchy was clear. You didn't talk to your boss's boss without your boss's knowledge and permission. Consulting seemed like it was a flatter organization. They kept talking about 'the team.' They took me along to review my findings with the CEO and I struck up a conversation, or actually the CEO did, but we talked for about five minutes. When we were done the partner told me, 'Never do <u>that</u> again. Your job is to speak when spoken to and otherwise zip it.'"

M ____ described her first year at Gemini. She had previously worked for a large insurer that was a Gemini client. She had worked on a client team and had volunteered to take the package from a reduction in force that was the result of the project. "The induction training was amazing. Two weeks with people from all over the world. We worked on a case as if it was a project and had to make a presentation to the client. I found out later that was the partner who had sold and managed that project. It was intense, but I gained a real understanding of insurance and consulting. I was assigned a project buddy on my first project. The discipline lead kept checking in with me over the first year. I had never experienced such hands-on management in my life, but I think I succeeded as a result. When I left I was leading and selling projects and that gave me the confidence to start this firm."

A BCG Senior Advisor I spoke with during the Covid pandemic:
"I spend most of my time educating teams about the financial services industry. I have a standard deck that I run through in half a day. I've contacted a few people I know in the industry and arranged meetings with the partner. I have even worked a little on some of those projects. The FinServ partner brings me along on pitches sometimes, usually second meetings. As a result of the pandemic, I'm on day-rate for now. I'm making pretty much the same money; the training sessions are on Zoom and I do them from home. It isn't bad, but I miss the project work. It is hard to imagine going back to a bank at this point, but I might do more independent consulting or join a firm with more project work."

I don't pretend that my conversations represent a significantly valid sample of mid-career consulting entrants who came from industry, but anecdotally I learned that:

Some firms hire from industry in the same stream with entrants from graduate school. This creates some dissonance because the two groups start from different perspectives. Other firms invest heavily in induction training that is based on skill and acculturation to put everyone on equal footing early. Gemini brought people together with the two-week Gemini Skills Workshop and two elective three-day workshops per year. It's hard to say where Katzenbach ended up with training. As a start-up we were very ad hoc and the partners had a preference for McKinsey trained people. They grew to be much larger before they were acquired, but I'm not sure the training progressed much further.

Consulting and industry are quite different workplaces. The consultant-client relationship is closer than most industry entrants feel about customers. The goals and pace of the work are different; consulting may be faster-paced, but owning long-term results is absent. Consultants often feel that consulting is completely different from any other workplace. The mid-career entrant from industry can feel that his or her expertise is not listened to; this can quickly lead to negative feelings about consultants and consulting and some industry entrants wash out earlier than expected.

Senior people from industry are often put in training or sales that some may find boring. A very senior person from the oil and gas industry who went to McKinsey "described telling the story over and over to more and more junior people."

Going out

Moving from consulting to industry can be extremely rewarding or totally frustrating. Like those who joined a consulting firm from industry, some of the ex-consultants I spoke with said they had trouble getting others to listen to their ideas. A consultant who joined BP told me:

> "It was easy because I knew most of the people. I did find that people looked at me differently now. My boss, who had been my client, had some unreasonable expectations. He expected that once I was on board I would 'hit the ground running' and things

274

would just happen."

A Gemini consultant who joined a pharmaceutical company in marketing said:

> "I wished at the time there had been more product/market training. I did not know the content of the products and customers as well as some of my new peers… I had a lot of catching up."

An engagement manager from a boutique consulting firm who joined a manufacturing firm told me:

> "It took some adjusting. My experience is that most big companies move a lot slower than consulting and one must adjust to the slower timeframe and pace. That said, with my latest position at a supply site, when we see issues that could impact supply, we need to move (and do move) at an urgent pace."

A principal from a Big 3 firm who went to an investment management firm was quite candid:

> ""The people management stuff I learned in consulting is transferable. The analytical thinking and presentation skills I developed often give me an advantage. I just need to rely on others for a depth of industry knowledge. I am still learning, but I am still behind my peers and hope I don't run out of runway."

A person with whom I have worked as both a client and colleague described her journey on the consulting road to industry and back again:

> "When I first joined [pharmaceutical firm] everyone looked at me with a certain awe. I was very sure of myself, and M_____ had hired me for that, I think. I came to understand that being the person that M____ held up to everyone as a paragon wasn't helping me get anything done. I had to work on building a network of my peers and had to learn to keep my mouth shut occasionally, which is not always easy for me. You know the joke about consultants 'having an opinion on everything without the hindrance of experience.' Well that was me. I did well there when I learned to ask others' opinions, but frankly, I never really recovered from

being M_____'s consultant. So when I went to [financial services firm] I interviewed about thirty people before I expressed any ideas about our marketing."

There are similarities between the experiences of those going out and those coming in:

- These are different workplaces where different content is valued and different behaviors are required.
- Getting listened to is difficult; being a know-it-all doesn't work.
- Pace of work is different.
- Training can ease the transition, but you need to educate yourself in the new business and culture.

There are people who manage to move back and forth between industry and consulting, but they tend to be rare. The few that I know have started out in consulting and moved to executive roles in industry. They come back into consulting as business developers or they start small consulting firms.

CHAPTER 30

MASTERING THE FRONT END (IT'S SELLING... SSSHHHHH)

T he first time I heard the euphemism "the front end" I thought it referenced the steering and suspension of a car. Consultants use this expression to avoid describing the part of their process that happens before the client agrees to pay them. In other words, selling. The most important criterion for promotion to consulting partner is new client acquisition, but the word *sell* is profane.

"We don't *sell,* "a senior partner once told me. The word *sell* was dripping with distaste and his face wrinkled like he had just been exposed to an open sewer pipe. "We acquire new client relationships. We are asked to *serve,* or to *solve new problems.* This *isn't* a used car lot."

I have sold enough in my life to be amazed at what a negative image salespeople have, especially the men and women of secondhand automobile distributorships. For a lot of people, not just consultants, salespeople are considered the lowest of the low. In my view, salespeople uncover what the customer needs or wants, and if what they offer can meet that need then a sale happens. I know that some salespeople don't behave according to my idealistic view of selling, but my experience has been overall positive (even on used car lots) so I'm not prepared to write off an entire business function. But to get back to the question at hand, consulting firms need to acquire new clients. How difficult this is and how frequently a firm needs to find new clients depend upon firm brand and reputation as well as client referral rates, average project duration, and rebuy rate (including extensions and expansions).

It may be easier for a McKinsey senior director to get a first meeting than it is for an independent consultant, but the independent consultant needs a much smaller sale than the big firm partner.

There are several models of new client acquisition:

- Partner
- Independent Salesperson
- Door Opener

The partner model

The partner model is the client acquisition model most frequently seen. In this model, the owners of the firm land the clients. Consultants are promoted from associate to engagement manager based upon their ability to bring in project work on time and budget. They are promoted to junior partner (sometimes called principal) based upon their ability to gain project extensions, expansions and rebuy rate. As described in the chapter "How to be Successful in a Consulting Firm," extensions are additional adjacent work for the same client buying center; expansions are new but similar work for another client buying center. Consulting firms measure rebuy rate as the percentage of clients who start another project within a given period of time, usually one or two years.

Consultants are promoted to full partner often by bringing in one large new client relationship or several smaller client relationships. Aspiring partners learn early to identify high flyers within the client system and maintain contact with them as they rise.

Large firms help this process through careful outplacement of consultants leaving the firm. Consulting firms hire top people, but the field isn't for everyone. Some don't like the travel; others aren't promoted to manager. Some managers don't make partner because they aren't bringing in new clients, i.e., they don't sell. Some just want a different experience inside a company. Large firms make sure that firm alumni get good jobs and that partners stay in touch with them. Alumni often later hire the consulting firm.

Consulting firms also promote partners based upon "thought leadership," those who write articles and books that build the firm's brand and/or develop new service offerings. In both cases the "thoughts" of the thought leader must lead to new clients.

Partner-generated billing can be substantial. I once did work at a large oil company that had three consulting firms that each billed over $200 million annually. Periodically this oil company would decide to "cut back on the consulting spend." What that meant was that they stopped using small firms and independents completely and cut the billings of two of the large firms down to $150 million. Usually the small firm austerity would last for two or more years, while the large firm austerity barely lasted a year. Driving that difference was the fact that the large firms each had one or two senior partners permanently assigned to the oil company and who took up residence on site. They were invited to meetings where they offered free advice, and were often present when a large complex issue arose, which was then turned into a consulting project.

One advantage of the partner model, especially for partners who have come up through the ranks, is that the "salesperson" is more likely to understand the project work.

Independent salesperson model

Some firms hire full-time independent salespeople to bring in new clients. Gemini Consulting used to hire IBM mainframe salespeople as Business Development Executives (BDEs). The BDEs sold big-ticket items of a quasi-intangible nature to C-suite executives.

The BDEs were supported by telemarketers that called division heads and CEOs until they found someone who would be willing to meet with the BDE. The BDE would have as many meetings as possible until they found a "red issue," a concerning problem to be solved that fit Gemini's capabilities. (At the time Gemini was doing quite a lot of "reengineering" or operational process improvement.) Then an operating partner, one who could frame the statement of work, or an analysis and design lead would move the sale into a full-fledged project.

CONSEQUENCES OF THE UNKNOWLEDGEABLE CONSULTING SALESPERSON

Some smaller firms hire salespeople to make cold calls; some hire rainmakers from another professional services firm - accounting or investment banking, for example. The skill of the independent salesperson is uncovering a need and building trust that the firm will be able to solve the problem. This necessitates understanding consulting service offerings just enough to recognize a problem that can be solved.

Independent salespeople get good at talking about consulting, but may not know enough not to overcommit. The hand-off doesn't always work, as this cartoon from my Gemini days illustrates:

The door opener model

Gemini Consulting front end was once described as a turbocharged big project engine.

For reengineering work it was at least a three-part model. I worked in two of these parts and will describe the sales process from one of my early projects.

Chris, a former IBM mainframe salesperson, was a business development executive (BDE) for process chemicals. He worked with the bank of telemarketers calling senior industry executives: "Chris is going to be in your area. Would you like to meet with him?"

GEMINI CONSULTING BUSINESS DEVELOPMENT MODEL

Chris then had a call with a senior executive who confided, "This division has just closed on an acquisition and frankly we're not sure the division head is up to the integration task." Chris showed a few slides about post-merger integration and scheduled another meeting with Mike, an Analysis and Design lead. Mike talked about aligning processes and ensuring that the value of the acquisition wasn't destroyed in the process. Chris and Mike had another meeting with the division head who'd been told to evaluate whether it would be helpful and if so hire them (corporate would pay). Who would say no?

The job of A&D was to analyze the problem and then to design a solution, which the client could decide to implement itself or hire Gemini to deliver in a Results Delivery (RD) project. A&Ds were eight to twelve weeks long and priced at about a 20 percent gross margin. RDs were six months to two years and priced at a 60 percent margin. The real purpose of an A&D was to serve as a door opener to sell an RD. In the best of times the conversion rate was 80 percent. The door opener strategy worked and kept the firm fed.

In the above scenario, the analysis created a plan to close one of three plants and consolidate associated warehouses, keep both brands and salesforces, and reduce functional staffs by 30 percent. The substantial savings allowed the company to provide a generous early retirement for some staff and retraining and redeployment for workers. The A&D led to an integration project that saved the client a documented $5 million. It was about a $750,000 project including A&D and RD and I was staffed on both. All from a door opened by Chris the BDE.

Other firms use different door openers such as a survey or other diagnostic tool, interviews, or a small quick-win identification project like implementing an inventory turn system that was successful in a similar firm. The principle is the same, i.e., perform a low-cost, low-margin service and use the opportunity to identify and sell a larger project. If the values of the selling consultants are attuned to being helpful and achieving results for the client, this is a perfectly acceptable way of acquiring clients.

How NOT to sell

Some consultants or salespeople care more about revenue than being helpful or achieving results. They sell by scaring the client. "This is the worst I've ever seen!" "You better hope that the board (or the analysts or your boss) doesn't find out about this." "I can't believe you are making any money at all."

Fear can manipulate clients into buying a single project. Some clients are under-confident enough that they allow themselves to be manipulated into buying several projects. But it is unlikely that they will like it or refer other clients to the firm.

Unfortunately there are a lot of consultants who sell this way, which may explain the poor reputation of the profession.

How to sell

I was never a rainmaker. While I did bring in new clients and some extensions and expansions when I worked for consulting firms, my largest sales accomplishment was in feeding myself as an independent consultant for many years. My experience tells me that selling consulting is a series of meetings:

- A first meeting, where the consultant demonstrates empathy for the client and **interest** in the client's business, and builds trust.
- A second meeting, where the client identifies a **problem** that concerns him or her.
- A third meeting, where the client and consultant contract and frame a statement of work (SOW).
- The diagram below outlines the tasks required at each phase.

QUESTIONS AND PREPARATION IN THE SALES PROCESS USE

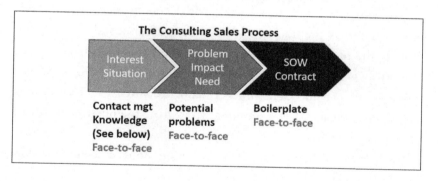

There is a lot of preparation for face-to-face meetings. Salespeople manage their contacts by staying in touch so they get a first face-to-face meeting to reinforce awareness and establish interest. In the second meeting, they help the client identify the problem and its impact, thereby establishing the need for consulting assistance. In the third meeting, the consultant and client ultimately arrange a SOW and contract.

It's important to note that there aren't literally three meetings. It may take ten first meetings before the client is ready to identify a concerning issue or sometimes all of these happen in one single meeting. But I think of these as phases of a sale.

The first meetings are the responsibility of the selling consultant, and often are landed by simply staying in touch with former clients and colleagues. There are many ways to get first meetings, however. Some consultants make speeches; some write books or give seminars or attend conferences. People come up to you at a speech or a seminar to give you feedback. You take their name and business card and make an appointment to reconnect.

Some use a website and search engine optimization to get first meetings, while others use email campaigns or LinkedIn ads and call programs. Some hire lead generators.

My entire process for getting first meetings was meeting with former clients and colleagues and asking them, "Who else do you think I should be talking with?" Sometimes that led to "rebuy" work with the same client. Sometimes it led to a meeting with a colleague or client of theirs. And sometimes the question led nowhere. The second meeting was usually the responsibility of the client. Sometimes it happened serendipitously when I called for a follow-up first meeting. "Oh, I was just thinking about you." Sometimes it happened when I had just seen a colleague of theirs. "I was speaking with Diane the other day and she mentioned you."

The important thing is that second meetings don't happen if you slow the flow of first meetings.

As I mentioned, the second and third meetings often flow together. If the client identified a problem I was familiar with or that I had solved before, we often came to a statement of work quickly. If not, a second "second meeting" could meld into a contracting session.

Sometimes the client would ask for a proposal. Some clients will send out blanket Requests for Proposals (RFP) to several consultants with whom they've met or in some cases to people they don't know at all.

My experience with blanket RFPs wasn't particularly positive. I wrote good proposals but rarely won the blanket RFP contest where I didn't have pre-existing relationships. In some firms where I worked we chose not to respond to "bake-offs" (named for the Pillsbury Bake Off of the 1960s). Bake-offs take lots of work and the odds of getting short-listed are small.

PETER BLOCK'S CONTRACTING PROCESS

1. Consultant connects around the context of the project *"I'm very enthusiastic to be here because____ How'd did this meeting come about?*	**Connecting**	
		2. Client explains the context of the meeting and may explain the initial definition of the problem *(if not the consultant asks "Please describe the result you are hoping to achieve?")*
3. Consultant summarizes definition of the problem, clarifying as necessary (Adds own opinions or similar problems faced by others if appropriate)	**Understanding the problem** **Client Needs/ Wants**	
		4. Client confirms definition of the problem asks for how the problem would be addressed
5. Consultant describes approach, offers, and requirements (including consideration, resources, attention, access), asks questions about concerns (exposure, loss of control)	**Consultant Offers/Needs** **Surfacing concerns**	6. Client explains risks to the project
7. *"Who besides you must be satisfied with the outcome of this improvement?"*	**Establishing the Client System**	8. Client describes any triangular contracting requirements
9. Consultant summarizes agreements about the scope and timing of the project, consultant requirements (e.g. client resources, consideration)	**Summarizing Agreements**	10. Client agrees the project parameters and authorizes the start of work
		Source: *Flawless Consulting*, Peter Block, 1999

I chose to respond only to those RFPs where I have a relationship and a reputation for the kind of work requested.

Ultimately, you get to a third meeting, a contracting session. In his book *Flawless Consulting*, Peter Block outlines an excellent process for contracting with a client, which I used many times. The process starts with connections about the work rather than talking about sports or other common interests. The consultant may direct the process, but the client does at least 50 percent of the talking. For the consultant, the secrets are to be authentic, and to be certain to state what you need from the client to accomplish this work.

The statement of work

The statement of work (SOW) is your contract with the client. It should include what you are trying to accomplish (outcomes or results), some idea of the plan (major activities, milestones and deliverables), and the basis on which you are charging the client (time, deliverables, percentage of achieved savings, etc.). The SOW should also include what is required of the client, and the process for reporting back on any current unknowns.

Extensions, expansions, and follow-on work

When a project ends , the consultant sometimes includes a pitch for additional work in the final presentation. Once, when my team finished a post-merger integration a senior partner wanted us to say something like:

"And we heard that you are planning other acquisitions. We could isolate targets for you and do due diligence."

Alas, this is why consultants have such a money-grubbing reputation. We didn't pitch this on that project. There was a small follow-on project (technically an extension) to help with the implementation of a two-brand strategy, which the client had requested . Our project's success did lead to similar work for another client division. There was some discussion at Gemini about whether this was an expansion (same work, different buying center), in which case our project manager would have gotten some credit. It was ultimately decided that the work was different and our project manager was only tangentially involved with the sales process. So our team disengaged.

Because selling is a criterion for promotion and bonus credit, some consultants get aggressive during disengagement. In my career my primary focus in disengagement was to be certain that the client could achieve the desired results. If so, I felt I could go back to the well again with a first meeting.

Selling consulting, like selling anything, is an endless process. Those who are successful tend to have high activity. If the firm or the consultant is also good at quality delivery it gets easier. I found that keeping a focus on being helpful and achieving results produced referrals, which fed me for many years.

CHAPTER 31

THOUGHT LEADERSHIP

Thought leadership is a phrase that is overused and misused in consulting. It has come to mean saying something smart at the right time or coming up with creative solutions to problems. I am not talking about that. Instead, I am referring to a different path to partner than direct selling. It involves original research or capitalizing on academic faculty research to develop new service offerings. It frequently involves publishing articles in the *Harvard Business Review* or similar publications and perhaps writing a book that gets good reviews and sells well. Thought leaders often do a lot of public speaking or appear on podcasts and YouTube channels.

Thought leaders and the service offerings they develop make the phone ring. They attract clients.

At Gemini, service offering development was controlled by the disciplines, i.e., strategy, operations, organization, etc. Some service offering development occurred as collaborations between disciplines. For example, I was on the post-merger integration team that developed a service offering later sold to many different industries. Gemini's Business Transformation service offering designed by Francis Gouillart and published in his book written with James Kelly, *Transforming the Organization,* was an example of thought leadership.

Business Transformation was called thought leadership at the time. It was composed of an analytical framework, the transformation map that showed the current state of every discipline and part of the organization and the desired state of that vector. Plans were developed and actions were taken. The book used a Cigna project as a case example.

BUSINESS TRANSFORMATION MAP

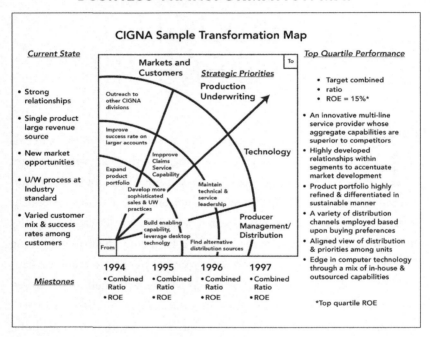

When Gemini Consulting alumni gather, Business Transformation is variously described as:

- "Misguided. I never met a client who said their business needed to be transformed. This was the sole reason for the decline of Gemini Consulting."
- "Brilliant, but misunderstood. Francis never said you had to or could do everything at once. Gemini Business Development Executives saw dollar signs in 'whale projects.'"

- "Brilliant, but ahead of its time. It forms the basis of 'digital transformation' today."

There are a few true thought leaders in consulting firms: Francis Gouillart at Gemini; Tom Peters, Bob Waterman and Jon Katzenbach at McKinsey; Fred Reichheld at Bain. These folks and others do come up with service offerings, but they also write books and speak about their ideas. Most ultimately leave their firms, join a university or go independent.

In fact, being a published thought leader is the single best path to continuing to work as a consultant into your eighties and nineties. However these cases are rare.

Thought leadership for the mid-career consultant or even the Pro means solving a client's problem in a unique but replicable way. There are three parts to that:

- Solving the client's problem means that the client must be not just satisfied, but enthusiastic about the results, perhaps even to the point of wanting to co-author an article in the *Harvard Business Review*.

- Unique means that the firm's partners haven't seen a problem solved this way before, and that most people think, "Wow, I never thought of that."

- Replicable means that others at your firm can understand what you did and copy it. It therefore must be easy to conceptualize, explain and deliver.

Thought leadership is consulting innovation. Like all innovation, it comes from *analogy*, seeing things in one context and transferring that insight to another; or from *visioning*, seeing a need that seems impossible to meet and imagining how meeting it might work. It comes from one of dozens of ideation techniques to arrive at an idea that is then tested, developed, and executed.

Thought leadership is <u>not</u> talking the most or loudest in a meeting, or saying "here's another idea" in the middle of a tight delivery. It is rarely if ever a designation that one uses to self-describe ("I'm a thought leader") nor a defensive response ("Hey, I'm just trying to contribute a little thought leadership here").

But if you want to be a consulting thought leader:

- **Read** a lot of business articles, trade press, and academic journals. All consultants should do this, but if you want to be a thought leader, be a researcher first.

- **Collaborate.** There are people who invent things on their own in a basement, but they are typically not the type of people who become management consultants. Collaborate with colleagues, with university and business school professors and with clients. Every Steve Jobs needed his Woz (Steve Wozniak). Every Francis Gouillart needed his James Kelly. (Kelly was the president of Gemini, a salesman, and widely assumed to have simplified and clarified Francis's ideas for the market.)

- **Experiment.** Find clients who will let you experiment, not with half-baked ideas, of course, but by gathering data that you may publish or co-publish later.

- **Teach.** The best consulting thought leaders refine their thinking and share their thinking by training other consultants and the world at large.

There are some who would say that the decision to become a thought leader is a "grow or go" decision at the partner career juncture, but I say this is something that mid-career consultants must decide much earlier. They must consider whether they want to continually sell as they progress or whether they want to develop client relationships through research and innovation and then teach others. Some thought leaders like Peter Drucker migrate to universities where they continue their research without going to client meetings. Some form research centers and run conferences, like Jim Collins. It is a different career ladder, a fork in the road for Journeymen, for which some are uniquely suited.

CHAPTER 32

SPECIALIZING IN ORGANIZATIONAL CHANGE

J udging by the questions I got in my last few years in consulting and the calls I still get in retirement, there is a growing need for specialists in organization change.

The first time I was called the "change guy," it was a thinly-veiled insult. "Okay, everybody listen up. This is Alan; he's the change guy. He's gonna help us *change*." The implication was that management had hired me to change a recalcitrant workforce. Of course, that's nonsense. It is impossible to change someone else. That's why the divorce rate is high.

Calling me the change guy was a dig from content consultants who regarded anyone who worked with people and culture as useless. "Here's Alan, the change guy. The competition is eating your lunch and your company is going bankrupt. He's gonna ask you how you *feel* about that."

Change managers used to be what systems integrators called the "user interface trainers" who came in at the end of a big system implementation to "show the dummies which button to push." Line managers used to make fun of you if you used the word "culture." Times have changed. Now everybody sounds like an organizational development guru. "We're on a journey to shape our environment to produce the optimum customer experience."

I am grateful to have worked in this field long enough to see people use the words "change management" without curling their upper lip. If you Google "change management" now, you'll come up with hundreds of certification courses.

Here I'll demystify change management, describe how I became a change guy and offer some tips to Journeymen who think they might specialize in change.

Making sense of change management

My change work often started with facilitating a group, sometimes the C-suite leadership team. My job was to create alignment around a new initiative. The initiative could be a new strategy or organization design. The company might need to develop new products or make more money with the same resources.

I interviewed people throughout the company to determine their views about the need for change and their ideas about what to do. There were meetings where I fed back the different points of view. We accepted the "points of agreement" and spent our time on the "points of discussion" (I never called them "disagreements" because such language tends to harden people's positions).

But as a colleague once said, "The thing about change management is that nothing happens unless someone changes - actually does something differently." So, getting people to agree to take action and then gently helping them follow through was, I found, more than half the battle.

Most of my work was around implementing two key processes:
- How a company innovates
- How they improve

I believe that these two processes underpin the health of any organization. Innovation starts a business cycle; a company creates or reinvents something. It perceives an unmet customer need or discovers a new technology that has use in its business. This leads to an "idea" that it can develop and then test and implement. Then the company must integrate the new product, market entry or operating process with its core business.

Later in the cycle when some element is under-performing or missing an opportunity, the company measures where it is and makes a plan to improve, and then measure again to quantify the improvement. Then it integrates the improvements with its core business and repeats the improvement process until the change needed requires innovation again.

Growth in revenue and profit comes down to how well a business innovates, integrates and improves continuously. There are other parts to organizational change management such as training and education, organization design and understanding incentives, but an aspiring change specialist should master this connected process:

Innovate-Integrate-Improve-Integrate-Repeat

How I became a change consultant
You will not get there the way I did.

My undergraduate degree is in theatre. I had no intention of going into business. I studied people because as an actor I wanted to portray them, but the habit of observing people proved helpful as a change consultant. Later, I waited tables, tended bar, drove a cab, and worked night shifts in factories to leave my days free for auditions. In these jobs I observed more.

Here is what I learned that you can use:

- **Immerse yourself in human behavior.** Develop empathy for the working person.
- **No experience is wasted**. Analyse and learn from it. Bring your entire life to your work.
- **Stars will always under-perform the ensemble.** When you're part of the cast there are no small parts — only small actors.

- **Presentations always require rehearsal**.

And my first real job as a booking agent taught me:

- **People are people.** Whether talking with a student lecture chairman or someone whose fame tongue-tied me, I learned that all people want to be heard.
- **Customers have needs.** If you ask, they'll tell you how to please them.

As a junior consultant I learned:

- **Successful change is about leadership engagement.** I've mentioned the ERF CEO who engaged and the transmission manufacturer who didn't. Time after time I've seen that getting leadership engaged makes change happen.
- **Skill at training, design and facilitation is a good foundation for change work.** At the Forum Corporation I learned how to design and do stand-up training. I used these skills a lot.
- **Learning by doing is the fuel of change.** For ten years, I worked behind Dr George Litwin, one of the leading lights of the organizational development field and author of *Motivation and Organizational Climate*. George had a habit of "throwing me in the deep end" so I would learn to swim or die. Painful yes, and more than a bit scary at times, but I learned more by doing than I have in the many courses I've taken.

Six tips to excel in change management

Here are a few tips that apply if you hope to do change work:

1. **Understand the business.** Organizational change is about getting a business result. Learn how the company makes money, what customers want, what suppliers can contribute, and what the constraints of operations are. Then you can communicate the "why of change" and are more likely to deliver a result that matters.

2. **Connect to people.** Work on developing your empathy gene by talking with customers, suppliers, leaders and line workers - people across all parts of the business. Find ways to be helpful, share credit and build trust by always doing what you promise.

3. **Develop process focus.** Determine what the customer values and what activities are needed to deliver it (and in what order).

4. **Experiment enthusiastically.** Both innovation and improvement are based upon the scientific method: state the problem, including the facts and measurements; make a hypothesis as to cause and solution; test it, try it, then fix it and try it again; and document both success and failure. Apply this to your work and your own development.

5. **Learn, baby, learn.** Learn the levers of organizational change, organizational structure, training, systems, or processes like innovation and improvement. Find ways to expose yourself to serendipity - get off the train at another stop, read a book you think you'll hate or talk to someone who is different from you. Take the time to reflect. Write down what you are learning and what you'd like to learn next.

6. **Always, always be authentic.** If the "little voice in the back of your head" is ever saying something different from the words coming out of your mouth, STOP. Get back to the truth. The only thing you have to offer to this work is you.

In the words of Mahatma Gandhi, "Be the change you want to see in the world."

An earlier version of this chapter was first published as "Becoming an Organizational Change Guy or Change Lady" in January 2018 in the Triaster Blog, http://blog. triaster.co.uk/blog/ Special thanks to Triaster, Michael Cousins and Brad Fagan for allowing me to include it here.

CHAPTER 33

STARTING A CONSULTING FIRM

I joined a startup, Katzenbach Partners, in 1999 as consultant number six and employee number seven. I left four years later when the firm was fifty people, but the firm grew to over two hundred before selling at the beginning of the 2007 financial crisis. In 2004 I launched Morton-Culler with Keith Morton. We had grand plans, but lasted for eighteen months. In both instances, I started with wide-eyed enthusiasm about small startup consulting firms, which I should have learned to temper from a conversation that I'd had twenty years earlier.

After business school I interviewed with seven consulting firms, including my first employer, Harbridge House Europe (HHE).

I still remember my interview with David Hussey, the managing director of HHE. Mr. Hussey, a very British man with the bearing of a warm-hearted university professor, explained the growth of HHE, its attention to its major client relationships and the ongoing development of capability in its staff of consultants.

I listened carefully, though with the somewhat starry-eyed demeanor of a new MBA. "Managing such a firm must be really challenging and exciting," I enthused. David Hussey smiled a long, silent worldwise smile and said, "Challenging certainly. But exciting? I rather think not."

I was a bit gobsmacked, but Mr. Hussey continued. "Alan, consider a group of people educated to the point of considerable ego. These are people whose opinion of themselves has reached the point where they believe other people should pay them for their advice. Now imagine managing such a group of people! Challenging? Exciting? No, I can tell you that managing consultants is an oxymoron, a complete and utter contradiction in terms."

Anyone who has managed consultants has felt like David Hussey from time to time, but surely all that is different when the firm is small enough or when I am the boss. Nope. Starting a consulting firm is one of the more difficult startups imaginable. Why? Because it's a perfect storm of service business challenges, client trust concerns, and firm design considerations.

Service business challenges

Consulting has the challenges of all service businesses, which offer something intangible while selling something specific. Service businesses are also people dependent. People use their minds to solve client problems and their hearts to keep clients happy. That raises the importance of who you hire and how you manage them.

Clients and trust

Developing client relationships is the most important task for a new firm. Often a consultant who leaves an established firm brings clients from that firm to his or her startup. This may be done with the old firm's blessing along with an agreement – or if not, the first few months of the startup are spent with lawyers.

Sometimes, however, relationships are not transferable. When Keith Morton and I formed our firm, I introduced him to three clients I had been working with as an independent. None of them accepted Keith. I now believe that had nothing whatsoever to do with Keith, but rather with the way I introduced him. I think my clients were concerned that I was replacing myself with another consultant and they resisted. If I had it to do over again I would introduce Keith as someone who brought a specific expertise, which would have defused their concern. The net lesson was that a client's trust is fragile and no existing client is a given.

Designing the firm – service offerings

Keith and I spent a good deal of time designing our firm. We offered a facilitated strategy process, an initiative to test strategic ideas called strategy pilots, and external relationship management initiatives to get closer to customers and suppliers. Keith and I both had interest in and experience with post-merger integration but decided that our little firm wouldn't have the credibility necessary to secure such work.

Katzenbach Partners started with team-based work that Jon Katzenbach was known for, but also strategic initiative work at a major pharmaceutical company and post-merger integration work at a telecom giant.

Designing the firm – clients

The problem many small firms encounter is sales. They typically start with a few client projects, perhaps enough to keep the partners and some associates busy, but expanding on that base is harder than imagined. Even experienced consulting partners, who used to do nothing but sell, get sucked into delivery. They miss the support systems of the larger firm that allowed them the freedom to nurture old relationships enough to find new clients and projects.

While I was at Katzenbach Partners there were periods of feast and famine and conflict among the founding partners about client development and internal processes.

Who will bring in the clients? How will we handle it when times get tough? Do we divide the profits from the firm equally or according to who brings in the business?

The founding partners agreed to split profits equally for three years and then to divide according to client/project origination. The firm had some ups and downs after I left, but expanded quite rapidly.

Founders also need to be clear about what industries they serve beyond "anyone who will hire us." Morton-Culler & Company focused on pharmaceuticals, media, and financial services because we were based in New York City and couldn't afford to travel extensively. Katzenbach Partners had similar market segmentation at first, but were much better funded than Keith and I were so travel was a non-issue.

Those I know who started small firms and survived did so serving industries in their location. An automotive specialist was based in Detroit; a firm targeting consumer products and manufacturing was based in Chicago; and a firm with relationships in the chemicals industry was within easy driving distance of DuPont, their largest client.

Designing the firm - values

Dr. David Maister of the Harvard Business School has written extensively on consulting and other professional services businesses. Maister identifies three value-laden goals espoused by almost all such businesses:

- Outstanding client service
- Staff satisfaction
- Financial success

Maister points out that while all firms should aspire to all three of these goals, the goals sometimes are in conflict and firm leaders should prioritize.

Choosing staff satisfaction as the primary goal might lead a firm to choose a greater mix of challenging "custom" work, which would require more senior resources and therefore be less profitable.

Choosing financial success (profit) as a primary goal would lead the firm's principals to seek work that reduced to a simple repeatable process that could be accomplished by more junior people. This would require more associate-level staff and systematic training and would likely utilize expensive senior resources in multiple sales and client management roles.

Choosing client service as a primary goal would lead a firm to seek one group of clients and attempt to provide whatever that client needed, even if that might fall outside the current capabilities of the firm. It might suggest a relationship management structure that puts a premium on the senior client relationship and links to many different "content specialists" both inside and outside the firm.

Each organization would likely be different. Differing cultural values would lead each firm to be staffed by different people in different organizational structures and profitability models.

The challenge is internal consistency, i.e., matching values with staffing and structure. Morton-Culler was led by staff satisfaction. Keith and I wanted to work on what we worked on. The few contractors that we hired during our tenure were experienced independent consultants.

While I was there, Katzenbach Partners hired many smart Newbies straight from university or graduate school. The firm gave these people unbelievable opportunity and many stepped up incredibly, but there was a broad-based pyramid without the routinized work.

Katzenbach was quite good at recruiting these new entrants, and their quality was truly amazing. I'm not sure that it was easy to find the work that these young consultants were best suited for. It also wasn't clear to me whether all the partners were prepared to invest the time required to develop this cadre of young consultants.

Designing the firm - the pyramid, fees and making money

Most consulting firms are time-based businesses. There are firms that sell products, like human resource firms that sell surveys or compensation comparative ratios, or IT firms that sell packaged software. There are employee benefit firms, which are owned by insurance companies and get commissions for health and welfare or life insurance, and pension plan investments. While these commissions provide revenue that isn't dependent on billed hours, it calls the firm's objectivity into question. Are benefits recommendations driven by what is best for the client or by the commission?

Most firms mark up consultant time. In a typical graduated hourly billing rate structure:

- Seniors/owners/partners bill at about two times compensation.
- Managers/junior partners bill at or about three to four times compensation.
- Associates/specialists bill at about four to six times compensation.

Profitability is determined by having the cheapest resource, the one with the greatest markup, do the bulk of the work. Firms structured with a broad base to the pyramid make the most money **if** they do the same project over and over and if they structure, routinize and document the work. In other words, if they follow "the book." Most startups don't have this luxury.

Managing the partnership

I was not privy to the partnership agreement of the founders of Katzenbach Partners, but they made things work surprisingly well.

Morton-Culler & Company had a detailed operating agreement. Keith and I specified who was responsible for each task, how we would make decisions, and how we would fund the business and distribute revenue. We virtually eliminated conflict on these issues. We even carefully laid out how we would dissolve the business in the event that we didn't make it as a firm. (This turned out to be helpful, almost too helpful. Perhaps because it was so easy, I didn't fight harder to continue.)

I have witnessed former partners in consulting firms give all their accumulated wealth to attorneys litigating the breakup. So I think it is worth the time invested to negotiate a good operating agreement.

Managing the firm

Depending on the size of the startup, one partner may be designated as managing partner to oversee administrative tasks such as payroll, taxes, staffing, office space, equipment, expenses, and billing. Or the startup may have brought with it project managers and administrators. Keith and I just divided up those tasks. Regardless, at some point you'll have to think about management.

Managers:

1. Hold staff accountable. They make sure the work gets out the door, the firm gets paid, and that staff does what it needs to do to make that happen.

2. Develop the knowledge and skills of staff to deliver the work better, faster and more efficiently over time.

As much as I sometimes fought with the founders of Katzenbach Partners, Gemini Consulting, and the Forum Corporation (I'm noticing a theme here), I will say that they all did a pretty good job of managing their firms.

MANAGING PROFESSIONALS

Professionals	Managers Should
Like variety	Rotate job assignments
Want participation	Seek their opinions
Expect autonomy	Treat them like winners
Are impatient	Be tolerant
Are goal-focused	Provide clear goals
Expect to be held accountable	Hold them accountable
Need feedback	Reward performance quickly
Need challenge	Support risk taking

The special needs of professional people

As David Hussey pointed out to me in that long-ago interview, managing consultants is hard. Professional people are a unique workforce with unique requirements of their managers.

The chart above shows that consultants are a demanding lot:

(I stole this from David Maister, who says he can't remember who he stole it from.)

Design a performance framework that speaks to these unique needs. How will you manage staffing to deliver variety of work? How will you manage delivery participation, autonomy and clear goals and still make money? Designing a consulting firm is challenging.

Design for:

- Internal consistency and balance – agree on the type of work you will seek and plan your hiring accordingly. Exciting ground-breaking work and a wide pyramid of junior people may not be compatible.
- Clarity of values - the order of values around service, satisfaction, and success must be aligned with the type of work and staffing. In addition, hire people who will do the work and treat people in the way that you would.
- A management system that includes involvement of your people, accountability, and people's development (expanding capability)
- You won't get everything right the first time; design for client value and continuous improvement.
- In these ways a consulting firm can achieve client service, staff satisfaction, financial success and competitive advantage. But it's a tough path.

CHAPTER 34

BECOMING AN INDEPENDENT CONSULTANT

I n my final working years and even in my retirement, I would get a call from a consultant, former client or a LinkedIn connection to talk with me about becoming an independent consultant. Sometimes they began by asking to "pick my brain," an expression my wife hates. "You have no brain left from all the people who pick it." "I never had much to begin with," I respond.

Blame it on the "gig economy" or even the way consultants make their work look effortless, but a lot of people see this life as easy street. Some want to escape corporate politics while others want prestige or to be listened to as they perceive external consultants are.

Some define a consultant as someone who "carries a black briefcase, is fifty miles from home, and has an opinion on absolutely everything without the benefit of knowledge or experience."

"I can do that job," they say. "I'll call Alan and pick his brain."

I always take the calls. I enjoy talking about consulting and what I've learned along the way, and helping people make tough decisions. So I thought it might be beneficial to share the content of those conversations here.

I often begin by asking why they want to become an independent consultant. The answers shape how I talk about the issues and in what order.

Some talk about the level of expertise they have acquired, for example, "I've been a Lean Six Sigma Black Belt in two companies now."

Some who work for consulting firms want autonomy and to keep "the multiplier," the difference between what they earn and the fees that are billed to the client.

Some have "moonlighted a little," which was "very lucrative and I thought I might be able to earn a comfortable living at this."

I start by telling these would-be consultants that I had been a management consultant since 1980 and that for many intervening years I worked for myself. Then I say,

> **"The single most important thing about becoming an independent consultant is having clients, real people who will hire you and pay you."**

I often begin here rather that launching into descriptions of what consulting is, or fees, or required investments because it focuses the conversation and, though it may seem obvious, many people forget to think about generating revenue.

"You need to have at least one person who will hire you at decent money for something that you already know how to deliver. This work will need to last at least three months and not require more than 75 percent of your available time."

Sometimes former clients will explain how they don't really need that because they are getting a "package" from a reduction-in-force, and "it's enough to live on for six months."

I tell them that, in my experience, it takes three to twelve months to develop client business from scratch and if they spend their severance to start a business they could easily find themselves broke with no business in six months.

> **"If you don't have a client, regardless of what your business card says, you are not an independent consultant. You are un-**

employed."

This is often a shock to people. But I come back to it several times during the conversation because I think it is that important.

What is a consultant?

There are many answers to this question, and some are punchlines to consultant jokes. But when I ask it of people, I am looking for several things:

How realistic are they about the work?

Do they define consulting as content-driven or process-driven?

What do they know about consulting industry structure and the nature of competition?

What are their core values?

The work

Consultants are problem-solvers. (On some level, most people get this.) Consultants solve problems that companies don't have the expertise or "bandwidth," available people on staff, to solve themselves. Or the clients are unsure of how to solve a new problem and want to work with someone to learn how to solve it.

I tell my callers that it is really important that they understand where their client is on this subject because it dictates the kind of consultant the client expects:

- An expert consultant who does analysis shares expertise of the twenty times he/she has solved your problem in the past, writes a report, and flies away.

- An "extra pair of hands," somebody who tells you what needs to be done and then does the work. Clients who hire the "extra pair of hands" consultant often want an employee without paid benefits whom they can fire easily.

- A collaborative consultant who works closely with a client team and builds company capability. The collaborative consultant builds the knowledge and skill of the client's people (competency) and adds the organizational processes and systems to support repeatable performance (capability).

Everyone says they want to collaborate. Most independents are "pair of hands" contractors, while most big firms are expert consultants despite what they say in their marketing and recruiting materials. I tell people that they need to be aligned with their client about what they will provide. And the place to do that is the statement of work.

The statement of work

The statement of work (SOW) is the contract with the client about what the problem is, how the consultant and client will work together to solve it, and how long the work will take. Typically the SOW doesn't include fees and conditions (these terms are included in the engagement contract) so that the SOW can be shared widely.

Sometimes preliminary research and analysis must be done before the problem and timeline are clear enough to write a SOW. I typically do these analyses on a time-and-materials basis. Some clients will not pay for initial research. Conflicts like this indicate that the client has the unspoken expectation that they are hiring an expert (or a magician) and that research and preliminary analysis are just ways to rip them off. I explain that it is better to hammer this out early rather than have it surface in the middle or end of the project.

Content vs. process

I know I have beat this drum senseless, but it is news to many seeking to become independent.

Content consultants share expertise, solutions or answers and process consultants teach how to solve a problem. Deciding what kind of consultant you are helps you define your business, how you will work with clients and therefore what kind of projects you are looking for.

It also helps to understand your competition. Big 3 and accounting firms tend toward the content side. Systems integrators and Human

Resource firms can be content or process. Strategy, marketing, and finance work is usually the content approach. Continuous improvement, innovation, or organization development work is most often a process approach.

I often illustrate the difference between these two types. Content people say that process people "don't have an analytical bone in their bodies." Process people describe content consultants as "seeing the world in shades of black and white."

I tell prospective independents of my journey from content consultant to process when I got frustrated with clients who didn't implement my findings, or in some cases even read the report.

I may tell the story I described earlier of the presentation discussion with a former McKinsey consultant:

He said, "The deck is the product!" I said, "The result of the change is the product."

Content and process consultants think entirely differently, and structure their projects differently.

For the aspiring independent consultant, you have to decide who you are and make sure that the clients who hire you know that what you offer is what they want.

Consulting industry structure and competition

Despite continuous consolidation, the consulting industry is still incredibly fragmented. One estimate puts global consulting north of $250 billion, divided across strategy (~$30 billion), operations (~$80 billion), human resources (~$35 billion), finance (~$80 billion), and technology (~$50 billion). Another estimate is in the trillions with no discipline breakdown.

I estimate that the top fifteen to twenty firms account for 50-60 percent of those fees. The middle-tier firms number in the thousands and probably control about 25-30 percent of the market. Independent consultants and one- to four-person firms number in the millions and their billings represent between 10-25 percent of the market.

The big firms compete on brand and for years have placed former employees in client organizations and nurtured their alumni relationships until the person is positioned to buy. McKinsey is best in class at this, but all the big firms do it. As an independent or small firm you will rarely compete against the big firms and then usually on relationship (working for a former employer, for example) and price.

Mid-sized firms compete on unique research or service offering. Relationships are always important. As an independent you may beat a mid-tier firm on relationship or the promise of duplicating the results of another firm's proprietary service offering.

Competing against other independents is about relationships, price, and pure salesmanship.

Service offerings – what are you selling?

This is an area where my intrepid wannabe entrepreneurs have usually spent a lot of time thinking. "I'm really good at value stream mapping" or "I've implemented a 360-degree feedback system that everyone really loves."

People who have worked inside companies often have successfully implemented consulting methodologies and gotten a lot of positive feedback for doing so. Sometimes one division will ask to borrow another division's star staffer because of this. The person may feel like they are getting consulting gigs already. "So why aren't I getting paid like a consultant?"

It may be true that the staffer is as competent as an external consultant. He or she also doesn't have to learn the client's business, the politics and the culture. The difference, of course, is that the "client" hiring you is paying nothing. Even in the rare company that cross-charges for the use of another's staff member, the "brown dollars" incurred don't mean anything. Marketing happens by word of mouth and there is no downside to hiring you.

So independent consultants need to think about describing service offerings in concrete terms with client benefits that lead to sales for "green dollars."

The other piece of advice I give in this area is focus. Callers often tell me ten things they are really good at. I tell them to pick three at most and keep them within the same discipline. So pick Lean and Six Sigma or Training and Performance feedback, but not Marketing and Finance.

Target clients

As important as it is to know what you are selling, to whom is the next most important question. I earned my living selling to large companies. As an independent my contacts were rarely at the CEO level, but rather at the division head or staff department head level. I did a fair amount of C-suite work in my career, but usually while working for or subcontracting to a consulting firm.

Lots of people tell me, "I want to work for small entrepreneurial companies because it's a lot of fun. No big corporations, but companies of $5 million in sales or less." I did work at this level and I admit that it is enjoyable and rewarding. One can have a huge impact. But when I worked in this segment, it was usually for friends and for very little money.

What I say to aspiring independents is, "Small companies pay small fees; it's all they can afford. Big companies pay big fees." Or if they aggressively insist that they'll be the exception and they don't want to work for "The Man" anymore, I recount what I said to a family therapist who poked me in the chest at a neighborhood party and said,

"I have more degrees than you. We use the same skills. Why is it that you get paid what you get paid and I get paid what I do?"

My answer was simple. "I guess because, if you are Michelangelo, you have a choice. You can sell your paintings on the street, or you can sell them to the Medici family. The Medici aren't very nice, but they do pay better."

There is a real need for consultants who can help clients in the mid-market deliver results quickly at reasonable fees. There are some great consultants who choose to work in this segment and find it very rewarding. They typically make a respectable income, but they aren't getting rich.

Finding clients – the front end

Like most independent consultants I started out working for my former employer. A consulting firm subcontracted me because they knew my work. Many people who leave big companies get hired back on contract for their first project. The danger is that this can lead to "pair of hands" type work, i.e., low money and low-impact results.

Over time a successful consultant needs to discover how to acquire new clients. Some write books and/or articles, which I found to be a long-term strategy. Blogs, vlogs, and YouTube channels are also possibilities. After you publish a number of writings people begin to think about your name. I found that short articles (one to two pages) are a great follow-up to a first meeting. Many chapters in this book began as that kind of collateral material.

Some consultants do public speaking - again long-term brand building. You must follow up and convert idle interest to a warm lead, to a hot prospect, and then to a statement of work.

Some use email campaigns or a telemarketing service to generate warm leads. Then they have to convert them.

I always used referrals. I talked to people who knew my work, often previous clients. I told them I was looking for work and asked if they knew anyone to whom I should be talking. Sometimes this led nowhere. Sometimes it led to work with their company. Sometimes they referred me to a friend, acquaintance, or business associate. I am religious about thank you notes to these people - real paper letters or handwritten notes, not emails and never texts.

Subcontract vs. direct bill

Small consulting firms often subcontract work to independents. This is a good way to get started if you know people at one of these firms. I started out doing subcontract work and the money seemed good at first. I quickly realized that the lead firm was marking up my time two to three times what I was getting paid. At first I was outraged, but I soon realized that this is a standard markup in consulting, whether consultants work for the firm or are subcontracted, and the lead firm found the business. (Remember when I said that having clients was the single most important element?) This isn't a rip off; that money pays for marketing and non-billable operating cost and profit.

I know many independent consultants who earn a very good living just doing subcontract work. However, be careful what you sign. Some firms tie you to a non-compete clause that will exclude you from working for any competitor or any client they have ever thought of working for.

I evolved into the Results-Alliance, a confederation of independent consultants and small firms who brought each other business and helped each other with projects. We had all worked together in the past and we liked working together. We paid each other finder fees and charged minimum markups in the 20 percent range. I thought that when I retired someone in the network would carry it forward. As fate would have it, my most active Results-Alliance colleagues either retired or went to work for other firms around that time. Results-Alliance simply closed down.

The revenue roller coaster

I tell people what I learned in my first iteration as an independent: devote 20 percent of your time to marketing even while you are working flat out. Don't cancel client marketing meetings for paid work or eventually you'll finish the project and have to spend months finding your next project.

Many consultants sell extensions and expansions to the same client over and over again. Repeat work is easier than starting from scratch, but after a while it tends to annoy even the most loyal clients. The gravy train ends and then you are stuck in the morass of starting over.

Fees – what should I charge?

"It depends." This usually is not a satisfactory answer. But it does depend on what the client will pay. If it is subcontract, there has to be room for markup. It depends on the size of the problem and the length of the project. If it is repeat business what did you charge last time?

Fees in consulting can range from $100 per day to upwards of $10,000 per day for a big firm partner.

I tell people to figure out what they want to get paid annually and divide that by 100-150 days per year. That leaves time for personal development and marketing. They should then test this number with other consultants they know and clients they might work for.

Investments and infrastructure

It often looks like independent consultants have no overhead and that they just keep all the money. When I was not on a client site, I worked from my home office. It was a real office without another purpose. It had a desk, file cabinets, computers, a printer, fax, scanner, photocopier, bookshelves, seats for guests, and two two-line phones.

Some people told me they can't work from home, "too many distractions." Once I had a client who called me three times the first day I worked from home. I finally asked him, "Joe are you checking up on me?" "Well. . . yeah, when I work from home, with the kids and the dogs and the TV I can only get in a couple of hours a day."

"Joe," I said, "There is no TV in my office nor even a radio. I have no games on my computers. I'm not on Facebook or Twitter. And I only bill you for hours I work." He stopped calling.

Joe's problem isn't unusual. If you are like this, get an outside office. Paying rent will be worth it.

I became good on PowerPoint, Word and Excel, but I subcontracted when there was a lot of that work. I did some larger projects and subcontracted to Results-Alliance members, but I had little patience chasing people for their time and expenses so I could bill the client.

I did all my own administration, kept track of my own hours, collected and totaled all my expense receipts and did my own billing. Of course, administrative tasks weren't billable hours, but I learned that if you don't bill clients, they don't pay you. If you aren't disciplined at administration, or hate it, it's worth hiring a part-time admin. My wife Billie was my paid admin when we were both single, and truthfully she was better than I was at that stuff. But Billie is my second wife and I didn't want to go looking for a third because I made her my secretary.

The first time I was an independent, I was structured as a sole proprietor, did my own taxes and saw no need for a lawyer. In my second round I became an LLC, had an accountant for taxes, and an attorney for contracts. I also carried $5 million in liability insurance, and several other kinds of insurance. I worked for large companies that required this and I had assets to protect.

I had two websites, belonged to several networking organizations, had a paid LinkedIn professional membership and a tech guy on call.

It is sometimes surprising to others that, while an independent consulting practice may not be the highest cost business to run, it most certainly isn't all revenue and no expense.

Personal development

One of the reasons I enjoyed consulting was that I loved the learning curve of starting work at a new company or in a new industry. I read lots of material about the company and the industry. I talked with many client people to solidify the knowledge. I often did research to help my understanding of the presenting problem. I grew tremendously in the first two weeks of work.

It wasn't enough.

As an independent consultant what you are selling is <u>You</u>. You must be current with contemporary business issues so reading the *Wall Street Journal* and a couple of business magazines is important. Reading *Harvard Business Review* or some other publication to be current with the latest findings of the academic business research is important. And you should attend a couple conferences a year and take whatever workshops that will increase your knowledge and skill.

The lifestyle implications

Don't burn yourself out.

Consulting is a challenging lifestyle. As an independent consultant the opportunity is always there to simply work all the time. Don't succumb to this temptation. As a wise mentor once said to me, "Alan, you can't help any clients if you're dead."

Consulting often involves five days of travel per week. Clients like to see you onsite. If you are lucky enough to have local clients, go home at night. If you are traveling all the time, talk with your client about working from home occasionally, every Friday perhaps. Fly on Monday morning rather than Sunday night.

When you work for a consulting firm, most of your friends are your teammates. You spend five days a week together, so maybe you'll socialize on the weekends. When traveling, getting to know your neighbors isn't so easy, nor is keeping in touch with friends. Make the time and don't leave it up to your non-traveling spouse to be the social director.

However, if you are an independent consultant, you have all the disadvantages of working for a consulting firm, i.e., never seeing your neighbors (or your spouse and kids) and not being able to join a book club or take a course during the week. But, unlike working in a firm, you have <u>no teammates.</u> You need to create your own network. Join a discussion group like Vistage Trusted Advisor or create your own local network of other independents.

The decision

As should be obvious by now, I encourage these "brain-pickers" to think deeply about the decision to become an independent consultant. Overall, about 30 percent have gone on to become independent consultants. It's not for everyone, but I enjoyed the autonomy, the growth, the challenge and, yes, the income. I never got rich, but I had a comfortable life and now a comfortable retirement.

Not all conversations get through all of this, nor do they all last an hour. Some new consultants send me links to websites or marketing materials for comment. I am always happy to respond. I tell them if it's helpful, use my feedback; if not, discard without a second thought.

Core Values

I often close by telling callers to be clear about the "why" of their business, which is often as important to clients as "what" you will do for them.

Someone once told me that my mantra "be helpful; get results" sounded like a country doctor, "patient care and positive outcomes." I liked that. I wish more consultants remembered the Hippocratic Oath, "First do no harm."

CHAPTER 35

EVERYTHING
I KNOW ABOUT
GETTING PAID,
I LEARNED FROM
COMEDIANS

"**B**ut how do you make sure you get paid?"

I was talking with one of the many people who call to "pick my brain."

This person had been offered contract work by his former employer.

"Look, I know how we manage our cash flow on the backs of our suppliers. Not the big ones mind you, but we make the little guys like me wait 90-120 days for their money."

I started to tell him how I managed to always get paid by my clients, but as I did, I wondered where I learned this. Ah yes. Comedians.

In the 1970s I was a booking agent for speakers, mostly on the college lecture circuit, but later for business meetings too. That exposure to business meetings was one of the things that sparked my interest in business, which led me to business school and a life as a consultant. But I digress.

Second City, the sketch comedy troupe from Chicago, had been doing college dates as part of performing arts programs since the sixties and comedians had been opening for rock bands on campus for years, but by the mid-seventies most comedians had figured out there was money at colleges. Dick Gregory did roughly 200 college dates a year. Yes, his work was political activism, but it was a stand-up act.

Jay Leno

I worked for the booking agency Lordly and Dame about the time comedy was taking off. L&D had a group of five agents that booked rock bands at clubs and colleges, and a lecture division, which hired me. One day Sam Dame, the founder, who booked entertainment at hotels in New England, called us all together.

"I've got a new act you should take a look at. (Sam called everything an "act" including Erica Jong and Margaret Mead.) He's a really nice kid. Selling Rolls Royces in Wellesley. He's a comedian."

Sam didn't like comedians – "Too needy. Comedians all had awful childhoods and now they're looking for the approbation of the world." So Sam recommending a comedian was news.

"No, really, he's a really nice guy. Funny. Clean and he'll work for a finiff." We mentally translated that to $500 a gig, a low money date, which was hard to find.

"I've asked him to talk to everyone when he drops off the check from the Balsams. Nice kid. His name's Jay Leno."

And so that Monday was the first time we all met Jay Leno. He didn't say much. And Sam was right - he was nice. We all introduced ourselves and said what our territory was. I was working the west coast territory at the time.

"Jeez, Alan that'd be tough," Jay said. "I'd lose a day going and coming, might have to get some more money and enough to cover the airfare, but I dunno, talk to me. If I have enough notice, I might put it together with something. Talk to me."

Then Sam said, "OK guys, here's the thing. Jay's flexible and all, but he needs us to help out with a couple of things. First, dates Sunday to Wednesday, maybe Thursday, 'cause Jay drives to New York for the open mic nights at the clubs."

Sam went on. "And I know you lecture guys send an invoice and the colleges pay whenever, but in entertainment we like to pick up checks at the gig – right, music guys?" There was general mumbled agreement from the rock agents.

So began Jay Leno's L&D career. Mostly Jay did dates in New England and the mid-Atlantic. But he always came in the morning after a date, handed Sam the check, and while he was waiting for Sam to cut his check he went down to "thank the salesman." He remembered everyone's name and what territory they worked. "Alan, west coast right? I might be going to LA in November."

At one of those impromptu meetings someone asked Jay, "How come you pick up the checks, Jay? Doncha think we're good fer it?"

"Well it's a habit, see, from the clubs. Ya do two shows a night in a club. The manager laughs like hell for the first show. But the second show he's heard it before. 'Not that funny' he sez. If ya tell him to bring the check in advance and he shows it to ya before ya go on, then after the show he's gotta give it to ya. But if you let him mail it in the morning – ah, well. . . 'Not that funny' sez he, and stuffs your check in his pocket." Everyone laughed.

So I learned to think about how to get paid in advance. Put it in the contract. I also learned the value of being nice.

Rodney Dangerfield

I booked Rodney Dangerfield at a college in Connecticut. This is before movies like *Caddyshack* and *Back To School* made him a star all over again. After the show, I took Marie, the young lecture chairperson, and her check back to Rodney's dressing room.

I knocked on the door and from inside I heard Rodney's voice. "Who is it?" I gave my name and was about to say "and Marie" when the door opened and there was Rodney in his undershirt and boxers.

"Ah excuse me," he said and closed the door. He opened it fifteen seconds later with an untucked shirt and pants on, mopping his face with a towel.

"Sorry, he said, "the place is kind of a mess. It's the maid's day off." Thankfully he never said, "I don't get no respect, you know what I mean."

After a few minutes of pleasant conversation Marie and I were about to leave when Rodney asked,

"Marie, could you give Alan and me just a moment?" She stepped outside and Rodney wrote me a commission check on the spot. "Take the money," he said. "I might forget to mail this and you wouldn't wanna book me next time. Thanks for arranging everything." Rodney put the check in a Thank You card, signed it, and handed it to me. Nice, beyond expectations.

Billy Crystal

The last comedy show I booked was Billy Crystal at New York University in 1979. Alex, the NYU student lecture chairman, was someone I really connected with. At the time Billy was on the TV show *Soap* and famous. He was also represented by William Morris. Somehow I booked the date.

The Saturday night crowd was huge and completely sold out. Billy was great. He did a bit with a girl from the audience crunching her hands in a bowl of potato chips with a mic attached, while he imitated Vic Damone doing a Saturday morning movie from Billy's 1950s childhood. It was hilarious. Billy closed with the old black jazz musician piece he had done on *Saturday Night Live* in 1977, "Can you dig it? I knew that you could."

My old boss Phil was the William Morris agent at the show. I didn't know he was coming. I don't think Alex knew either. He wasn't there before the show, just showed up after the show for the check. There was one check written to Lordly & Dame.

I think I had asked Alex to cut two checks, one to Billy, one to Lordly & Dame. Maybe I forgot. Maybe NYU couldn't handle the two check transaction. Nonetheless, Phil was furious. A lot of nasty things were said.

I offered workarounds, adding, "The first thing Monday Sam will write a check to you guys. You know he'll do that; you worked for him. That's who he is."

"Alright, he said. "But <u>you</u> are going to tell Billy and he's gonna see how much you guys are making."

So we all went backstage. Billy was signing autographs, and Phil pulled Billy aside and explained the situation before Alex or I could say anything.

I tried to jump in to explain. Alex tried to jump in. Phil spoke loudly over both us.

Billy interrupted him. "Phil, Phil, . . . PHIL! So what exactly is the problem here? NYU is not stiffing us. Lordly & Dame won't stiff us. When things don't go as planned we adapt. So Alan will take the check and send a new check on Monday. The banks are not open tomorrow, right? Or did something change in New York last night?"

Then he shook Alex's hand, thanked him, and went back to the crowd. We left and Sam sent a check to the William Morris Agency first thing on Monday.

Lessons from comedians

I didn't tell this whole long story to the guy asking about how to get paid as an independent consultant. Here is what I said:

- First of all be NICE - never be arrogant. Don't put anyone down. Never give someone a reason to lose your check or bury approval forms at the bottom of a pile.
- Find out the process for payment in advance and befriend those people. I often include the accounts payable people in interviews so I have a name if something gets held up.
- Then make clear arrangements for payment in the contract.
  - Big projects often bill a fixed amount upon signing and then monthly.
  - Explain the terms. Net thirty is usual. Be clear about the payment process and put that in the contract.

- I avoid putting penalties for late payments or discounts for early payments. It just looks desperate and makes someone wonder, "Does this guy have a lot of his clients stiffing him?"
- Send thanks - at least emails but cards are nice too - when you receive payment.
- And if things do not go as planned - Adapt.

CHAPTER 36

CONSULTANT DREAMS AND FANTASIES

I have a friend, a Pro consultant who worked until his late seventies. He described himself as a "Dalmatian" after the black-spotted white firehouse dog, "first one on the firetruck when the client rings the alarm." Consultants often call themselves "road warriors," but the consulting road is hard. Even with the video calls and other remote work options generated by working during Covid, clients still want consultants on site. At some point, every consultant recoils at yet another Sunday night flight or chokes on one more 10 p.m. grilled chicken salad at the Marriott and vents frustration to a colleague.

"Y' know. This'd be a great job if it wasn't for the travel."

This exclamation launches a common shared-dream contemplation, "How can we earn money without showing up?"

Let's face it. Consulting travel does wear thin after a while. You are rarely home for the kids' weekday events. You can't sign up for the evening clubs or classes that people with normal jobs attend. And when, at the occasional weekend party, a well-meaning neighbor says something like, "All that travel must be really _exciting_!" Well, this is why consultants seem to have the best jawlines. It's from all the clenched teeth responses. "Well it isn't _really_ like vacation travel."

So in the late-night hotel restaurants after a full day's work and in the Friday night airport lounges waiting for yet another delayed flight, consultants engage in a fantasy together. It's called "money without showing up" or "money without billable hours" or simply "getting off the road," and it generates the passion of the downtrodden. It's hardly the stuff of a John Steinbeck novel, but it does often have the angst of the Eric Burton and the Animals song:

"We gotta get out of this place, if it's the last thing we ever do.

We gotta get out of this place. Girl, there's a better life for me and you."

The conversation moves to earnest brainstorming; after all, we consultants fancy ourselves "problem-solvers." I've heard and participated in these visionquests enough that the ideas generated fall into several broad categories.

"Get clients where we live"

This is a great idea if the clients you typically serve are headquartered close by your home. Automotive consultants who live near Detroit travel less than those who live in New York City. Of course, even Detroit-based consultants will have to travel to do work for BMW or Toyota. Automotive plants and suppliers are not all located within driving distance of the Motor City.

There are some consulting firms (Point B, North Highland Group) that take pride in local offices serving local clients. And this strategy is often behind many consultants who leave big firms with global staffing to "go independent."

There are some disadvantages to the "serve local clients" strategy:

- **The variety of the work is less** because cities tend to specialize in certain industries: New York City is financial services, big Pharma, and media; San Francisco is financial services, biotech, and high tech. Smaller cities have less choice; if you live in Hartford you better be fluent in insurance.

- **Consulting locally still isn't a "normal work life."** Consultants, especially associates in big firms, work long hours. Having a "hometowner" doesn't necessarily mean that you don't stay at a hotel with the rest of the team or that you see your family more.

Still, the first time I became an independent consultant it was so I could see my children grow up. I managed my schedule by working for clients in my hometown of Pittsburgh and those in cities one hour away by air (New York, Chicago) or were short drives like Cleveland.

Do non-client-facing work from the office or from home

Consultants do a lot of research and analysis, which doesn't have to be done in the team office on the client site. When I started in consulting, major consulting firms had research departments and libraries, so there was a reason to be in the office more. Now everything is networked and/or available online.

One way that big consulting firms have dealt with travel frustration is to actually tell clients that consultants need to be in the office one day per week. When I was at Gemini Consulting there was a program called 5-4-3, i.e., five days delivering value to clients, four days on client site, three nights away from home. We travelled on the first flight on Monday morning and flew home on Thursday night. There were always clients and consulting project managers who didn't believe we were actually working if they couldn't see us, but 5-4-3 made things more bearable for a while.

Consider travel as a factor in staffing

Some consulting firms staff globally, so if you live near an airport you might go from a project in Baku, Azerbaijan to one in San Jose, California. Some firms have a more local staffing model. Still others staff humanely by giving you an easy travel assignment following the "travel-bear gig." This works with generalist consultants and in times of relative flush project work and staff supply. However, all bets are off when all the staffing group can supply is a warm body: "Look, I know availability isn't a skillset, but it's Arthur or nobody – got it?" Or when there isn't project work the conversation between staffing and consultants becomes, "This is what there is right now. Are you aware that we are laying off people who are on the beach?"

"Bring the clients to us"

This comes up all the time when consultants are dream-whining. "Why can't they travel instead of us?"

There are business ideas that do bring clients to a consultant's offices: seminars, conferences, and now webinars, the latter not even requiring clients to travel. However, these are typically businesses entirely different from consulting. Consulting firms often use seminars, conferences, and webinars as marketing tools rather than stand-alone businesses.

There is a story told by Jim Collins in his book *Built to Last* about how Peter Drucker once advised him NOT to go into consulting because if you staff up to consult, then you have to "feed the beast." Collins, however, could staff with a minimal research team to write the book and hire an event planner to run the occasional conference for CEOs to share research, bringing clients to Collins in his home city.

Seminars and webinars are tools of the training business. They intend to achieve learning, not a business result. Conference centers are hotels, with as much attention to linens, workout rooms and food as any content delivered.

Still having clients travel to see you *is* a powerful dream for most consultants.

In the late 1980s, I was a vice president in a small consulting firm. We'd had a very good year and the managing partner invited the entire staff to Negril, Jamaica for a week to celebrate. We stayed in a small Jamaican-owned cabin resort in the middle of the seven-mile white sand beach. This wasn't to be a complete vacation, he told all of us – we would work on next year's plan from 7:30 a.m. to noon. The afternoons and evenings we would be free to enjoy the sun and fun of Negril. To prove that he was serious, he invited several clients to visit mid-week to work with us, planning the next year in their engagements. The client planning sessions went well and our people abided by the half-day schedule.

Most of the team left to go back home on Saturday, but I stayed on with the managing partner for a few days. We didn't really abide by the half-day schedule anymore, and, in fact, we partied a bit. We drove around Negril and the neighboring towns and we dream-shared a lot.

In Lucea (pronounced Lucy) we stumbled on a piece of property for sale. It was a five-acre palm-treed plot on a limestone ledge about fifteen feet above the stunning turquoise water. There were concrete stairs down to a small white sand beach. We called the seller and while I have no memory of how much it cost, it seemed reasonable. We saw a local architect, who could hook us up with a local contractor. The architect explained how we could get water and sewer pipe into the lot through the limestone and how the town would give us a tax abatement deal for ten years if we hired just fifteen local people as serving staff for our conference center. The deal was moving very fast.

Then I asked an inconvenient question. "Shouldn't we ask our clients (who had just visited us to plan next year) if they would send people to our conference center?" We made a few calls.

This was a typical answer:

"Oh, good God, no! I pulled off this boondoggle once. I could never do it again!"

We demurred and went back to consulting.

"Money for results"

Consultants always talk big about "getting a piece of the action." They fantasize about gain-sharing agreements and taking an ownership position. A few, like Bain Capital, actually become private equity firms and take the gains from turnarounds instead of fees. Bain Capital also takes its losses and there is the rub for most daydreaming consultants. They want the upside but aren't willing to take the risk that produces the reward.

In 1984 to 1987, I was engaged at British Airways during its turnaround from a nationalized industry to the "world's favorite airline." During that engagement, the client asked the project leader in a public meeting how much of our £2 million project fees he would be willing to take in stock from the planned public offering. He said, "We'll just take the fees."

For years, those of us in the room have lamented our "if only" loss because the stock came out at fifty pence and rose to thirty-seven pounds in the first nine days. Of course, none of us used our own money to buy stock. Nor would we have taken no pay if the stock tanked. But all of us imagined that the consulting firm would have shared the windfall with the consulting team that produced the result (not likely).

I worked on some gain-sharing projects over the years. In these projects, a client negotiates a deal that gives the consulting firm a share of money saved or revenue produced on the project in return for a below-market rate consulting fee. It always seemed like such a great idea.

Invariably, such an engagement became contentious. Some clients argued, "That was our idea! I'm not going to pay you for it." A few clients failed to make the changes that might achieve a result, e.g., not taking people off payroll or pulling the trigger on a bulk supply agreement. Some consultants set unrealistic cuts or unsupported strategies in the hopes of a score.

Occasionally a well-structured contract ended up paying the consultant more than the going consulting rate for a gain-sharing project. Usually that client never bought that way again.

"Money while we sleep"

Eventually, the "money without hours" musing always gets around to a product-based business. Professional services geeks like consultants seem to always want to sell something tangible. They fantasize about how "once you cover the costs it's all gravy – money rolls in when you're napping on your sailboat."

Anyone who has ever sold a product understands that this is naïve, but products are sexy; they give you something to identify with in a way that a service offering doesn't. Consultants really don't know much about products, so the brainstormed ideas are often "productized service offerings" such as:

- Diagnostic surveys used in the entry phase that are packaged and sold to other consultants or clients
- Packages like consultant-in-a-box, interview guides, frameworks, analysis tools, Excel calculators, newsletters, articles, books, webinars, and subscription websites. The latter are usually marketing tools and given away, but consultants see a gold mine with no mining needed.

Sometimes consultants come up with an idea that works, earns money and allows them to stay home a little more. Sometimes a product idea becomes a marketing tool. But most times, we daydreaming consultants went back to work, billing hours and flying out on Sunday night to come home again on Friday.

SOME FINAL THOUGHTS: THE FUTURE OF CONSULTING

In 2014, I posted an article entitled "The Uberization of Consulting" on LinkedIn, the business-oriented social media site. It was my second post on LinkedIn; the first was a sad goodbye to a former client and LinkedIn connection who had passed away.

I had been reading about "Uberization" - is that even a word?

It used to be called dis-intermediation, i.e., replacement of the middleman with technology (the internet). Think Amazon eliminates Borders, Netflix eliminates Blockbuster.

By 2014, the sharing economy wasn't particularly new. Airbnb was founded in 2008, Uber and Kickstarter in 2009. GoFundMe followed in 2010 and Lyft in 2012. But as a late adopter, these firms had just crossed my radar.

I marveled how Uber replaced taxicab infrastructure, and Airbnb did the same for hotels. Kickstarter and GoFundMe offered crowd-source funding previously done by banks, private equity, venture capital and "Aunt Martha."

Historically, in the taxi industry someone owned the cars, hired the drivers, set up the sales frontend (a phone number and a radio dispatcher), took all the risk and made all the profit.

Then, smelling a new way to make money, the government got into the act. Cities started regulating the taxi business by selling medallions (licenses to operate) and limiting the number of players. Then they escalated the medallion price until it became a tremendous source of revenue and a big barrier to entry, much like liquor licenses.

Full disclosure: this probably interested me because I drove a cab for a while in Boston in 1969. In those days, medallions cost $150 and drivers were employees. The owner owned the cars, took care of all maintenance and insurance, bought all gas, paid the drivers $1/hour and 40 percent of the waybill (usually $3-5 per ride). Airport rides ($15-20) were a big deal and tips (usually 10 percent) were nice but not critical. (An elderly lady once gave me a cookie as a tip. It made my day.) Payments were in cash, with the meter and a log as a check against almost non-existent driver fraud. Feedback from a customer was difficult; an unhappy rider had to call the dispatcher who told the owner and maybe it got passed on to the driver.

Today the city gets hundreds of thousands of dollars for a medallion, and drivers are independent contractors who time-lease the cars from the owners. Drivers are also responsible for gas and a share of maintenance, and get to keep what is left after all expenses including a protected "royalty" for the medallion. Airport rides are still a big deal ($40-$150) and tips (20-30 percent) are the only way a driver takes home enough to feed a family. To share feedback, a customer must remember the cab number and hackney license number of the driver before calling the dispatcher. Then, of course, an unhappy rider wonders if it ever got through to the owner and driver.

Uber uses technology – Smartphones, GPS and the Internet - to replace the dispatcher and phone at the front end. Its drivers are private contractors who own the cars, and are responsible for "shared ride" insurance, gas and maintenance. Payments are electronic and two-way feedback (both yours to the driver and hers to you) is instantaneous.

In 2014 my Uber experience had been positive. Cars were clean and well maintained, drivers were courteous, and service was speedy and inexpensive. I didn't really worry about how Uber was taking advantage of its gig economy drivers, who all seemed very nice. Later some male Uber drivers were accused of sexual assault and other bad behavior and Uber co-founder Travis Kalanick resigned in a media storm over a toxic culture in 2019. (I mostly use Lyft now.)

But in 2014 I puzzled through this business model.

The status quo of consulting

Consulting is a time-based service business not unlike taxis.

The government hasn't gotten involved in the licensing game – there are no expensive medallions - but those firms who can afford it build big brands through advertising. (You've seen the billboards in airports and full-page ads in business magazines.) Big firms use brand-awareness with the general public and the universities and business schools who supply them with junior consultants. The business schools do "feed the beast," providing fresh recruits to go "up or out."

What if technology could automate more of the front end? What if technology could provide income without billable hours on client site? What if this cost saving would allow for less "up or out" churn in the workforce?

Enter Uber-ization

The Uberization model replaces the army of juniors with senior people, i.e., those who like to solve a variety of client problems but aren't interested in the partner/salesperson role. These senior "independents" partner with the client to teach – rather than just do.

This model also uses technology - Dropbox, Googledocs and email for sharing docs - instead of a big fancy office and the infrastructure it requires. Intellectual property is shared among principals and alumni networks or available online through Slide Share, Flevy or Google.

Can these "independents" use social media – LinkedIn, for example - to replace or more likely augment the front-end, relationship-driven sales process?

I founded such a network – Results-Alliance – and we did a few projects. But while the Results-Alliance network shared the client development tasks and delivered work together, we missed the opportunity of the shared economy.

The front end of most shared economy companies is an app or website. Uber and Lyft are accessed by phone, and rental companies like Airbnb and VRBO use both phone and website access. Financing companies like Kickstarter and GoFundMe often involve multiple pages on a website.

It is hard to imagine how the sales of consulting would be done by a Smartphone app, but online services for independent consultants have expanded exponentially. Technology in the form of online prerecorded webinars, chat bot texts, and emails could attract clients and set up first meetings. There are now management consulting podcasts and video streaming services that teach methodologies and analytics. This is a variation on the seminar/webinar business development strategy, but a subscription model or advertising model may create a "money without billable hours" revenue stream as well as a new way to generate clients for independent consultants and small firms.

Online service offering distribution has exploded. There are more than twenty consulting content aggregation firms like Flevy.

Clive Mallard, a Gemini Consulting colleague, started The Independents' Consultant, an online consulting skills training company for independent consultants to use for new hires and their own self-development. I also know of an organizational development consultant whose entire business is conducting three video interviews with members of the client system and recommending one or more consultants. She charges the client a flat fee and receives a finder's fee from the consultants. Evidently she copied this model from psychotherapists.

Since its founding in 2013, McKinsey Solutions combines the firm's industry and functional research with data science to offer core consulting methodologies as standalone products and prepackaged solutions to a variety of clients including mid-market function heads and executives. Solutions started as a way to "productize" the business for clients who might never afford the firm's full services. The Solutions product extended the "long tail" of service offerings that were commoditizing, i.e., being taken in house by clients. Solutions is now described as a "platform" that includes podcasts, blogs, client community forums and much more. I'm told that some partners in the firm's classic advisory business still resist the disruptive nature of this division, but McKinsey Solutions has grown to be 50 percent of the firm's headcount.

So it would seem that there are multiple opportunities going forward to provide consulting subscription business models like McKinsey Solutions, or combinations with other industries like Bain Capital, which uses consulting methodologies to turn businesses around but takes a financial stake in the outcome.

Perhaps the biggest change on the horizon for consulting is Artificial Intelligence. I don't see chat bots doing interviews, but currently there are AI programs on the market that transcribe voice to text, useful for transcribing interviews, and AI may further automate surveys. There are programs to manage contacts, and do data analysis that a horde of analysts used to stay up all night to do. Soon there may be algorithmic, autonomous, automatic systems that do much of the work of big data marketing, and operations and logistics optimization.

When I started in consulting there were libraries of hard copies of industry data and previous projects. During my years in the field these were replaced by central databases and files on individual consultants' external hard drives. One can easily imagine AI, database , and communications technologies making information available not just to consultants but to clients as well. How will the role of the expert consultant evolve in this ubiquitous information environment?

Based upon what this technology laggard knows today here are some places AI might change the way that consulting is sold and delivered. **The bolded inputs could be done by AI.**

HOW AI MIGHT AID CONSULTING

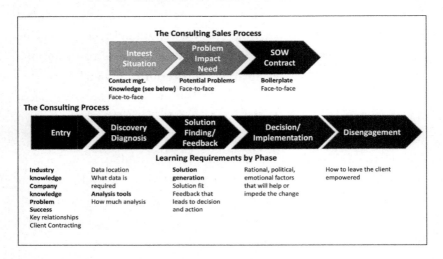

Consulting will still be about change, and change will be about people. Companies may need new information about new customers or competitors. Businesses may need new ways to finance growth and create sales. Leaders will need new ways to communicate direction and attract followers. Organizations will need new ways to innovate, improve and integrate those changes. Some of that work may be automated, but not the judgement, creativity, and empathy that help people change, i.e., create insight, inspire action, and achieve results. This will require a real live breathing consultant who offers expertise, implements new processes, provides answers, asks questions, and generates ideas and results. The next twenty years in consulting promise to be very exciting. Almost makes me want to continue working just for the experience.

Almost.

Looking Back

I know former consultants who are quite cynical about the value of consulting. They often grumble about the way they were misused by their employers, how they worked too hard, were seldom listened to, and unfairly passed over for bonus or promotion. They also disparage clients as dependent on consultants to do the work that they should be able to do for themselves. They see all the negatives of the profession and miss the joys.

In contrast, as I look back from my retirement, I really enjoyed my time in consulting.

I am grateful for each of my thirty-seven years in the field, for all the ups and downs, failed projects and mistakes that I learned from, as well as times when I was able to genuinely help a client make a change and achieve a result.

I am grateful for the learning, the variety of work, and the smart, flexible problem-solvers I met in client companies, consulting firms and those who were independents.

To any individual or company I failed, I apologize. To those I was able to help, thank you for the opportunity.

My advice to any in the field, or who are contemplating entering it, is simple:

If you choose this career, know that the skills and knowledge you'll need **change** over time **from doing the work, to doing and managing, to selling, managing and doing.**

Consulting is **helping people change. Strive to be helpful.**

You need to **learn continually**, new industries, new methodologies, new technology, but that in itself is worth the ride.

Clients want results - more revenue (innovating), more profit (improving), or improved people stuff (integrating, organizing or developing). **Stay focused on achieving results.**

And always be prepared to find wisdom in unusual places.

Additional Resources

This book espouses my point of view about consulting, which was shaped by my experiences over a lifetime career. I have referred to other consultants and authors who have helped to form this viewpoint or who have provided useful tools. I enclose a list of these and other resources here.

Books

On Consulting

Block, Peter. *Flawless Consulting 4rd Edition*. San Francisco: Pfeiffer, 2011. Chapter 4 on contracting is brilliant. There is also a *Flawless Consulting Fieldbook*. Pfeiffer, 2000, and *The Answer to How is Yes*. Pfeiffer, 2003. These discuss how to get clients to act.

Edersheim, Elizabeth Haas. *McKinsey's Marvin Bower*. Hoboken, NJ: John Wiley & Sons, 2004. Marvin Bower was responsible for building McKinsey & Company and professionalizing consulting.

Maister, David H. *Managing the Professional Services Firm*. New York: Free Press/ Simon & Schuster, 1999. David H. Maister is the definitive resource on how a consulting firm works.

Maister, David H, Charles Green, Robert Galford. *The Trusted Advisor*. Twentieth anniversary edition, Free Press, 2021

Mostraghimi, Raamin, and Varun Bhartia. *The ABCs of Consulting*. Very Young Professionals, 2018. Ostensibly a children's book, but really a consulting parody. The perfect gift for a consultant with a newborn. ("C is for carry-on luggage.")

Phelan, Karen. *I'm Sorry I Broke Your Company: When Management Consultants Are the Problem Not the Solution*. San Francisco, CA; Barrett-Koehler Publishers, 2013. A somewhat irreverent view of the field with the central message: Remember that businesses are human enterprises, and people working together to provide a product or service to other people. Don't treat them like machines.

Schaffer, Robert H. *High Impact Consulting*. San Francisco, CA: Jossey-Bass / Wiley, 2002. Robert H. Schaffer shows how to keep a helpful mindset and achieve results. Schaffer's other books, *The Breakthrough Strategy* and *Rapid Results*, describe his methodologies.

Schein, Edgar H. *Humble Consulting: How to Provide Real Help Faster.* Oakland, CA: Barrett-Koehler Publishers, 2016. Dr. Schein was a leading light of organizational development, and how to change organizational culture. This book presents effective values-based consulting.

On Change

Gladwell, Malcolm. *The Tipping Point.* New York: Little, Brown and Company, 2006. Gladwell explains how change happens when a critical mass of opinion leaders adopt an idea.

Heath, Chip, and Dan Heath. *Switch: How to Change Things When Change is Hard.* New York: Crown, 2010. A good explanation of how to manage the emotional limiters to change.

Kotter, John P. *Leading Change.* Boston, MA: Harvard Business Review Press, 2012. Also *The Heart of Change* written with Dan S. Cohen. There are a lot of books about change models that talk in terms of steps or phases. Kotter describes the requirements for successful change.

Litwin, George H., John Bray, and Kathleen Lusk-Brooke. *Mobilizing the Organization: Bringing Strategy to Life.* London: Prentice Hall / Simon & Schuster, 1995. A book to which I contributed that tells the stories of some of the most important change projects of my early career.

Phelan, Karen. *Who Moved My Holy Hand Grenade: Everything I needed to know in business I learned from Monty Python and the Holy Grail.* New Jersey, USA: Lineson Publishing, 2013. A humorous sendup of change management theory, which contains some very helpful advice, in spite of itself.

On Strategy

Ansoff, H. Igor. *Corporate Strategy.* New York: McGraw-Hill, 1965. There are many excellent books by Ansoff on strategic management, but this is the one that started it all.

Frisch, Bob, Logan Chandler. "Off-sites that Work." *Harvard Business Review*, June 1, 2006. A perfect roadmap for preparing for and facilitating a strategy off-site.

Kim, W. Chan, and Renée Mauborgne. *Blue Ocean Strategy.* Boston, MA: Harvard Business School Publishing, 2004. INSEAD professors demonstrate how to differentiate your business so that you have no competition.

Porter, Michael. *Competitive Strategy.* New York: The Free Press, 1980. Porter details the industry analysis that should help businesses decide whether or not to enter an industry and how to differentiate their business.

On Quantitative Continuous Improvement

Deming, W. Edwards. *Out of the Crisis.* Cambridge, MA: MIT Press, 1982. Dr. Deming, the guru of the quality movement, has the best prescription for managing Continuous Improvement.

Gawande, Atul. *The Checklist Manifesto.* New York: Picador/Macmillan, 2010. Using medical examples, Gawande describes how to ensure outcomes by making sure that that all important activities are completed on time.

Gonick, Larry, and Woollcott Smith. *The Cartoon Guide to Statistics.* New York: HarperCollins Publishers, 1993. A fun way to learn statistics that sounds like an oxymoron. It isn't.

Lynch, Richard L., and Kelvin F. Cross. *Measure Up: Yardsticks for Continuous Improvement.* Malden, MA: Blackwell Publishers, 1991. A good description of how to choose the best metrics.

Spear, Steven J. *The High Velocity Edge: How Market Leaders Leverage Operational Excellence to Beat the Competition.* New York: McGraw Hill, 2010. Spears earned his PhD writing about the Toyota Production System. Building upon this example he describes how to accelerate change.

On Innovation

Christensen, Clayton. *The Innovator's Dilemma: When New Technologies*

Cause Great Firms to Fail. Boston, MA: Harvard Business Review Press, 2015. This is one of a four-book series that includes *The Innovator's Solution, The Innovator's Method,* and *The Innovator's DNA.* This series is chock full of cases about companies that successfully navigated disruptive innovation and those who didn't.

Drucker, Peter F. *Innovation and Entrepreneurship.* New York: Routlege/HarperCollins Publishers, 1985. One of the most read of Drucker's books that provides no-nonsense how-tos for running an innovative business.

Hamel, Gary. *Leading the Revolution: How to Thrive in Turbulent Times by Making Innovation a Way of Life.* Boston, MA: Harvard Business School Press, 2000. Hamel has written many excellent books. This one is memorable for the detailed blueprint for the Royal Shell innovation funding, internal venture capital system.

Kelley, Thomas, and Jonathan Littman. *The Art of Innovation: Lessons in Creativity from IDEO, America's Leading Design Firm.* New York: Doubleday, 2001. Stanford University's Human Centered Design model described in detail.

Michaelides, Dimis. *The Art of Innovation: Integrating Creativity in Organizations.* Cyprus: Performa Productions, 2007. Michaelides offers an artistic presentation that drives innovative thought through image and symbol.

On Organizations, Teams, Management and Leadership

Butler, Ava S. *Mission Critical Meetings.* Tucson, AZ: Wheatmark, 2014. Tips and tools for running meetings.

Collins, Jim. *The Good to Great* series (*Good to Great, Built to Last, How the Mighty Fall, Great By Choice, Turning the Flywheel*). New York, NY: Harper Business 2001-2020. Peter Drucker advised Collins not to form a consulting firm because then he would have to "feed the beast," continually looking for clients. Collins' research has arguably made a more significant contribution than if he had been on a client acquisition flywheel.

DePree, Max. *Leadership is an Art.* New York: Penguin/Random House,

2004. Easily my favorite book on values-based leadership by the CEO of Hermann Miller.

Frisch, Bob. *Who's in the Room? How Great Leaders Structure and Manage the Teams Around Them.* San Francisco, CA: Jossey-Bass, 2021. Leadership decisions about change and about hiring consultants. Frisch makes the point that these decisions are often made by an executive and a few close advisors, "the team with no name," and that improving process and structure will lead to better decisions.

Heskett, James L. *Managing in the Service Economy.* Boston, MA: Harvard Business School Press, 1986. The first of several books by James Heskett that explain the unique challenges of service businesses.

Katzenbach, Jon R., and Douglas K. Smith. *The Wisdom of Teams.* Boston, MA: Harvard Business Review Press, 1993. This is the definitive book on teams. Katz has many excellent books on a variety of leadership and organizational topics. *The Discipline of Teams.* New York, NY: John Wiley & Sons, 2001 is a follow-on book with an excellent chapter on virtual teams.

Kleiner, Art. *The Age of Heretics: A History of the Radical Thinkers Who Reinvented Corporate Management.* San Francisco, CA. Jossey-Bass 2008. This book describes the historical research and practice of what we now think of as contemporary management theory. I read an earlier edition of this book and was so impressed that I summarized it for training new consultants. This edition bears a forward by Dr. Warren Bennis.

Litwin, George H., and Robert A. Stringer, Jr. *Motivation and Organization Climate.* Boston, MA: Harvard Business School Press, 1968. Organizational culture has become both a ubiquitous buzzword and an excuse for an inability to change. Litwin and Stringer demonstrate how relatively easy it is for managers to create a high-performance climate.

Pugh, Derek S. and David J. Hickson. *Writers on Organizations.* London; Sage Publications, 2007. This book has 1-3-page summaries of organizational and management theory. I used the summaries to educate new MBAs on organizational and process consulting.

Senge, Peter. *The Fifth Discipline.* New York: Currency, 1990. Senge explores the integration of systems thinking and participative management.

Sinek, Simon. *Start with Why: How Great Leaders Inspire Everyone to Take Action.* New York, NY: Portfolio/Penguin, 2009. There is a series of Sinek's books, *Find Your Why, Leaders Eat Last,* that are excellent, but this one is the first and the best at helping leaders make change.

Ulrich, David. *Human Resource Champions: The Next Agenda for Adding Value and Delivering Results.* Boston, MA: Harvard Business Review Press, 1996. I used David Ulrich's models on two HR restructuring projects to great effect.

Newsletters/ Websites and Blogs

Top Consultant newsletter http://news.top-consultant.com/uk/newsletter.htm A UK-based newsletter with good articles on the industry, job postings and available training.

The Independents' Consultant http://theindependentsconsultant.com/ New associates training for independent consultants.

Flevy http://flevy.com Tools, frameworks, articles, and much more from this business document provider.

Consultants Mind https://www.consultantsmind.com/ Consulting blog and available tools.

Triaster Blog, *http://blog.triaster.co.uk/blog* Triaster Consulting, led by Michael Cousins and Brad Fagan

On Human Enterprise, http://www.onhumanenterprise.com/ blog of Niko Canner and Incandescent Consulting

Visual Capitalist, https://www.visualcapitalist.com/ a subscription website with some of the best graphics for information that I've seen.

APPENDIX

British Airways

The British Airways drive to privatization was the first large-scale change project in which I was involved. It was arguably the most successful. For years I looked for another client like BA and I'm told by many other project colleagues - including John Bray, Dr. George Litwin, Dr. Warner Burke, and Dr. Donald Tosti - that they too have looked in vain for such a client. On his website, Dr. Nick Georgiades, the consultant who became BA Vice President of Human Resources, talks wistfully about his five-year tenure at British Airways. So I am not the only one who talks about BA "far too much."

To be clear the reason none of us ever found such a dream project again was that the British government under Mrs. Thatcher spent lavishly to ensure the success of the first and most visible privatization of that period. In addition to funding the massive effort to change the culture and behaviors of BA leadership and staff, the government underwrote a large rebranding effort that included £52 million to repaint planes and launch an enormous advertising campaign.

BA 1984-1987: The Transformation Leading to Successful Privatization

In 1983, an article in the *Financial Times* (FT) called British Airways "a national disgrace - the world's least profitable airline and the airline with the worst service record of any airline flying on the North Atlantic." By 1987, British Airways had completely transformed itself. It was the most profitable airline in the world; it received the best customer service ratings of any airline on the Atlantic routes and underwent privatization through a widely distributed, oversubscribed, public offering of stock that was issued at 50p but was bid up to £37 in the first week.

How British Airways got there is one of the most extraordinary change efforts of our time.

Externalities and the driving need for change

British Airways was created in 1976 from the merger of two failing nationalized carriers: British European Airlines (BEA) and the British Overseas Airways Corporation (BOAC). These airlines arose after World War II from the remnants of the RAF bomber corps (BEA) and the Spitfire fighter group (BOAC). The merger was widely perceived to be a failure. The employees of the two airlines came from remarkably different backgrounds and even in 1984, they occupied different buildings at London Heathrow Airport and had distinctly different logos and marketing materials.

In 1983, when the FT article came out, the airline had just lost an astounding £1 billion on less than £3 billion in revenue. The article referred to recent customer service surveys that ranked BA dead last in on-time performance and customer satisfaction, and carried damning quotes from important customers who swore they would never fly the airline again. This came at a time when the traffic on North Atlantic routes was growing by 20-30 percent per year due to increased business between the booming US and UK economies. The competition on the North Atlantic routes was among major European and US carriers, not discount airlines. (Sir Freddy Laker's Laker Airlines and People Express had all but failed and Sir Richard Branson's Virgin Airlines had not yet been founded.)

At the time of the article, Jan Carlzon's Scandinavian Airlines System (SAS) had transformed airline service. Virtually all other airlines were flying near full, and BA's load factor was 60 percent, despite a £5 million television ad campaign where actor Robert Morley implored Americans to "Come home - all is forgiven," and Britons to "Fly the flag - please."

BA had 58,000 employees, almost twice the number of any of its competitors, yet its service queues at Heathrow were interminable, and passengers were either ignored or rudely herded like cattle.

The unwanted FT publicity was an embarrassment to the government of Tory Prime Minister Margaret Thatcher. Mrs. Thatcher had campaigned on "stopping government waste" and here was unbelievable inefficiency, called "Bloody Awful" on FT's front page. In 1983 Mrs. Thatcher announced that she had appointed Sir John King (later Lord King of Wartnaby), industrialist and the former ambassador to the United States, to be Chairman of British Airways to turn the airline around before privatization early in 1987.

Sir John King's first act as Chairman was to offer a two-year salary severance package to any BA employee who wished to leave. Over 20,000 employees took the package. Prior to this offering, 48 percent of BA's employees had never worked anywhere else. Afterwards there were 37,000 employees, 84 percent of whom had worked only at BA.

The first members of the change team

Sir John's second management act was to hire Colin Marshall (later Sir Colin, then Lord Marshall, of Knightsbridge) as Chief Executive. Colin Marshall was an experienced British travel industry executive who had worked as a management trainee purser on the Orient Steam Line, and a divisional manager for Hertz Car Rental before being hired at age thirty to turn around Avis Car Rental of Europe.

Colin Marshall brought on Nick Georgiades, an independent consultant, as VP Director of Human Resources, and Mike Levin, a former US Organization of Secret Service (OSS) psychologist, as his personal consultant and aide-de-camp.

Nick, Mike and Colin later sought out Dr. George Litwin and John Bray, both founders of the Forum Corporation, a management training firm. Also on board were representatives of the Hay Group for executive compensation, and Pilat, an Israeli performance management consultancy.

Together this change team conducted initial research on the conditions that created the state of affairs at BA. They discovered that:

- Executives were held accountable for neither profit nor service levels. They were compensated solely on length of service.

- The performance appraisal system was also based upon length of service.
- No one had the words "customer service" in their job description.
- There were no processes in place for customer service emergencies in the terminals. For example, at Heathrow, one of the most fogged-in airports in the world, there were no processes to adapt loading procedures to foggy conditions, which accounted for the large numbers of late-gate departures.
- Employees had no conception of the skills and knowledge required to run a service business.

The change team articulated a new vision of what the airline would have to become to transform sufficiently to privatize:

- Customer friendly
- A profitable enterprise
- A winning team and a great place to work

Colin Marshall said this would require "visible leadership who were focused on customers and serving the people who served them."

The change team conceived of a change model called the "three-legged stool," the inclusion of three separate but equal streams of change work:

BA CHANGE MODEL

The Three-Legged Stool

THE NEW BA

Executive Compensation

Performance Appraisal

Leadership and Service Education and Training

Executive Compensation to align how executives are measured and paid with desired results

- **Performance Appraisal** to align how all other employees are measured and paid with desired results
- **Leadership and Service Education and Training** to communicate the direction and give employees needed new capabilities.

The Hay Group worked on Executive Compensation, Pilat worked on Performance Appraisal, and George Litwin's company HRI and John Bray's Forum Development Group worked on Leadership and Service Education and Training.

The Executive Compensation stream

Executive Compensation was ultimately changed from length of service to a salary and bonus system where 40 percent of compensation was "at risk," depending on goal achievement. Sixty percent of bonus compensation was paid on business goal – e.g., profit, market share, customer satisfaction etc., as appropriate. Forty percent of bonus was paid on feedback from peers and subordinates as to whether the executive led according to the vision and values of the new British Airways: Customer Focus, Empathy and Empowerment, Trust, and Personal Responsibility.

The Performance Appraisal stream

The Performance Appraisal stream began work on defining employee jobs around customer satisfaction and profit. It then introduced a performance-based performance model and a new computerized performance appraisal system that adjusted for "rater bias."

The Leadership and Service Education and Training stream

This stream produced many programs aimed at various knowledge and skill deficiencies identified over the three-year project period. Further, because training included two-way change communications, this stream surfaced much needed work in other areas not anticipated in the somewhat simplified "three-legged-stool" model. This work included process improvements in customer service, organizational redesign, and a series of change projects in all aspects of the business. These projects were nominally a part of the Managing People First Programme (MPF), but they took on a life of their own and drove much of the results achieved in the entire change effort.

So the work of this stream often began in a formal training program, but continued outside the classroom until it was integrated into day-to-day operations of the business. It is most easily understood by describing programs in the chronological order in which they began.

The Passenger Group Management Programme

Colin Marshall's first exhortation was to "FIX THE TERMINALS." Customer service in Heathrow was terrible. Ticketing queues were long, service personnel were rude, 60 percent of gate departures were late, and half of the late departures sat on the tarmac because they missed the air traffic control take-off window.

Because no one had customer service in their job description, a new job was created, the Passenger Group Coordinator, or PGC, who was responsible for coordinating service as well as the logistics of loading passengers. Front line supervisors (Grade 7, part of the represented workforce) were told that their job was being abolished. They could take a generous severance package or apply for a new more highly paid position (Grade 8, still represented) for which they would go through an assessment center to "determine suitability." The new job requirements included customer service and empowering leadership. Supervisors who elected to apply for the new position were given two full weeks of intensive training (including a weekend to which spouses were invited) before the assessment.

The program schedule went from 7 a.m. until 11 p.m. every day and covered basic supervisory and customer service skills as well as leadership skills and feedback.

In the end, 97 percent of existing supervisors applied for the new position, and 98 percent of those who were trained passed the rigorous assessment center.

Putting People First

Putting People First was a one-day program for all employees that explained the principles of customer service and how to manage one's emotions to provide service. Time Manager, a Danish firm that had worked at SAS, ran the program. They adapted their time and calendar management materials to communicate the message of serving customers and those who serve them. Time Manager ran large sessions of 50 to 200 people with break-out groups. The time management materials may not have been the most appropriate methodology, but the fact that every employee heard the message about customer service and the emotional labor it required had a significant impact.

Managing People First

Managing People First targeted the top 2000 leaders inside British Airways. It was a one-week resident program, with a demanding daily schedule (7 a.m.to 11p.m.). There were several components:

- Peer and subordinate feedback collected by questionnaire and delivered by computerized reports, with leadership coaching by facilitators. This feedback was delivered daily in teaching units corresponding to the leadership values of the new BA: Vision, Empowerment, Trust, Personal Responsibility
- Specific leadership development content customized to individual need
- Work in teams on self-selected change projects. As mentioned earlier, this work was planned during Managing People First and carried out after the program.
- Teams presented their change program plans to Colin Marshall, who came to every single MPF program.

The Cabin Crew Programme

The Cabin Crew Programme was a "mini-MPF" for all cabin crew. This program focused on improving cabin service and redesigning in-flight cabin service processes to reduce the number of cabin crew needed on flights, while actually improving service levels.

How BA Makes Money or The Green Beret Programme

This program was designed to teach all managers from supervisors to executives how to read financial statements and make budgets. It evolved from the first pilot program into a way to generate cost saving and revenue development ideas that were then implemented by those in the class. Soon the easy financial improvements were made, but each succeeding group challenged itself to try to save or improve more than the last. The program became a "boot camp" experience producing tangible results in more and more difficult arenas. People competed to attend and it became The Green Beret Programme, named for intensive training of US Army Special Services.

The Seeds Programme - The change agent development programme

The Seeds took its name from the Chairman Mao expression "plant but a few seeds and a thousand flowers will bloom." Facilitators of Managing People First selected individuals as the Change Agents for the BA Way. They were selected according to the passion with which they engaged the MPF course, and positive impact they had on others – the bravery of their words, the degree to which others listened when they spoke, and the degree to which others took action as a result of their words.

Slightly more than forty Seeds surfaced out of 2000 leaders in MPF. In this program, Dr. George Litwin and Dr. W. Warner Burke of Teachers College, Columbia University taught three core skills:

- How to deliver an inspiring speech about the BA Way – vision and values
- Organizational process skills – specifically, how to intervene in

a small group's process that was "stuck" and get them back on track

- How to give tough behavioral corrective feedback to an executive, senior to them, about the way that executive was living the values

The Seeds helped the change teams and drove change in other ways. Not surprisingly, by 1987 many of them were in senior positions running the new service-focused, profitable airline they had created.

Results, Critical Success Factors, and the post-1987 British Airways

As described earlier, British Airways became customer-focused, efficient and profitable in a three-year period. The published 1986 results showed that BA had earned almost £500 million on revenues of around £5 billion. In 1986 its customer service ratings routinely exceeded every airline except Singapore Airlines and Swiss Air, and in the last month of the year BA was the highest rated airline for customer service, beating even those formidable competitors.

British Airways managed the news of its success extraordinarily well and so when the public offering came in the spring of 1987 (at the hottest time of the hot 1980s market) many people who had never owned a stock had "flutter on the flag." Consequently the stock went from 50 pence to 37 pounds in the first week. The stock ranged between £15 and £20 for the first year before settling to around £9 for subsequent offerings.

Now decades later, this change effort has been written about and used as a model for countless others. Its critical success factors include:

- The driving need to change –"privatize or die" and the embodiment of this in Mrs. Margaret Thatcher
- The colossal investment made by the British government
- Colin Marshall's focus aided by Mike Levin's aggressive determination
- The Passenger Group Management Programme's "early wins" in the terminals

- Putting People First's large group meetings, which everyone in the airline attended, that communicated the consistent message of customer service
- Managing People First's universal leadership language
- Results created in MPF's change teams
- The Seeds Programme's development of change agents among opinion leaders
- Hard metrics and results focus developed in the Green Beret Programme Executive Compensation, and Performance Appraisal streams

In the years since 1987 British Airways has been on a roller coaster ride along with many other airlines. Deep discounting airlines have provided intense competition and any company is only as good as last quarter's numbers. In some years profits have been up and in other years down, but customer service has remained stable and consistently among the highest in the industry. Even today, BA continues to represent a pride of accomplishment among employees, shareholders, and the general British population. It is a model of what can be accomplished by a group of dedicated employees. For many, British Airways will always be *The World's Favorite Airline.*

ACKNOWLEDGEMENTS

In my life, I have had lots of help. I am not an easy person to help so let me express my gratitude to all who have helped me or tried to help me even if I seemed less than grateful at the time.

Thanks to Dr. George H. Litwin, a mentor who provided me with many exciting clients including the British Airways project I talk so much about. Thanks also to the late Dr. Richard W. Taylor; our work together inspired much of the continuous improvement content of the book.

I'm grateful to all those who have supported my writing over the years, subscribers to my blog, LinkedIn, beBee, Medium, and Dennis Pitocco and my colleagues at BIZCATALYST 360°.

The following people helped me bring this book to fruition:

I thank Bob Frisch of Strategic Offsites Group, Robert Shaffer of Shaffer Consulting and Roopa Unnikrishnan of Center 10 Consulting, all of whom read an early draft and gave feedback that sharpened my audience focus. Thanks especially to Bob Frisch and Roopa Unnikrishnan for their kind words reproduced in the front matter and excerpted on the back cover.

I am grateful to Sandy G. Hickerson for early review and feedback and for much advice on self-publishing. I also thank Aiman Ezzat and Ashwin Yardi of Capgemini Group for arranging a detailed review of a later draft and to Sanjay Negi of Capgemini for that review and his feedback. I appreciate Joe Barnes, Jere Cowden, Kaye Foster, Naresh Jessani, Brad Martin, Florence Woo, and Bob Yardis for their recommendations.

Thanks to Sean Riley of Kelly Consulting who, along with several current and former BCG, McKinsey, and Gemini consultants (not named by their request), for input to the chapter on mid-career transitions.

I am grateful to Art Kleiner and Wallace Mohlenbrok for a substantial developmental edit, which changed the structure and flow of the book. Thanks to Lisa Monias of South River Design Team for the cover design and for the interior design and to my son Zac Culler for designing my blog logo and publisher imprint. Thanks to Jay Seldin for the author photograph.

Most of all thank you to my wife, Billie Smith Culler. Billie earned her living as a business writer and editor for more than twenty years. I am extremely fortunate that she has been my first reader, my first and second to nth editor. She has shown amazing patience when I whined, resisted, and ignored her editorial advice only to accept it from someone else later. She has encouraged me, pulled me out of discouragement periodically, and supported my writing, even when it took time away from our time together. Thank you, Billie! This book wouldn't have happened without you.

Even though I had a great deal of assistance with this book, any errors are my own and probably due to my obstinate rejection of offered advice.

Thank you also to all my clients and consulting colleagues who made my thirty-seven years in the field a good run and a wild ride.

ABOUT THE AUTHOR

"When I began thinking about work I was in a play."

Alan Culler studied theatre as an undergraduate. There he learned to observe people in order to portray them. That skill turned out to be quite useful later as Alan became an organizational change consultant.

"What I didn't learn was how to get work as an actor."

So Alan went to work as a booking agent for celebrity speakers. He learned to sell, which fed him as a consultant. He also learned that "the famous and powerful are just people who want you to listen and help if you can." This turned out to be useful later when talking to CEOs.

With no roadmap, Alan decided to become a consultant and went to the London Business School. He worked for five firms: Harbridge House (acquired by Coopers & Lybrand, now part of PwC); The Forum Corporation (now Achieve Forum, part of Korn Ferry); HRI, (Dr. George Litwin's firm, which had the British Airways contract, was acquired by Forum to form Strategic Action Services); Gemini Consulting (now Capgemini Group); Katzenbach Partners (McKinsey spin-off, startup, ultimately acquired by Booz & Company, Strategy &, now a part of PwC).

Alan Culler first became an independent consultant in 1987 and again in 2003, ultimately spending twenty-three years of his thirty-seven-year consulting career working for himself in a variety of structures - sole proprietor, partnership Morton Culler & Company, and Results-Alliance LLC, a confederated network of independent consultants.

In 2018 Alan retired to write stories and songs. Forthcoming books are *Change Leader? Who, Me?* and *Wisdom from Unusual Places.*

Alan Culler now lives in New Jersey with his wife Billie and black

Labrador Retriever, Pip. They take every opportunity to see their five adult children and five grandchildren.

You can read more about Alan at https://www.alanculler.com and read more of his writing at https://wisdomfromunusualplaces.com.

INDEX

Printed in Great Britain
by Amazon